AF446733

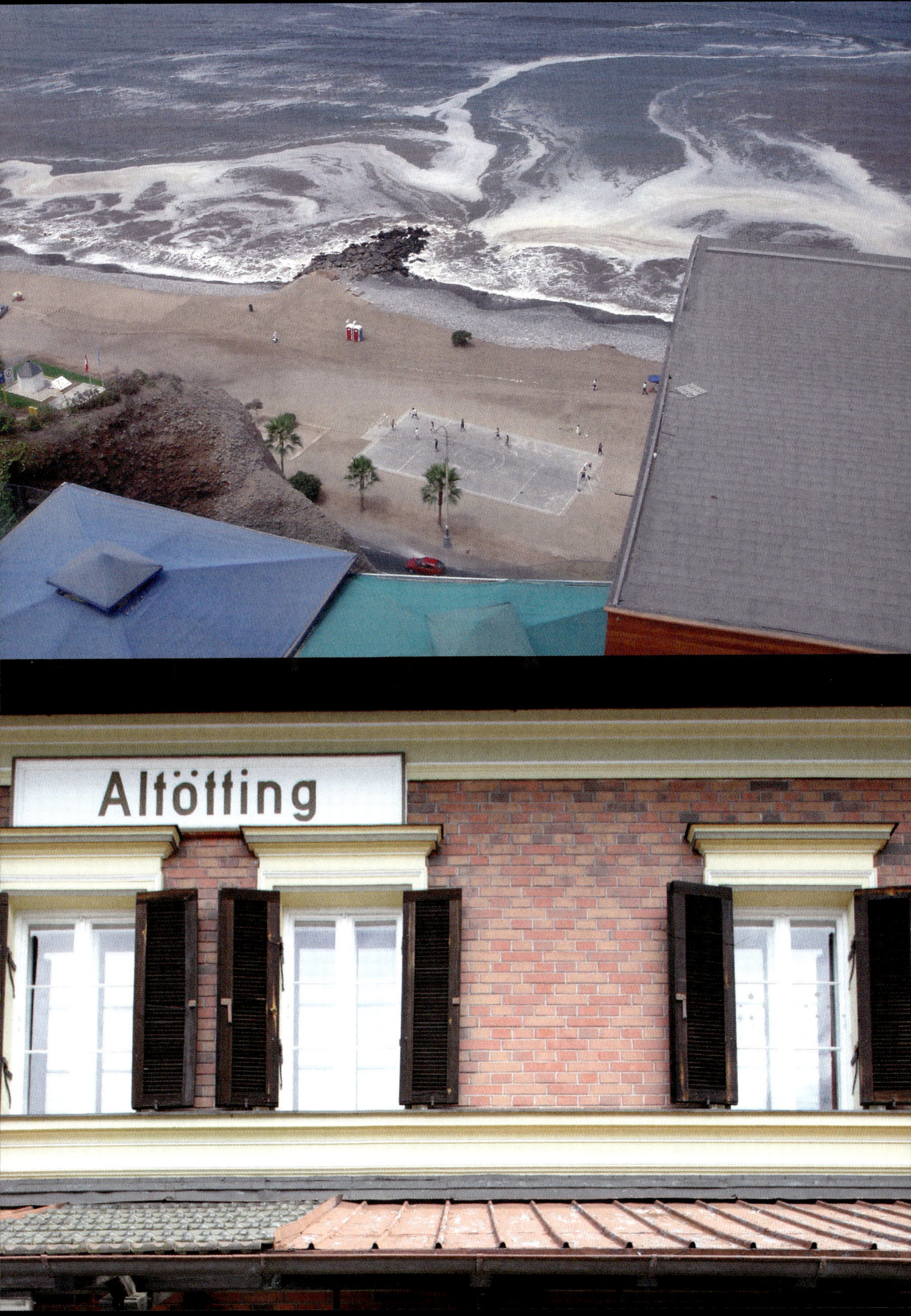
Altötting

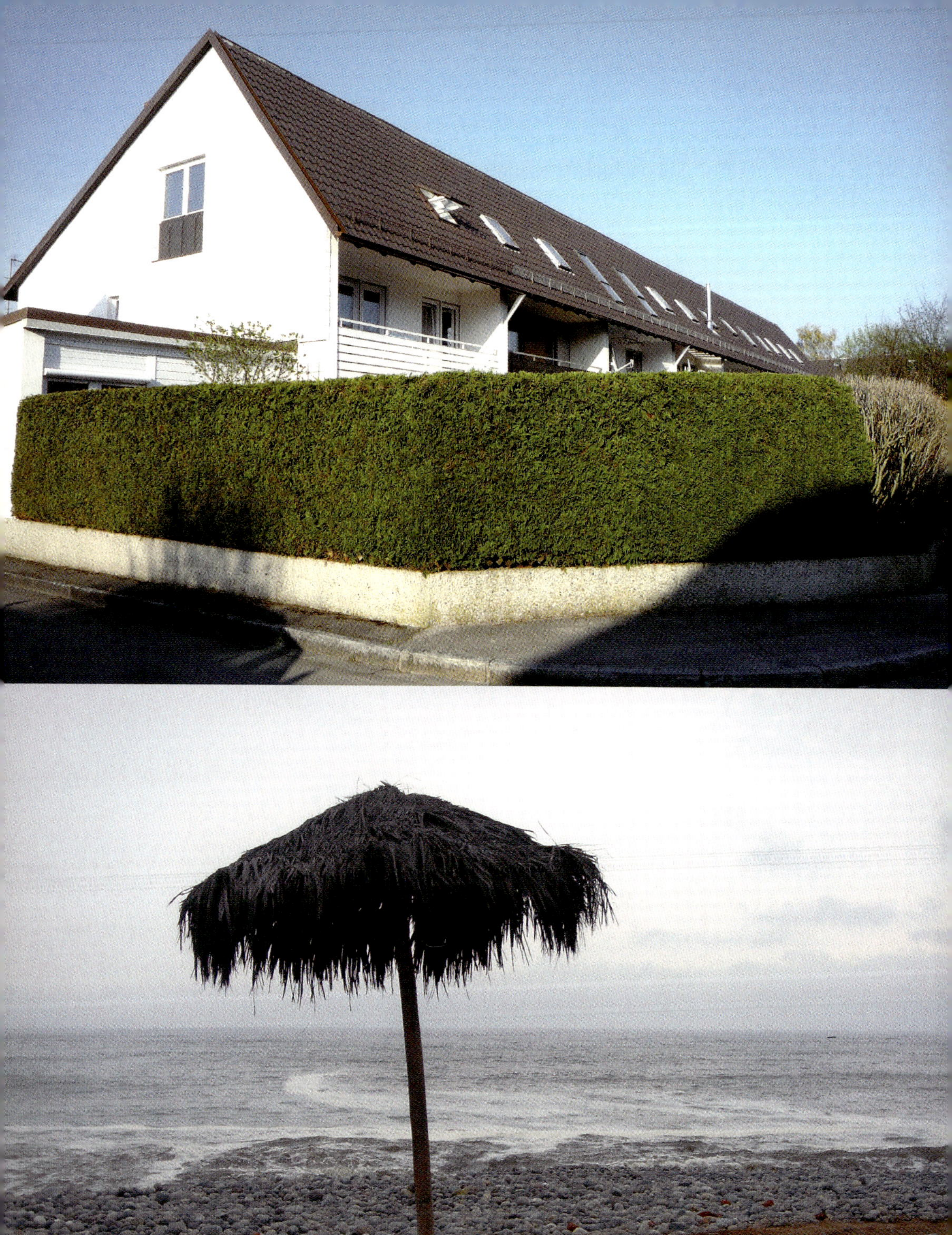

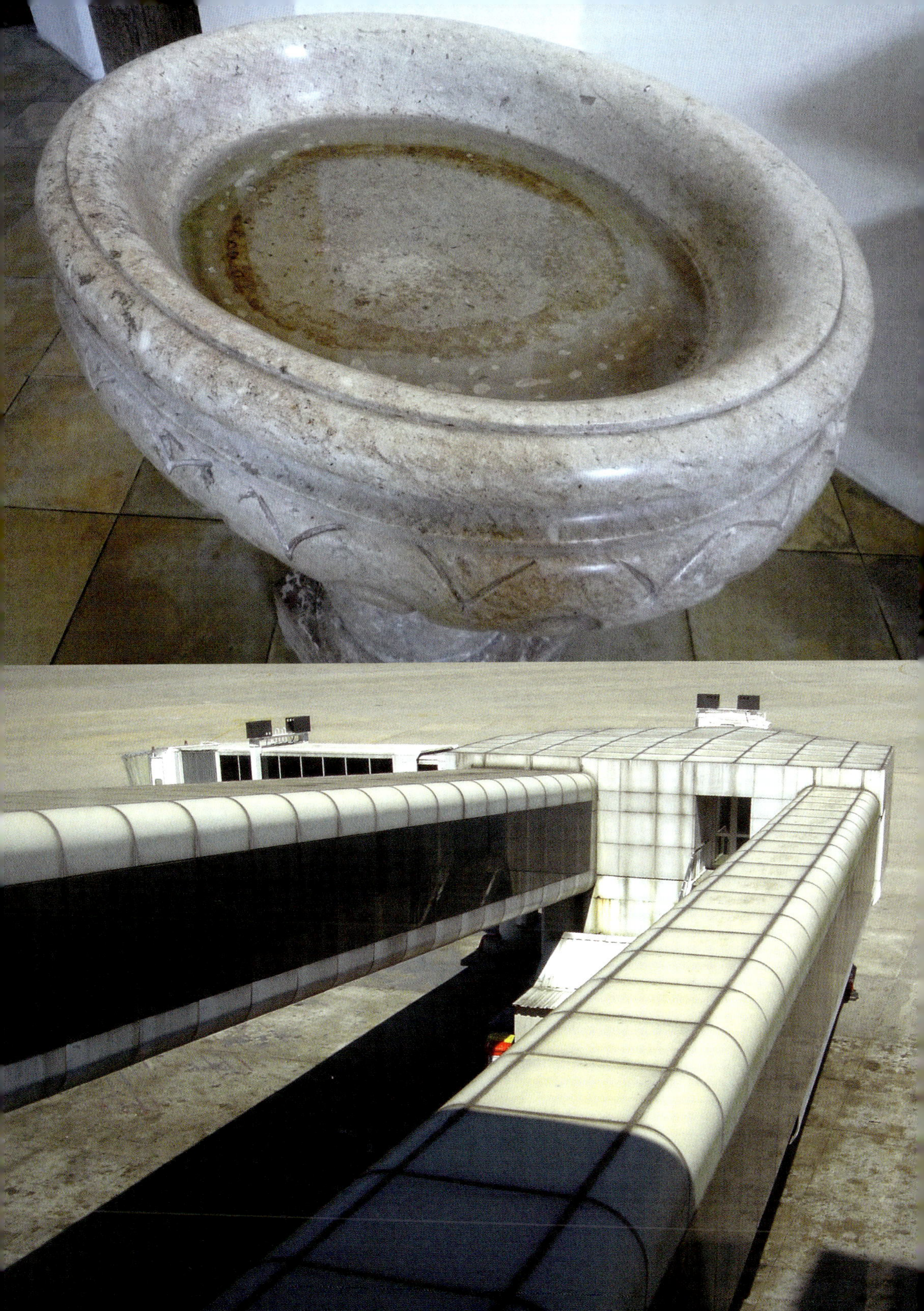

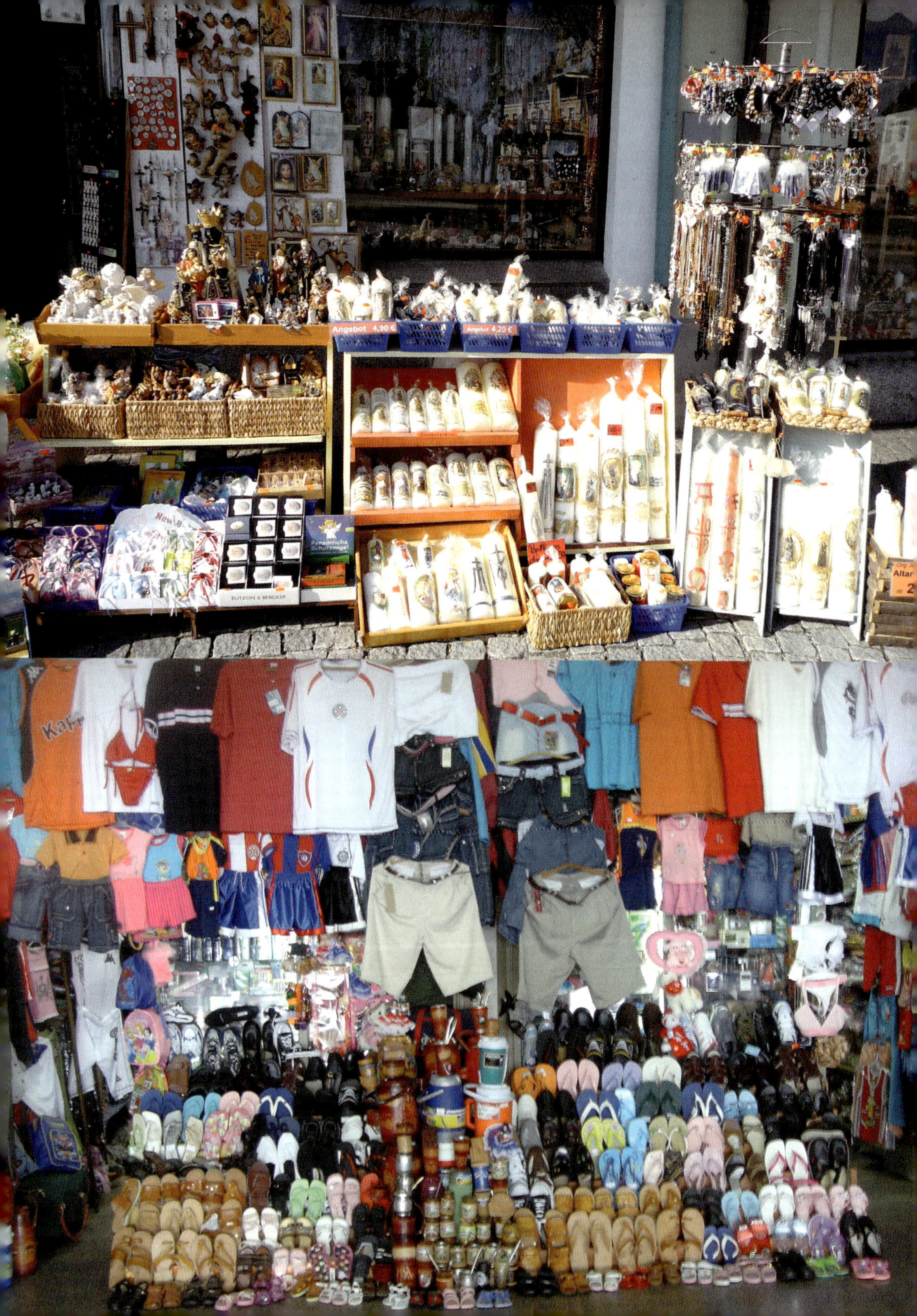

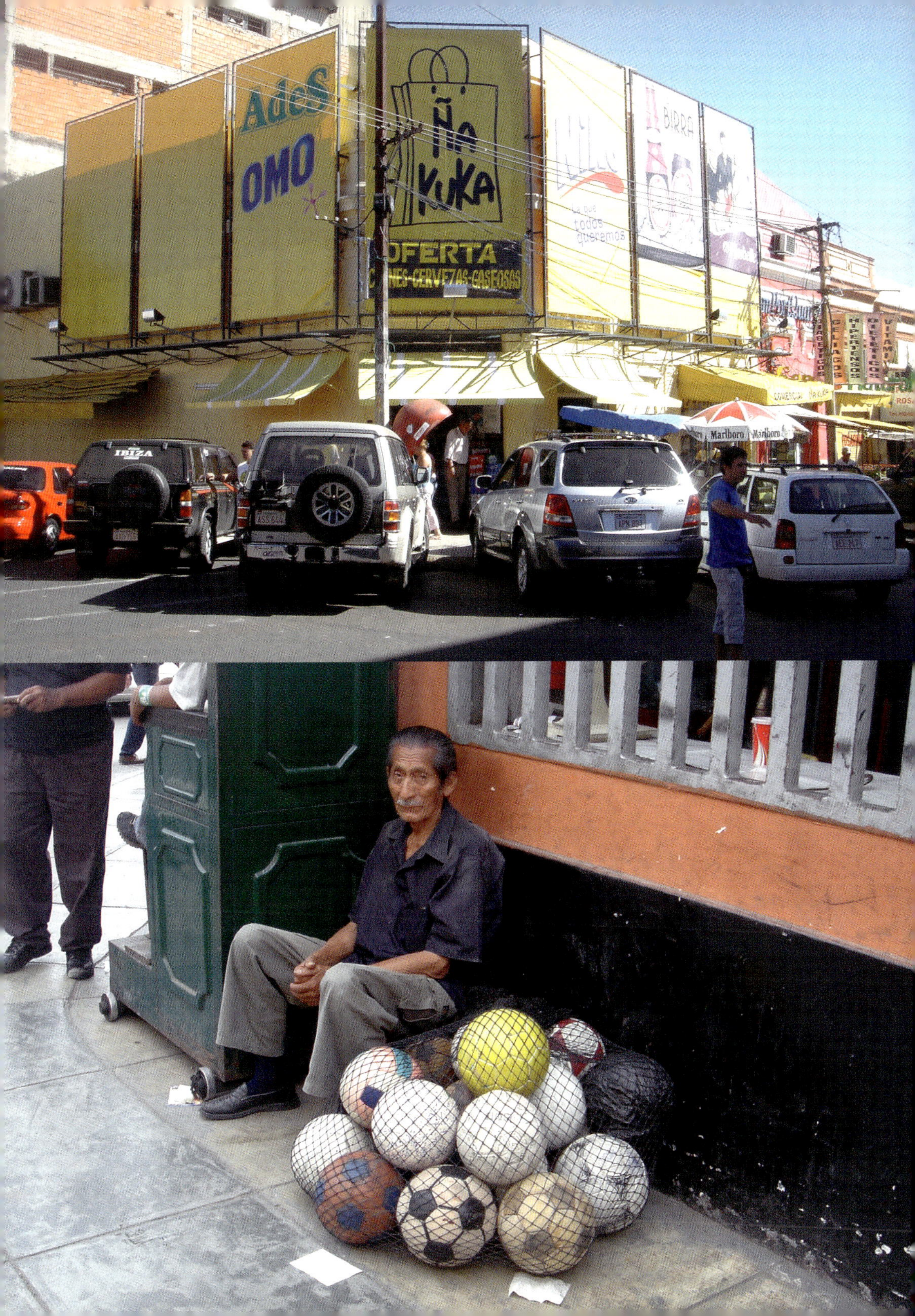
AdeS
OMO
Ña
Yuka
OFERTA
CIONES-CERVEZAS-GASEOSAS
Nils
La que
todos
queremos
BIRRA
Marlboro
Marlboro
IBIZA

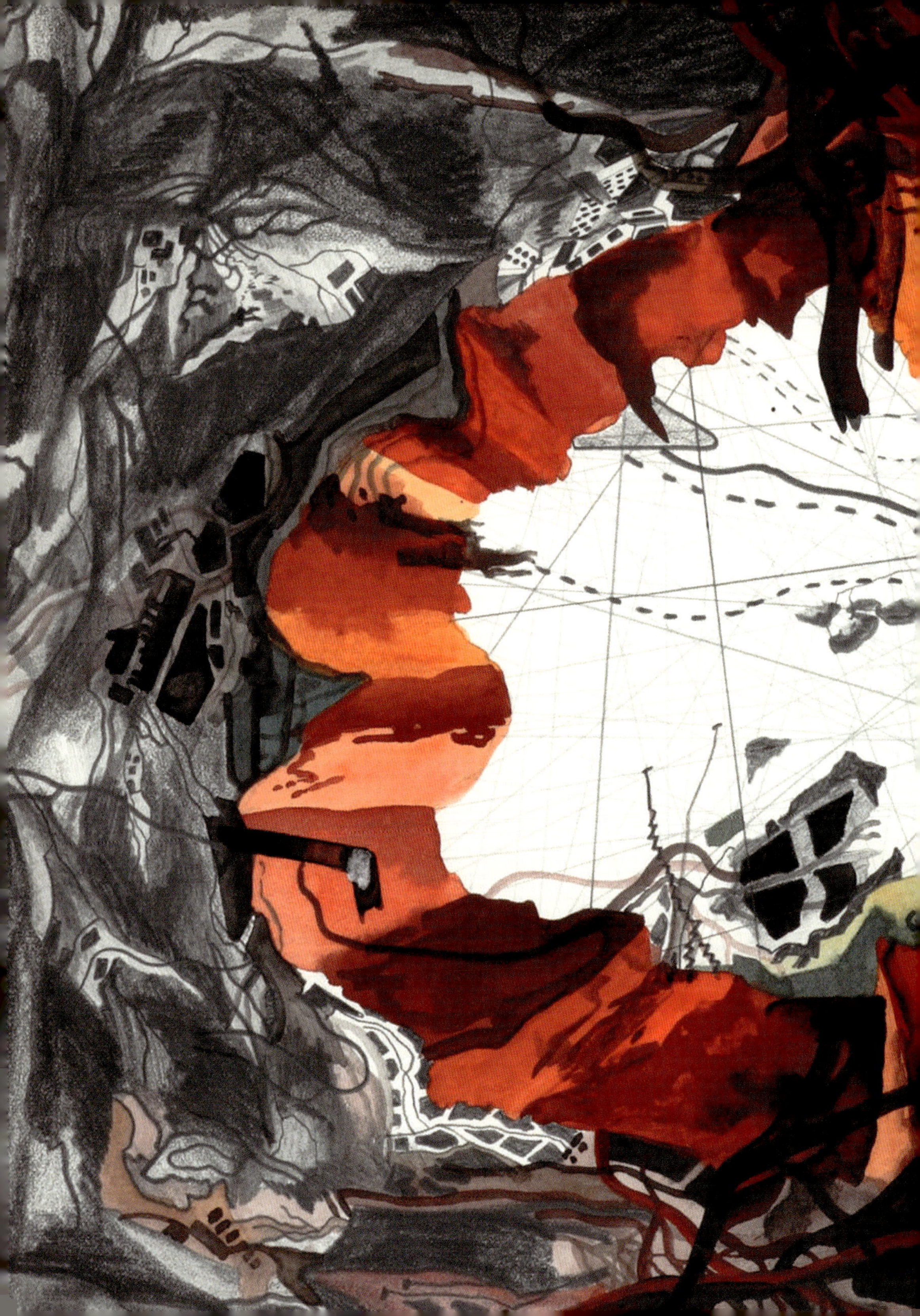

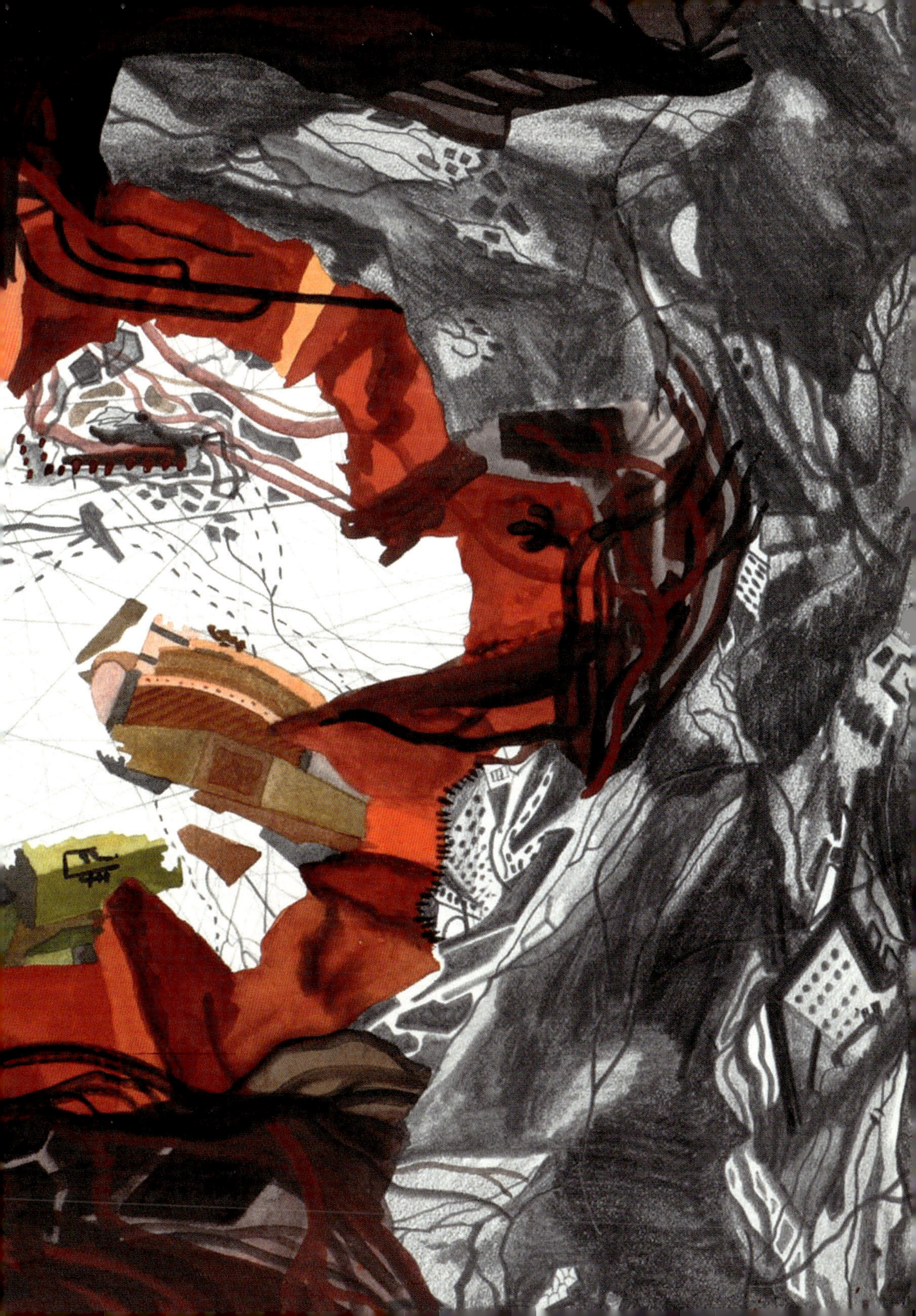

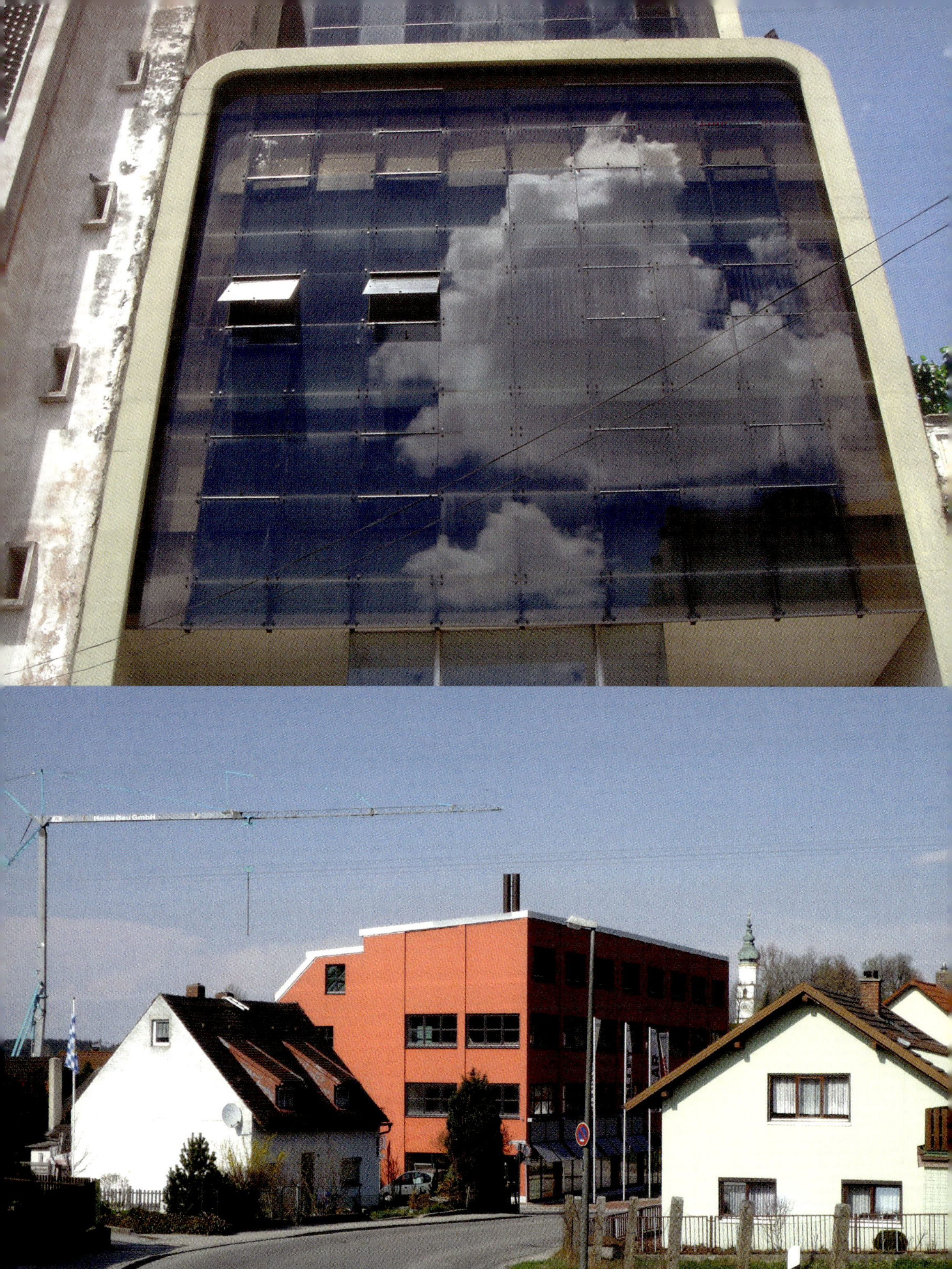
Heise Bau GmbH

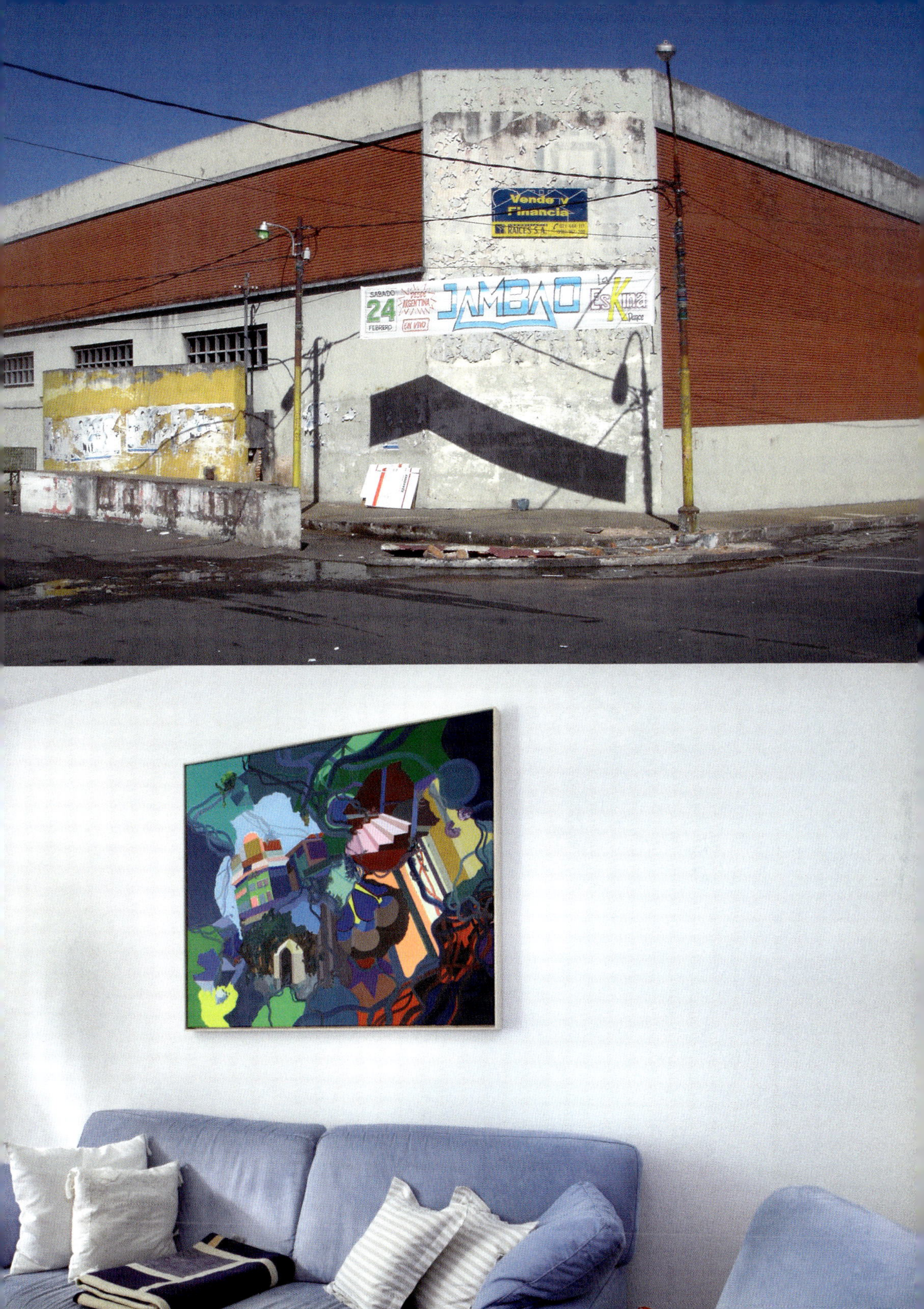

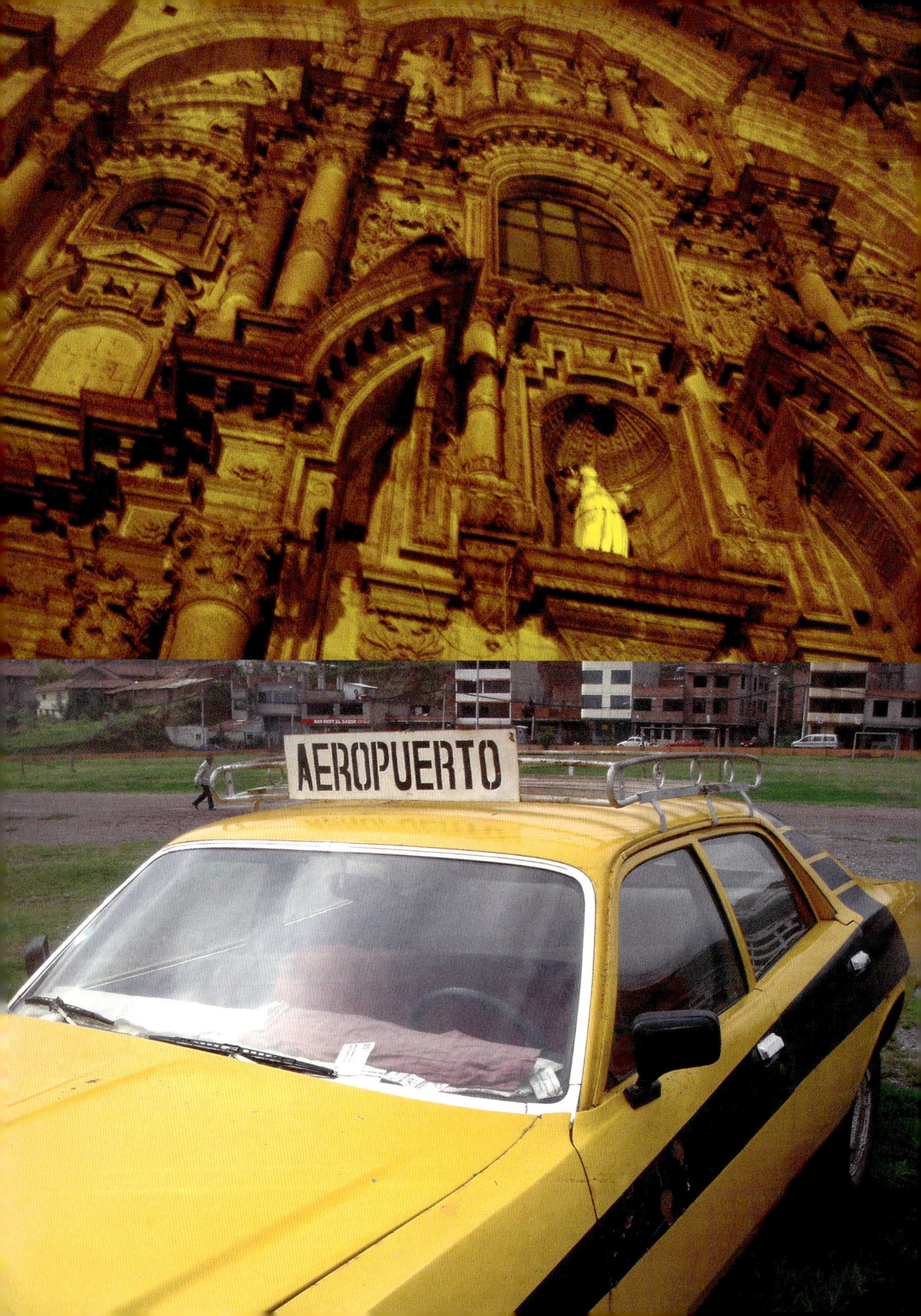
AEROPUERTO

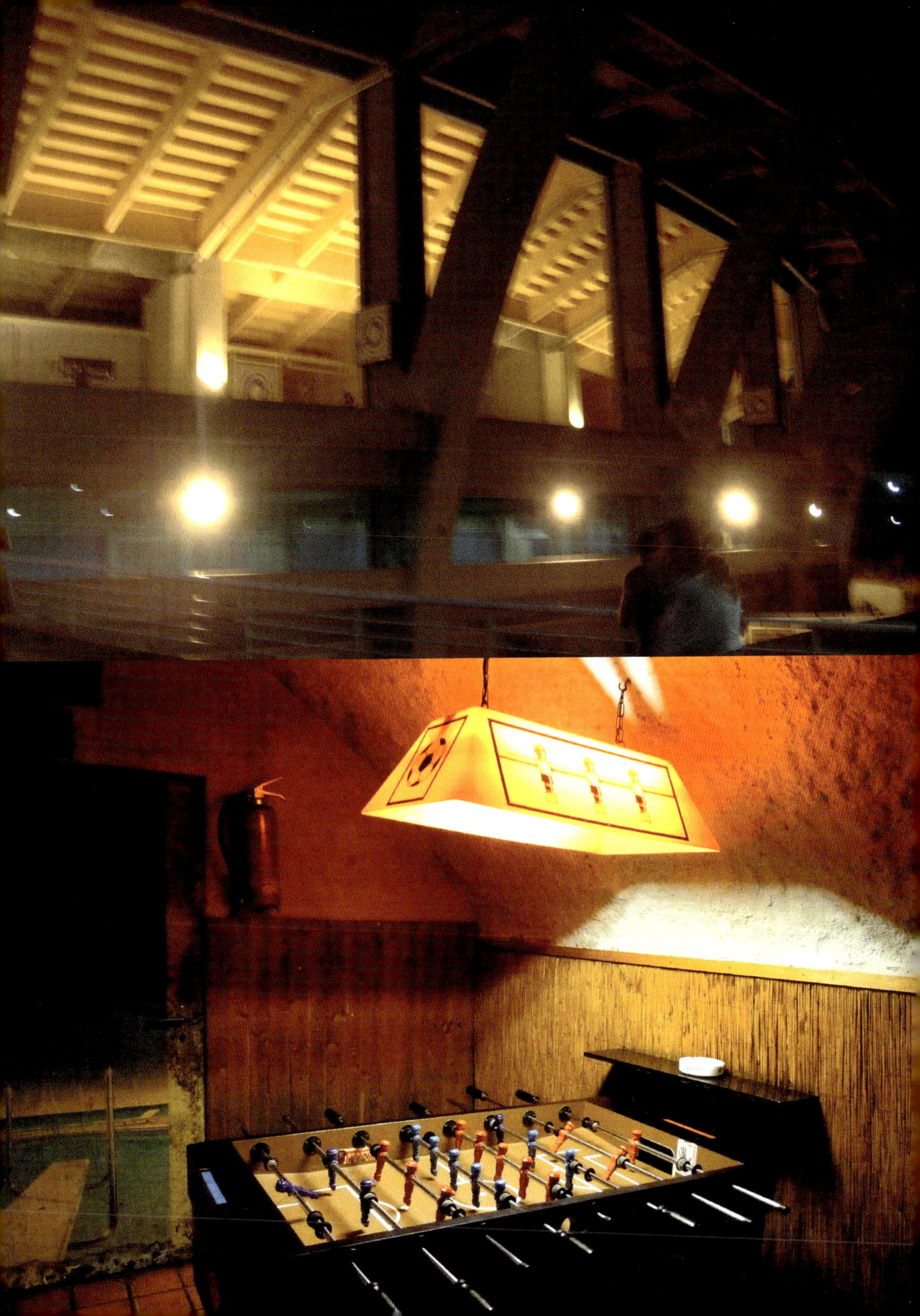

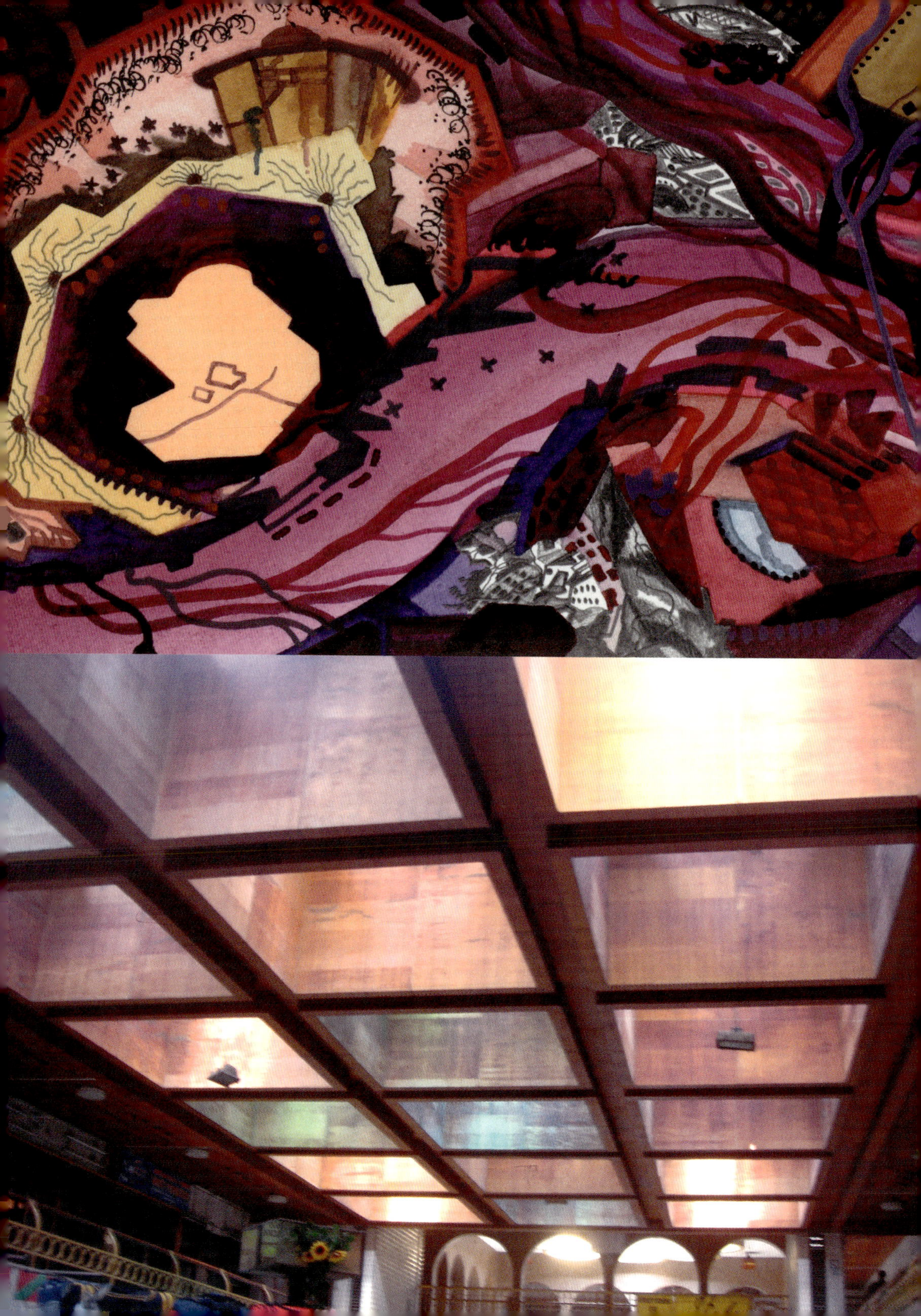

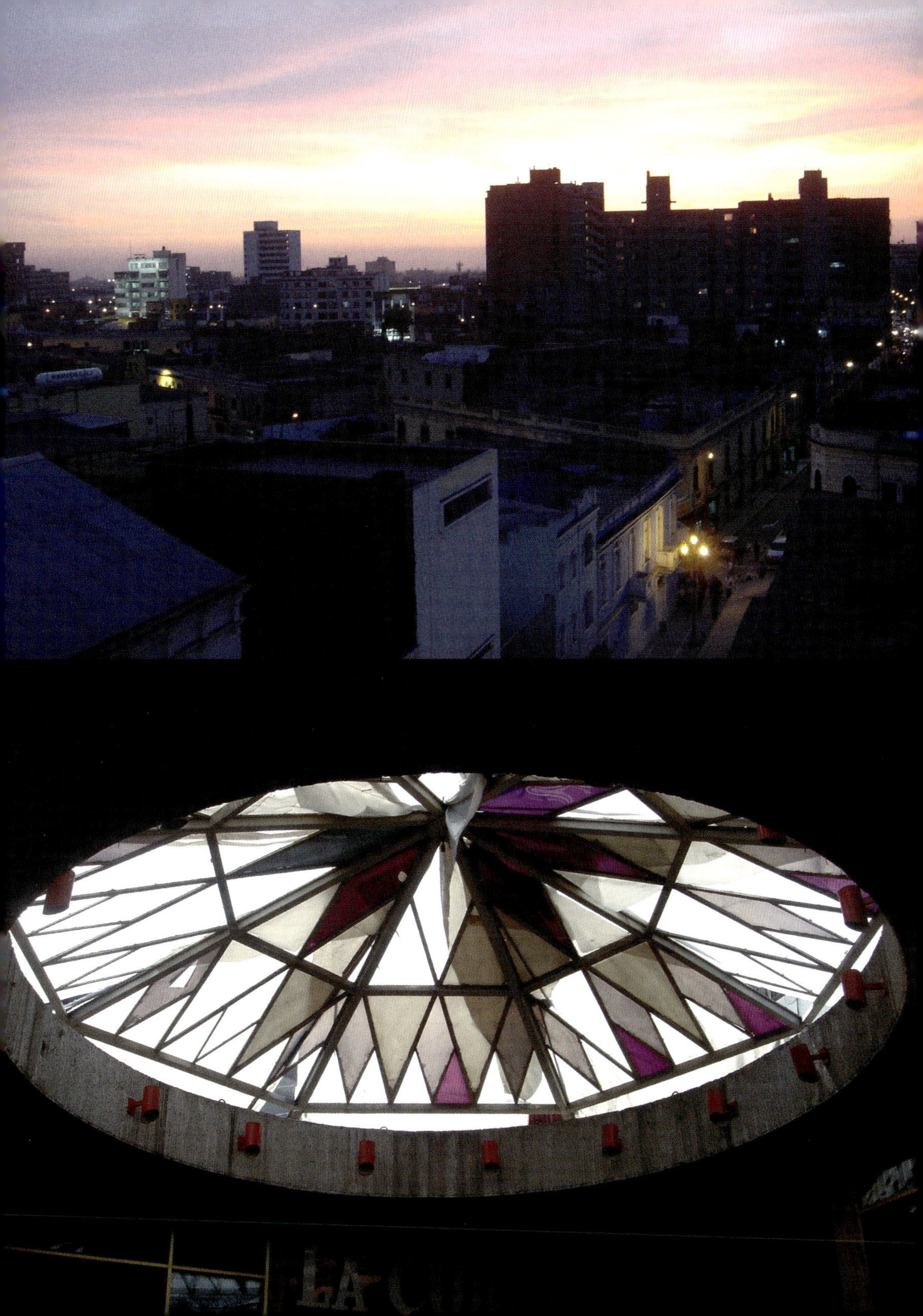

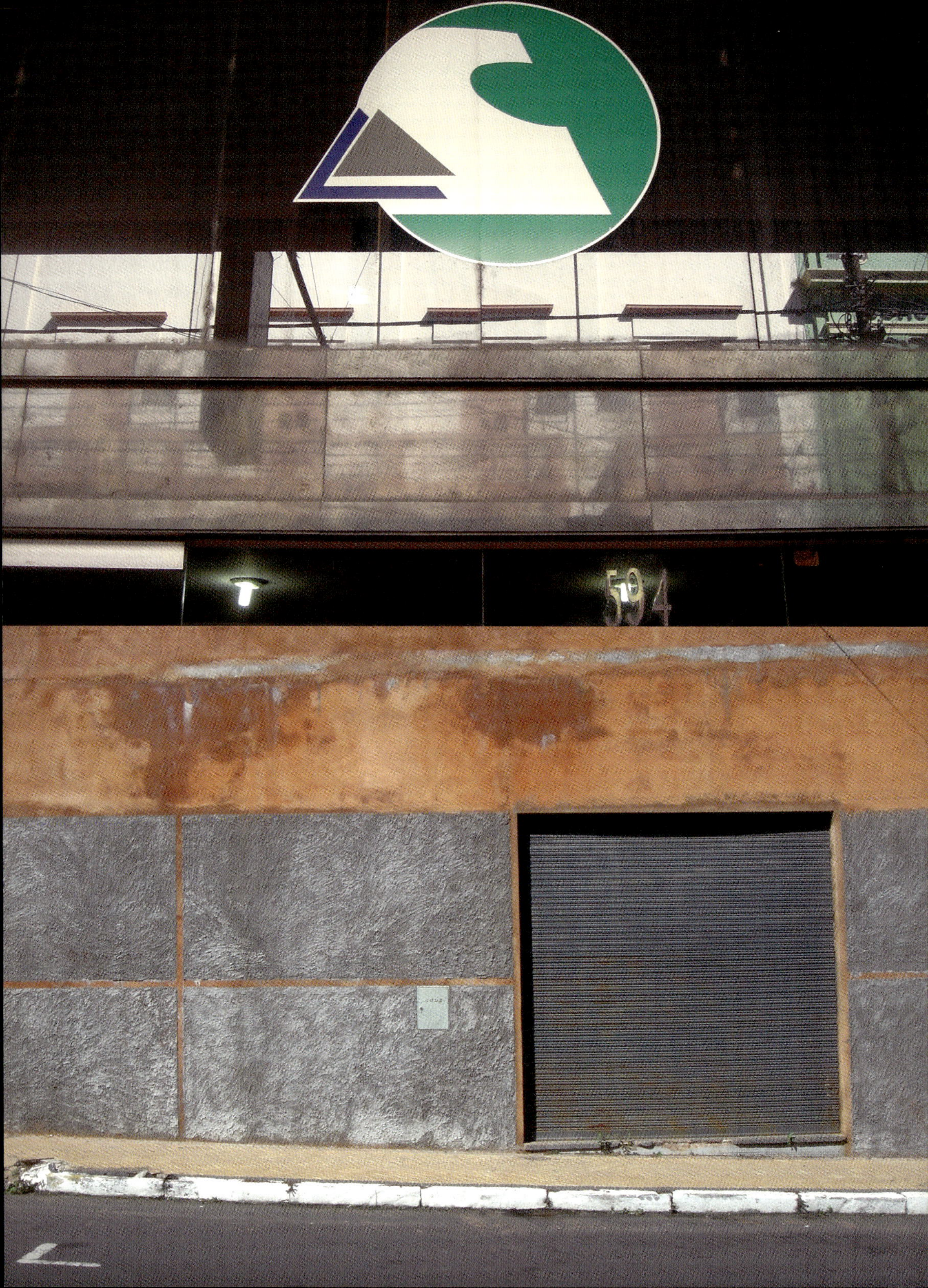

594

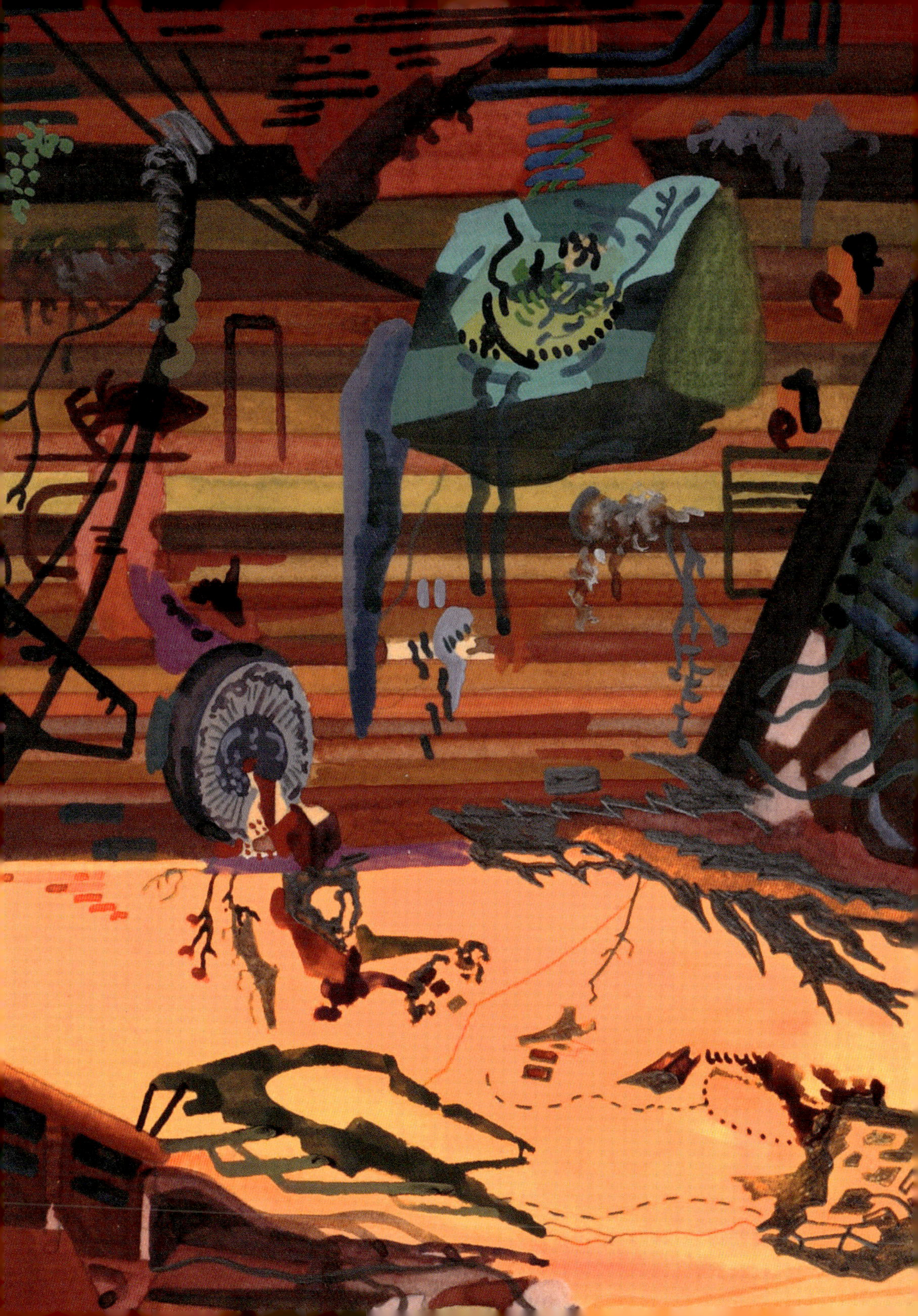

VORWORT | FOREWORD

Franz Ackermann in der Stadtgalerie von Altötting

Altötting – das „Herz Bayerns", ist seit über 1200 Jahren geistliches Zentrum und 500 Jahre bedeutendster Marienwallfahrtsort im deutschsprachigen Raum. Die Gnadenkapelle mit der Schwarzen Madonna und der sie umgebende weitläufige Kapellplatz sind zur Wallfahrtszeit das Ziel unzähliger Pilger aus Bayern, den Nachbarländern und auch ferneren Regionen.

In unmittelbarer Nachbarschaft zum „Bayerischen Nationalheiligtum" hat sich während der zurückliegenden zwanzig Jahre die ehemalige Missionsausstellung der Kapuziner als „Stadtgalerie" ebenfalls zu einem gut frequentierten Besichtigungsziel entwickelt. In Zusammenarbeit mit namhaften Künstlern, Künstlergruppen, Galerien, Museen und Kunstsammlern werden hier jeweils vom Frühjahr bis zum Herbst wechselnde Ausstellungen bildender Kunst gezeigt. Dass die Ausstellung „Lima, Altötting" von Professor Franz Ackermann als „außergewöhnlich" gelten darf, liegt einerseits in der Präsentation von Werken dieses international renommierten zeitgenössischen Künstlers in unserer kleinen Wallfahrtsstadt und zum anderen in der künstlerischen Gleichbehandlung der hier gestalteten Schauräume. Grundprinzip bei allen Projekten Ackermanns ist die nicht-hierarchische Betrachtung aller Ausstellungshäuser – nichts „von der Stange", sowie alles neue Arbeiten. Das Interesse an seinen panoramaartigen Einbauten in der Stadtgalerie Altötting war dementsprechend nicht nur in Kunst- und Kulturkreisen groß. Dem Künstler, den Sponsoren und allen weiteren Beteiligten gilt daher der besondere Dank für die Realisierung dieses, den Werkprozess und die Ausstellung dokumentierenden Katalogs.

Franz Ackermann, geboren 1963 in Neumarkt-St. Veit, ist in Altötting aufgewachsen, verbrachte hier ab der 6. Klasse seine Schulzeit und die ihn nicht zuletzt auch aus künstlerischer Sicht prägenden Jugendjahre. Am Altöttinger König-Karlmann-Gymnasium erhielt er wohl die entscheidenden Impulse mit der Förderung seines künstlerischen Talents im Leistungskurs Kunst unter seinem Fachlehrer Alto Hien und dessen Lehrerkollegen Manfred Bugl und Herbert Stern.

Heute sind das Reisen und die „Sehnsucht" nach der großen, weiten Welt für Franz Ackermann unverzichtbarer Teil seines künstlerischen Schaffens. Nicht minder bedeutend ist ihm die Rückbindung an seine bayerische Heimat, insbesondere an das „Herz Bayerns", den Wallfahrtsort Altötting, mit seinen spezifischen Gefühls- und Erlebniswerten. Folglich sind ihm die regelmäßigen Besuche bei seiner hier lebenden Mutter, die Kontakte zu den Jugendfreunden und die Teilnahme an den ortstypischen Festen im Jahreskreis stets wichtig geblieben.

Möglicherweise bringt die Inschrift am Jagdschloss Esting zum Ausdruck, welche Erkenntnis den erfahrenen Weltenbummler und „herausragendsten Vertreter zeitgenössischer Malerei" innerlich bewegt:

„Außerhalb Bayerns gibt es kein Leben … und wenn, dann kein solches!"

Herbert Hofauer

Erster Bürgermeister Altötting

Franz Ackermann at the City Gallery of Altötting

Altötting, the "Heart of Bavaria," has been an intellectual center for over 1,200 years. As the most important Marian pilgrimage town in the German speaking world, it has also been a lively pilgrimage destination for over 500 years. During pilgrimage season, the Gnadenkapelle (Chapel of Grace) with its Black Madonna and the spacious chapel square are visited by countless pilgrims from Bavaria, neighboring states and countries, and more distant regions.

The past twenty years have seen the development of the former mission exhibition of the Capuchins, which lies in direct proximity to the "Bavarian national shrine," into the "City Gallery"– which is now a well-frequented point of interest for visitors. In cooperation with well-known artists, artists' groups, galleries, museums and art collectors, this location features changing visual art exhibitions.

The fact that the exhibition "Lima,   Altötting" by Professor Franz Ackermann can be characterized as "exceptional" is due both to the presentation of works by this internationally renowned contemporary artist in our small pilgrimage town as well to the equal artistic attention given to the spaces in which they are displayed. A basic principle underlying all of Ackermann's projects is the non-hierarchic handling of all exhibition venues – his shows are never "off the rack," but consist of all-new works. The interest in his panorama-like installations in the City Gallery of Altötting was commensurately great and went far beyond artistic and cultural circles. The artist, the sponsors and all further participants deserve special thanks here for their contributions to the realization of this catalogue, which documents the working process and the exhibition itself.

Franz Ackermann, born in Neumarkt-St. Veit in 1963, grew up in Altötting. He went to school here from the sixth grade onward, and the period he spent here also included his formative years in an artistic sense. It was at the König-Karlmann-Gymnasium in Altötting that he received what were probably his most crucial impulses, through the nurturing of his artistic talent in the art major class led by art teacher Alto Hien and his colleagues Manfred Bugl and Herbert Stern.

Today, travel and a "longing" for the wide world constitute an essential element of Franz Ackermann's artistic creativity. No less important to him, however, is the connection to his home in Bavaria, especially to the "Heart of Bavaria," the pilgrimage town of Altötting, with its specific worlds of emotion and experience. Consequently, regular visits here to his mother, contacts to childhood friends and participation in typical local celebrations throughout the year have always remained important to him.

Possibly it is the inscription at the Hunting Lodge of Esting expresses the inner realization motivating this experienced world traveler and "most outstanding representative of contemporary painting":

"There is no life outside of Bavaria … and if there is, then it's nothing like this!"

Herbert Hofauer
First Mayor of Altötting

KÜNSTLICHE PARADIESE

Über Franz Ackermanns Kunst im Allgemeinen
und seine Arbeit für Altötting im Speziellen

1. TROPIK UND ENTROPIK | Man nehme eine Sandkiste und fülle zweierlei Sand hinein, eine Hälfte mit hellem, die andere mit dunklem. Dann nehme man ein Kind und lasse es in der Kiste im Kreis herumgehen, wieder und immer wieder, und im Lauf der Zeit werden sich die beiden, ursprünglich so leicht zu unterscheidenden Materialien zu einem diffusen Grau vermischen. Nun bitte man das Kind, rückwärts zu gehen, doch anders als bei einem Film, den man umgekehrt abspult, wird sich kein Ausgangszustand wiederherstellen lassen. Im Gegenteil: Ob vorwärts oder in Gegenrichtung – die beiden Sandflächen werden sich weiter vermengen, hinein in die völlige Ununterscheidbarkeit. Robert Smithson, der Veteran der Land Art, hat sich dieser kleinen Geschichte gern bedient, um vom Wirken der Entropie zu erzählen. Menschliche Tätigkeit bringt die Welt nur durcheinander, ihr Gesetz ist die Unordnung. Der zweite Hauptsatz der Thermodynamik lässt es unausweichlich erscheinen: Was geordnet war, gerät aus den Fugen, was differenziert war, vermischt sich. Menschliche Arbeit ist Reduktion von Komplexität. Und jede Reduktion von Komplexität fügt der Welt neue Komplexität hinzu. Nichts zu machen.

Franz Ackermann ist ein Reisender. Das Unterwegssein ist, man hat es oft betont, die Essenz seiner Kunst. Hier, im Irgendwo, entstehen die Skizzen und Skripts, die in bester altmeisterlicher Tradition das Disegno liefern, die zeichnerische Grundlage dafür, dass es später Gemälde gibt, Installationen, Raumausstattungen von ausladender Geste und panoramatischer Weite. Ackermanns Eingriffe in den Ausstellungsort sind buchstäblich Environments, wie man das einst in den Sechzigern nannte, multimediale Darbietungen in schillernder Facettiertheit, in denen sich die Umgebung widerspiegelt. Das ökologische System wird ästhetisches. Nicht, dass Ackermann dem Entropischen entkäme. Seine „Mental Maps", wie er die Ergebnisse seines Reisens nennt, kämpfen wie überall mit der Erosion des Spezifischen, und die Hochhäuser und Straßenecken, die Parks und Highways sehen in Singapur aus wie in Sao Paulo. Entsprechend sehen sie auch auf Ackermanns Notaten einander ähnlich, und kein Ausflug an den Äquator ist gefeit vor dem Entropenkoller.

Dazu kommt der Aufenthalt an den „Nicht-Orten", wie Marc Augé sie in einem einflussreichen Buch der frühen Neunziger beschrieben hat, in den Flughäfen, Hotels, Verkehrsmitteln und Fast-Food-Stationen, in denen man immer mehr Lebenszeit zubringt und die ihrerseits geprägt sind von der Unzuständigkeit von Übergangszonen. Derlei Notwendigkeiten, wie sie die postmoderne Ubiquität mit sich bringt, kleidet man gern in eine drastische, weil von der Bedrohung schwärmende und das Authentische forcierende Metapher: man nennt es Nomadentum. Die jettende Existenz der Gegenwart allerdings ist keineswegs vom Hunger bedroht und die Wasserstelle in einigen Kilometern hat prinzipiell eine andere Dimension der Notwendigkeit, als der nächste Internet-Anschluss. Den Hirten und Herden, die das Nomadentum verkörpern, ist es von vornherein gerade nicht einerlei, wo sie sich befinden. Ihr Blick ist streng justiert auf die Möglichkeiten vor eben dem Ort, der ein anthropologischer Ort ist, und damit das Gegenteil jener Diffusion, die die Nicht-Orte kennzeichnet.

Kunst ist, wie jede menschliche Aktivität, Kontingenzbannung. Die Tatsache, dass etwas jederzeit auch anders sein könnte, genau das meint Kontingenz, soll ungeschehen gemacht werden. Kontingenz ist Komplexität und Arbeit gegen sie ist Reduktion von Komplexität. Dass das nicht zu haben ist, ist oben bereits beschrieben worden und letztlich müsste man als Künstler an dem Mechanismus verzweifeln. Franz Ackermanns Arbeit ist auf eine erstaunliche Weise diesem Problem nahe. Darin liegt die Eminenz seines Werkes. Es ist eine Art von dichter Beschreibung, die seine Blätter, Tafeln, Bühnen entfalten, eine Beschreibung, die der Welt, von der sie handelt, dezidiert entspricht. Die Einfalt der Wirklichkeit wird gekontert von der Vielfalt und es ist schlechterdings nicht zu entscheiden, ob diese Bilder das Immergleiche illustrieren, oder ihm in der Facettierung, Ausfaltung und potpourrihaften Vermengung von Eindrücken die trotzige Behauptung von Verschiedenheit entgegensetzen.

Der Leitgegensatz unserer Zeit heißt Ausdifferenzierung versus Entdifferenzierung. Bringen, so gilt die Frage, der Kapitalismus, die weltweite Kommunikation und die Vernetzung das Dasein des Erdenbürgers durcheinander oder sperren sie es in das stählerne Gehäuse der Gleichförmigkeit? Ist Entwurzelung oder ist Uniformierung unser Schicksal? Sind alle anders oder alle gleich? Tendiert die Realität zur Parzellierung ins Kleine oder zur Nivellierung ins Große? Lebt die Welt von den Emanzipationen, Entmarginalisierungen und Aufwertungen des Peripheren oder ist Globalisierung ihr Schicksal? Nicht, dass Ackermanns Arbeit dieses Problem lösen könnte. Aber wie kaum ein zweites bringt sie es auf den Punkt, indem sie die Frage aufwirft, die Frage aufzeigt, sie buchstäblich zeigt mit ihren ureigenen piktoralen Mitteln.

2. DRAUSSEN UND DRINNEN | Deutlicher denn je hat Franz Ackermann in der Stadtgalerie Altötting ein Panorama ins Werk gesetzt. Die Paneele, die die Wände zur Gänze umkleiden und die den Fond bilden für die in sich zentrierten Spektakel der Arbeiten auf Papier oder Leinwand, setzen einander unermüdlich fort, sie reichen sich gewissermaßen weiter und gestalten ein Kontinuum, das nirgends beginnt und nirgends endet. Ein Effekt des Allover wird gesetzt, eine Welt in der Welt wird formiert, mit ihr motivisch verbunden, vor allem aber auch rhetorisch. Ein solches Panorama setzt sich zur Realität metonymisch in Bezug, als Ausschnitt, der in seiner Fragmentiertheit doch wieder als Ganzheit funktioniert. Die Welt ist alles, was der Fall ist, wie der berühmte Anfangssatz von Ludwig Wittgensteins „Tractatus" weiß. Auch in Franz Ackermanns Welt ist alles der Fall, ein Alles en miniature, stellvertretend für die Totalität der Dinge.

Am 25. Mai 1793 eröffnete Robert Barker am Londoner Leicester Square die erste Panorama-Rotunde und damit einem ganzen Jahrhundert eine neue Aussicht. Bevor das Kino kam, erfüllte das Rundbild die Spektakelbedürfnisse einer sich demokratisierenden, die Massenunterhaltung forcierenden und Amüsement gegen Geld zur Verfügung stellenden Epoche. Es war der Innenseite eines Zylinders appliziert und versprach mit seiner 360-Grad Perspektive die Totale dessen, was zu dem Moment, wo man sich in ihm befand, zu sehen sein konnte; die Leinwand, die die Dinge vor Augen stellte, setzte das Bild in eines mit seiner Umgebung.

Abgeschlossenheit und Augenzeugenschaft, Absorption und Theatralik brachten sich simultan zur Geltung. Es war eine durch und durch artifizielle Ganzheit, die das Panorama in Szene setzte, doch es war eine Ganzheit, zu der man sich nicht durch eine spezielle ästhetische Haltung disponieren musste; diese Ganzheit war einfach da, als hermetisches Allüberall einer künstlichen Gegenwelt, die doch nichts anderes vorführte als das, was man kannte und wiedererkennen konnte. Zugleich befand man sich in der privilegierten Position eines festen Standpunktes, in einer fixen, architektonisch wie bildperspektivisch garantierten Mitte; die Wirklichkeit dieses Rundbildes war also konzentrisch; und sie war auf jene eindeutige Weise erhaben, dass sie sich auf eine Plattform bezog, der gegenüber sie sich in Aufsicht darbot. Das Panorama war von vornherein ein Exerzierfeld für die Kontingenz der Welt und dafür, wie man sie bannt: Es wechselte je nach Nachfrage und ökonomischem Kalkül die Szenerien, doch jede Veränderung brachte sich aufs Neue mit der Evidenz des Anfangs- und Endlosen zur Geltung. Das Panorama war die Instanz par excellence für die Gültigkeit des Hier und Jetzt: Was es an Sujets, Themen und Motiven anbot, hatte sein tatsächliches Pendant in der Wirklichkeit des Optischen; und wie es diese Dinge zeigte, fügten sie sich ein in das Kontinuum, das das Bild selbst war und damit wiederum als real vorführte.

Hätte es dieses Prinzip nicht seit mehr als 200 Jahren gegeben, Ackermann hätte es erfunden. In perfekter Widerspiegelung macht es das Draußen der realen Welt zum Drinnen der artifiziellen. In aller Paradoxie: Das Panorama gibt einen Vorschein dessen, wie kompliziert die Welt ist, indem es selber kompliziert ist und doch auf eine Weise Komplexität bannt, dass der Mechanismus der Reduktion erst richtig augenfällig wird. Schon 1806 stand in Millins „Dictionnaire des beaux arts" die folgende Beschwerde zu lesen: „Kann man sich etwas Absurderes und Unangenehmeres vorstellen als in einem Panorama all die Wagen zu sehen, all die Leute zu Fuß oder zu Pferd, die immer im Begriff sind, sich zu bewegen, und doch immer auf der Stelle bleiben; die Kutscher, die in alle Ewigkeit ihre Peitsche schwingen, die Pferde, die sich immer aufbäumen; die Hunde, die unentwegt aufeinander losgehen; die Kinder, die ständig fallen, ohne jemals die Erde zu berühren etc. etc." Das Panorama lieferte pure Gleichzeitigkeit, aber diese Simultanität konnte gegen es verwendet werden als willkürliche Stillstellung; zu detailverliebt, ausgeschmückt und episch war seine Schilderung, als dass noch Momenthaftigkeit zu greifen gewesen wäre. Ausschnitthaftigkeit ist eine Bedingung, mit der jedes Bild zu kämpfen hat, aber erst jetzt, in der Perfektion einer eigenen Welt, die das Panorama inszenierte, war es als Problem erkannt. Das räumliche Kontinuum, die räumliche Totalität, die das Rundumbild erreicht, macht umso deutlicher, dass das Theatralische auch eine zeitliche Dimension hat. Ihr Preis ist die Stillstellung.

Das Fugel-Panorama in Altötting, beispielhaft für die Gattung und singulär in Deutschland, versucht eine Lösung, indem es Narration einführt. Ein Erzähler, der Radio-Sprecher Gustl Weishappl, ist engagiert worden, um dem Allüberall des Blicks auf Golgatha und die Kreuzigung mit jener Abfolge zu kommen, die sich ergibt, wenn etwas gelesen und gesagt wird.

Texte funktionieren kontinuierend und ergänzen damit das Koexistierende der Bilder. Die Besucher hören zu und sehen hin und wähnen sich, funktioniert die Illusion, mitten im Geschehen. Die Stillstellung der Zeit ist aufgeweicht. Jetzt, in der Zusammenarbeit von piktoraler und literaler Sprache, ist eine Ganzheit erreicht, doch auch sie ist synthetisch, artifiziell, Ergebnis einer Hybridisierung.

Franz Ackermann hat sich für seine Altöttinger Installation explizit auf Fugels „Weltberühmtheit Europas", wie es in den diversen Werbe-Utensilien so schön heißt, bezogen. Keine Beschriftungen stören den Gesamteindruck, kein Werk wird als Solitär ausgewiesen. Gleichsam organisch gehen die Sujets, Themen und Motive ineinander über, weiten sich ins Dreidimensionale und reichern sich mit realen Gegenständen an, dem Boot, den Broschüren, wie es auch bei Fugel Objekte der Realität gibt: Sie schaffen das sogenannte „Faux Terrain" des Panoramas, das falsche Gelände, das im Kontext des Künstlich-Künstlerischen dadurch zu einem falschen wird, dass es mit richtigen Gegenständen arbeitet. Mit der Referenz auf das Fugel-Panorama ist das Ackermann-Panorama nichts anderes als geerdet. Und die Entropik, die die Grund-Bedingung eines Schaffens in der Welt im Allgemeinen und in Ackermanns Oeuvre im Besonderen abgibt, bekommt eine ungeahnte Topografie. Das Durcheinander der Welt wird versetzt mit Heimat.

Als Marc Augé sein Buch über die „Nicht-Orte", die „Non-Lieux" publizierte, lag das Prinzip Ortsspezifik, der berühmte Schwanengesang aus den Achtzigern, in den letzten Zügen. Site Specifity hatte noch eine Art Refugium für den anthropologischen Ort abgegeben; sie war das Relikt der unverwechselbaren Lokalität, bevor sie abgelöst wurde von jenem Prinzip des Abstellens von Dingen als Kunst, das mit dem Begriff Drop Sculpture witziger bezeichnet wird als es gemeint ist. Im Ganzen nun ist Ackermanns Installation ortsspezifisch. Und der anthropologische Ort, der sich jetzt auftut, ist der ureigene, ist der buchstäbliche Ort, aus dem der Künstler kommt, der Ort, der eine Kleinstadt ist, mit seinem Milieu, mit seinen Bekannten und Verwandten und den Erinnerungen an die Kindheit und die verlorene Zeit. Natürlich ist das nur einmal möglich, dann, wenn Ackermann in seinem Heimat-Ort ausstellt. Doch die Zusatzgratifikation, die sich dabei ergibt, die weitere Dimension, die sich ermessen lässt und die sich ausmessen lässt, bleibt dem Oeuvre insgesamt erhalten.

3. SCHICHTEN UND SCHICHTUNGEN | Ackermanns Display für Altötting hat, apropos Dimension, seinen Zug in die Tiefe. Bei aller Planimetrik, dem Ausbreiten und Ausweiten in eine panoramatische Horizontale, gibt es auch ein Stück Stratifikation. Es ergibt sich in den Schichten und Schichtungen, im Hintereinander und Übereinander von Bildern und Bildteilen, in den Durchblicken, Perforierungen, Gemengen, die die Simultanität mit dem Wissen um die Verschiedenheit ihrer Herkunft versetzen. Verschiedene Lagen kommen zusammen, Sedimente gleichsam, als hätte es verschiedene Zeiten gegeben, zu denen sie entstanden sind und die sie nun Revue passieren lassen. Tatsächlich sind es diverse Momente, die hier aufscheinen,

Ackermanns Reise die Panamericana entlang, die einen Gutteil der Motive bereitstellt, aber auch Relikte von anderen Präsentationen, dazu die Intervention in den speziellen Raum der Stadtgalerie sowie die jeweiligen Aktualisierungen, die die Rahmung besorgt. In der Transparenz in sich wieder opaker Details, in ihrer Monochromie und ihrer Zartheit, in den Partien von Figürlichem und der Integration von Textteilen gemahnt Ackermanns Arbeit an das Prinzip Palimpsest, an jenes altehrwürdige Medium, dem es nicht zuletzt zu verdanken ist, dass sich antike Spuren erhalten haben. Palimpseste sind Seiten mit verschiedenen Lagen von Schrift aus verschiedenen Epochen, Überschreibungen eines ausgedienten durch einen aktuellen Text. Der berühmteste Palimpsest ist die mittelalterliche Handschrift natürlich christlichen Inhalts, die ein längst ausgedientes Pergament verwendete, das wiederum mit antikem Gedankengut, nämlich Ciceros „de re publica", beschriftet war; nur so hat sich der politische Traktat überhaupt für die Nachwelt retten lassen. Palimpseste sind jedenfalls uralt, ihre Entdeckung indes ist genuin modern.

Ackermanns Installation ist materiell und medial ein Palimpsest. Darüber hinaus ist sie es metaphorisch. Sie funktioniert als Palimpsest, weil sie mit einer Art mentaler Markierung arbeitet, eben mittels „Mental Maps", wie Ackermann es selbst nennt. Thomas De Quincey hat die Idee, dass auch das Gedächtnis als Palimpsest strukturiert ist, in die Kulturgeschichte eingeführt: So schreibt er, im Jahr 1845, folgendes: „What else than a natural and mighty palimpsest is the human brain? Such a palimpsest is my brain; such a palimpsest, O reader, is yours. Everlasting layers of ideas, images, feelings, have fallen upon your brain softly as light. Each succession has seemed to bury all that went before. And yet in reality not one has been extinguished." Nichts ist gelöscht im Palimpsest des menschlichen Hirns, alles bleibt erhalten an Ideen, Bildern, Gefühlen, und dadurch wird es nicht weniger als ewig, everlasting.

Charles Baudelaire war einer der fleißigsten Interpreten De Quinceys, dessen „Bekenntnisse eines Opiumessers" Einzug gefunden haben in Baudelaires narratives Poem „Die künstlichen Paradiese". Hier hat der Literat ein Kapitel eingefügt, das eben den Titel „le palimpseste" trägt. Baudelaire erinnert darin an einen Literaten, der all seine Manuskripte zerstörte, sie, wie es heißt, einem „effroyable holocauste" zuführte, bevor sie jemals die Chance auf Publizierung hatten. Die Begründung fürs Autodafé ist folgende: „Warum nicht? Was wirklich wichtig daran war, ist, dass diese Dinge geschaffen worden sind; sie sind geschaffen worden, also gibt es sie." Sie sind sowieso eingedrungen und haben sich sowieso eingebrannt in das Gedächtnis, und dort bleiben sie unabhängig von aller Realisierungsform erhalten. Denn: „Le palimpseste de la mémoire est indestructible". Der Palimpsest der Erinnerung ist unzerstörbar.

Der Palimpsest ist nicht nur eine buchstäbliche Erscheinung, in der sich Ackermanns Arbeit darbietet. Der Palimpsest ist eine Metapher, und sie gemahnt an eine Erinnerung, in der sich visuelle Erfahrung und Angelesenes, Spuren von Gesehenem und alltäglicher Austausch sedimentierten. Der Palimpsest, der Ackermanns Bildwelten sind, funktioniert notwendig nach Maßgabe ihrer medialen Bedingungen; er funktioniert simultan. Doch was darauf alles zu

sehen ist, verdankt sich dem Vielerlei diverser systematischer Alter. Gerade in der Gleichzeitigkeit ist zu sehen, was es an Ungleichzeitigem gibt. Beides, das Gleich- wie das Ungleichzeitige,
gibt der Zeit ihre Fasson.

Künstliche Paradiese: Das wäre der Begriff, Baudelaire abgelauscht, für Ackermanns
Inszenierung für Altötting. Gegenwelten in aller Artifizialität hat er ins Werk gesetzt, die für
den glücklichen Moment die Realität und ihre Kompliziertheit in die Buntheit bannen, in ein
farbenstarkes Spektakel, das vergessen macht, wie auschnitthaft es notwendigerweise ist
und wie vermittelt seine Unmittelbarkeit. Künstliche Paradiese, paradis artificiels: Wer sie
betritt, tut das im Wissen darum, dass wir vertrieben sind aus dem einen Paradies, aus dem
Garten Eden, denn der Prozess der Erkenntnis ist unwiderruflich. Doch immerhin hat das
Paradies einen zweiten Eingang, und an diesem Tor wird nicht ab-, sondern hereingewiesen.
Der Wächter ist ein Künstler.

ARTIFICIAL PARADISES

Franz Ackermann's Art and His Work for Altötting

What am I doing here?
Arthur Rimbaud writing home from Ethiopia,
cited after Bruce Chatwin, "The Songlines"

1. TROPIC AND ENTROPIC | Take a sandbox and fill it with two types of sand, one light, the other dark. Then take a child and let it walk around in a circle in the sandbox, again and again. In the course of time the two different materials, which at first were so easy to distinguish, will become mixed in a diffuse gray. Ask the child to go backwards. Unlike playing a film backwards, this will not return the system to its original state. Regardless of whether the motion is backwards or forwards, the two sands continue to mix, to the point of complete indifferentiability. Robert Smithson, the veteran of Land Art, liked to use this little story as a means of describing the principle of entropy. Human activity only makes the world more mixed up, its law is that of disorder. The second law of thermodynamics makes it appear inevitable: that which was ordered will go to pieces, that which is differentiated will become mixed. Human work is the reduction of complexity. And every reduction of complexity imposes new complexity on the world. Nothing to be done about it.

Franz Ackermann is a traveler. Being on the road, many a critic has observed, is the essence of his art. Here, somewhere, is where the sketches and scripts are created, which in the best old-masterly tradition provide the disegno – the drawing that serves as the basis for the painting – for installations and spatial designs of expansive gesture and panoramic breadth. Ackermann's interventions in the exhibition space are literally environments, as they used to be called in the sixties, multimedia offerings of scintillating many-facetedness in which the surroundings are reflected. The ecological system is rendered aesthetic. Not that Ackermann could escape the entropic pull. His "Mental Maps", as he refers to the products of his travels, struggle with the overall erosion of the specific. The high-rises and street corners, the parks and highways in Singapore look like they do in Sao Paulo. Correspondingly, they are also similar in Ackermann's jottings, and no excursion to the equator is immune to the entropic madness.

And then there are the sojourns in non-places, as Marc Augé described them in his influential book of the early 1990s, in the airports, hotels, public conveyances and fast-food stations in which one increasingly spends one's time, and which are marked by the unspecificity of transit zones. There is a fondness for clothing these necessary developments of postmodern ubiquity in a drastic metaphor, romantically expressing their threats and stressing authenticity: the new nomadism. And yet the jetting existence of the present is in no way threatened by hunger. Getting to the next watering place several miles away has a necessity of fundamentally different significance than finding the next internet access point. The attitude of the shepherds and herds of true nomadism toward the place where they happen to find themselves at present is in no way one of indifference. Their gaze is strictly focused on the possibilities of the place, which is an anthropological place, and thus the opposite of the diffusion that characterizes the non-place.

Art, like every human activity, is the banishing of contingency. The fact that something could at any time be different, and this is precisely the meaning of contingency, is to be undone. Contingency is complexity, and work against it is the reduction of complexity. That this end is not to be achieved has already been established above, and thus the artist is also being driven toward despair by this mechanism. Franz Ackermann's work is very close to this problem in an astonishing way. Therein lies the eminence of his work. There is a sort of thick description that is unfolded in his graphics, panels and settings, a description that decidedly corresponds to the world it deals with. The simplicity of reality is countered by variety, and there is absolutely no way of deciding whether these images illustrate its unchanging sameness or stake a defiant claim to its diversity in its many-facetedness, variance and potpourri-like mixtures of impressions.

The reigning opposition of our time is that between differentiation and undifferentiation. Do capitalism, so the question, and its worldwide networks of communication mix up the existences of the people of planet earth, or do they lock them up in the steel and glass towers of uniformity? Is our destiny that of being uprooted or of being made uniform? Is everyone different or is everyone the same? Does reality tend toward small-scale subdivision or large-scale leveling? Does the world live from the emancipation, demarginalization and upvaluation of the periphery, or is globalization its destiny? It is not that Ackermann's work could solve these problems. But like hardly any other it distills them to their essence by raising the question, by literally showing the question using its unique pictorial approach.

2. OUTSIDE AND INSIDE | More than ever before, Franz Ackermann has spread his work out into a panorama at the Stadtgalerie Altötting. The panels covering the walls in their entirety and surrounding the centered spectacle of works on paper or canvas continue one another tirelessly, passing seamlessly from one to the next and creating a continuum with no beginning and no end. The effect of an allover is established, a world in the world is formed, linked to it motivically, but most of all rhetorically. This sort of panorama relates to reality metonymically, as a cutout whose fragmentation nonetheless functions as a whole. The world is everything that is the case, as the famous first sentence of Ludwig Wittgenstein's "Tractatus" states. In Franz Ackermann's world as well, everything is the case, an everything in miniature, standing for the totality of things.

On 25 May 1793 Robert Barker opened the world's first panorama rotunda in London's Leicester Square, opening with it a new vista for a whole century as well. Before the advent of cinema, the panorama painting fulfilled the need for spectacle of an epoch that witnessed the spread of democracy and understood the limitless opportunities offered by mass entertainment providing amusement for money. Mounted on the inside of a cylinder, the panorama, with its 360-degree perspective, offered the totality of the visible at the moment in which one was inside its all-encompassing world. The canvas put everything before one's eyes, making the image into the surroundings; one witnessed a self-contained world of absorption and theatricality. The totality set in scene by the panorama was thoroughly artificial, and yet it was a totality that did not require one to adapt a special aesthetic posture; it was simply there, as the hermetic allover of an artificial parallel world, which nonetheless did not present anything other than what one knew and what one could recognize. At the same time one found oneself in the privileged position of a firmly established standpoint, in a fixed, architecturally and perspectively guaranteed middle. The reality of the round painting was concentric, and it clearly offered an experience of the sublime in its orientation toward a platform offering an ideal view. From the very beginning, the panorama was a parade ground for the contingency of the world and for the way in which it is banished. The scenery changed according to popular demand and commercial acumen, and yet every change emphasized anew the absence of a beginning or an end. The panorama was the authority par excellence for the validity of the here and now: the subjects, themes and motifs that it offered had their factual counterpart in the reality of the optical, and in the way it showed them they ordered themselves into the continuum that the picture itself was and in turn presented as real.

Even if this principle had not been around for more than 200 years, Ackermann would have invented it. In perfect reflection he makes the outside of the real world into the inside of the artificial one. Paradoxically, the panorama provides an intimation of how complicated the world is, being itself complicated and yet banishing complexity in a way that makes evident the mechanism of reduction. In 1806 one could already read the following complaint in Millin's "Dictionnaire des beaux arts": "It is hard to imagine anything more absurd and unpleasant than seeing all of the wagons in a panorama, all of the people on foot or on horseback, who are always just setting off into motion and who nevertheless remain perpetually rooted to the spot; the coachmen who are eternally swinging their whips, and the horses that are always rearing up; the dogs that are continuously charging at each other; the children who are always falling without ever touching the ground etc. etc." The panorama delivers pure simultaneity, but this simultaneity could be raised against it as an accusation of indiscriminately freezing the image. Its depiction is too enamored of detail, too elaborate and epic for any spirit of the moment to be made tangible in it. Every image must in some way come to terms with the fact that it is a cutout, but now, in the perfection of a self-enclosed world that the panorama sets in scene, this problem was recognized as such. The spatial continuum, the spatial totality achieved by the panorama makes it all the more clear that there is also a temporal dimension to the theatrical, which here is sacrificed at a high cost: that of immobility.

The Fugel Panorama in Altötting, exemplary of the genre and singular in Germany, attempts to find a solution by introducing a narrative. A narrator, the radio announcer Gustl Weishappl, was engaged to complement the allover gaze upon Calvary and the Crucifixion with the sequentiality that arises when something is read aloud. The texts function as a continuing progression, complementing the coexisting images. Visitors listen and look and can imagine that they are in the midst of the occurrence, that is if the illusion works. Now, in the collaboration of pictorial and literal language, completeness has been achieved, and yet it is synthetic, artificial, the result of hybridization.

In his Altötting installation, Franz Ackermann has explicitly referenced Fugel's "world-famous European attraction", as it is quaintly referred to in various promotional materials. No work information disturbs the overall impression, and no piece is presented as a solitary artwork. The subjects, themes and motifs are organically interwoven, expanded into the three-dimensional and enriched with real objects – the boat, the brochures. As in the Fugel panorama, there are also objects of reality: they create the so-called "faux terrain" of the panorama, which in the context of the artificial-artistic becomes a falsification by working with real-life objects. For the Ackermann panorama, the reference to the Fugel panorama is nothing more than a ground wire. Thus entropy, which generally represents the fundamental condition of creating in the world and specifically does so in Ackermann's oeuvre, is accorded an unexpected topography. The confusion of the world takes on an element of homecoming.

At the time when Marc Augé published his book on "non-places", the "non-lieux", the principle of site-specificity, the famous swan song of the 1980s, lay in its final throes. The site-specific had provided a sort of refuge for the anthropological place; it was the relic of unmistakable locality, before it was displaced by the principle of setting things out as art, which with the concept of "Drop Sculpture" is labeled more wittily than it is meant. Altogether, Ackermann's installation is site-specific. The anthropological place that is established is the one that is most intimately the artist's own, literally the place from which he originates, the small town, with its milieu, its friends and relatives, its memories of childhood and times forever lost. This is, of course, only possible once, when the artist exhibits in his hometown. And yet the additional gratification that arises thereby, the additional dimension, which can be assessed and surveyed, remains conserved in the oeuvre as a whole.

3. LAYERS AND LAYERINGS | Ackermann's display for Altötting also exerts, with regard to dimension, a pull into depth. Despite all of its planimetry, its spreading expansion into a panoramic horizon, there is also an element of stratification. This arises in the layers and layerings, in the positioning of images in front of one another and on top of one another, in the views, perforations and mixtures, which combine simultaneity with knowledge of the difference of their origins. Various strata come together, like sedimentations, as if they had come into existence at various times and were now being surveyed as a whole. The moments captured here are in fact of diverse origin: Ackermann's journey along the Pan-American Highway supplies many of the motifs, but there are also relics of other presentations as well as the intervention in the unique space of the Stadtgalerie and the updatings occasioned by the setting. In the transparence of details in themselves opaque, in their monochromaticism and fragility, in the figurative elements and the integration of textual passages, Ackermann's work recalls the principle of the palimpsest, that venerable medium which is to be thanked for having conserved so many traces of antiquity. Palimpsests are pages with multiple layers of writing from various epochs, the overwriting of an outdated text with one of current relevance. The most famous palimpsest is a medieval manuscript, of course featuring Christian content, that made use of a very old and outdated parchment upon which a treatise from antiquity was written, namely Cicero's "De re publica". It was thanks to this reuse of writing material that his text was preserved for posterity. Palimpsests are very old, but the discovery of them is genuinely modern.

Ackermann's installation is a palimpsest with regard to both material and medium. More, it is such in a metaphoric sense. It works as a palimpsest because it works with a sort of mental tagging, with "Mental Maps", as Ackermann himself refers to them. Thomas De Quincey introduced into cultural history the idea that memory is also structured like a palimpsest. In 1845 he wrote the following: "What else than a natural and mighty palimpsest is the human brain? Such a palimpsest is my brain; such a palimpsest, O reader, is yours. Everlasting layers of ideas, images, feelings, have fallen upon your brain softly as light. Each succession has seemed to bury all that went before. And yet in reality not one has been extinguished."

Charles Baudelaire was one of De Quincey's most diligent interpreters, and he incorporated "Confessions of an English Opium-Eater" into his narrative poem "Les paradis artificiels". Here he inserted a chapter carrying the title "le palimpseste". In it Baudelaire reminisced on an author who destroyed all of his manuscripts, sacrificing them in an "effroyable holocauste" before they ever had a chance of being published. The justification for the auto-da-fé was the following: "Why not? What was really important was that they were created; they were created, and so they exist." They have penetrated and burned themselves into memory, and there they remain, independent of any form of realization. "Le palimpseste de la mémoire est indestructible".

The palimpsest is not only a literal form of appearance in which Ackermann's work presents itself. The palimpsest is a metaphor, reminding one of memories in which visual experiences are sedimented, traces of what has been seen and read in everyday life. Palimpsests, which Ackermann's image worlds are, necessarily function within the framework established by their media: they function simultaneously. And yet everything that is to be seen in them owes its existence to the variety of diverse systematic ages. It is precisely in this simultaneity that one can see how much unsimultaneity there is. Both, the simultaneous and the unsimultaneous, give time its contour.

Artificial paradises: that is the concept, cribbing from Baudelaire, for the work Ackermann sets in scene in Altötting. In all of its artificiality, his integration of so many contrary worlds into his work banishes for a happy moment reality and its complexity through a vividly polychromatic spectacle that allows one to forget how much cutting and pasting has been done and how mediated its immediacy is. Paradis artificiels: those who enter them do so knowing that we have been expelled from the one paradise, from the Garden of Eden, and that the process of knowledge is irreversible. And yet paradise has a second entrance, whereby comers to this gate are not sent away, but invited in. The gatekeeper is an artist.

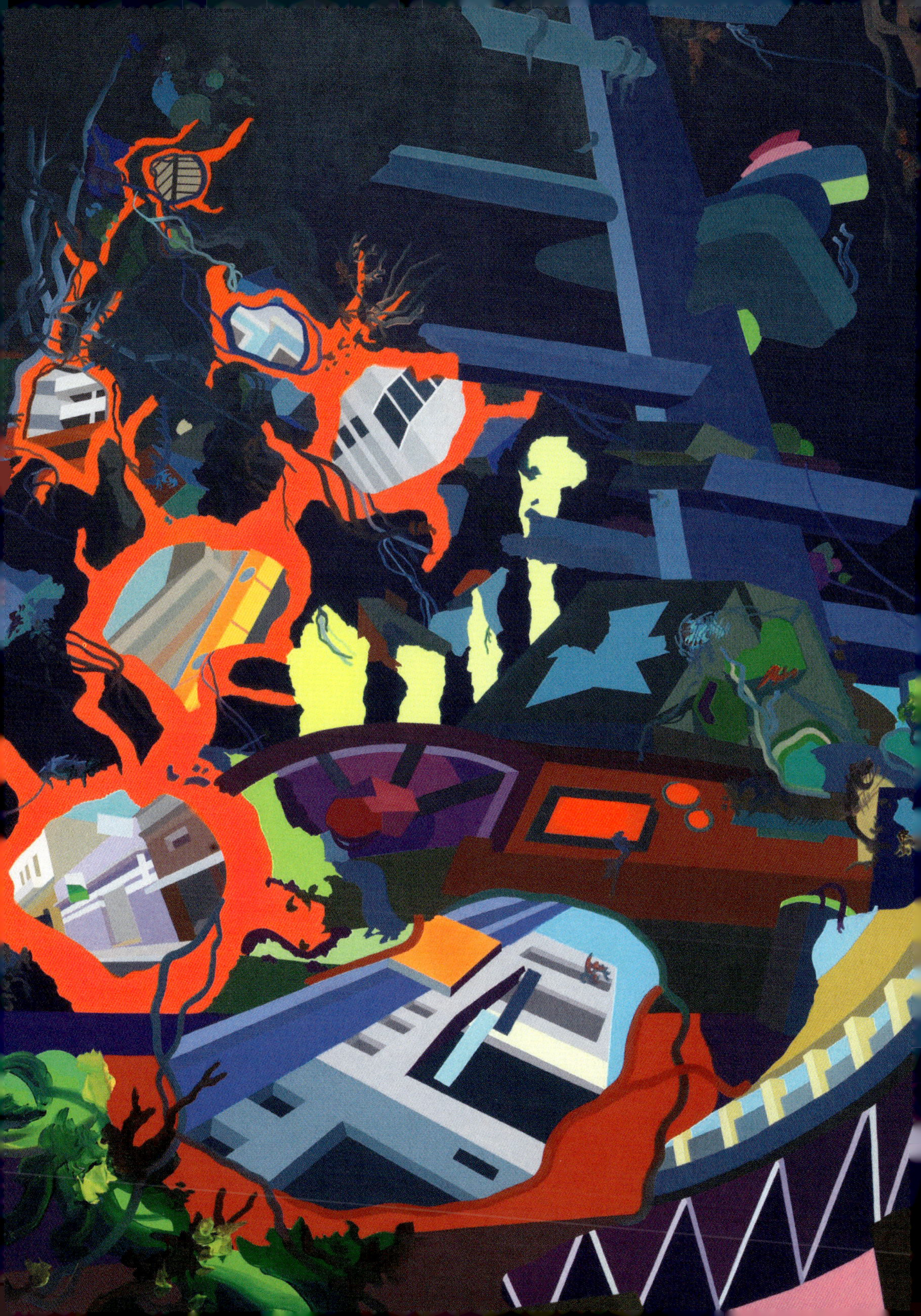

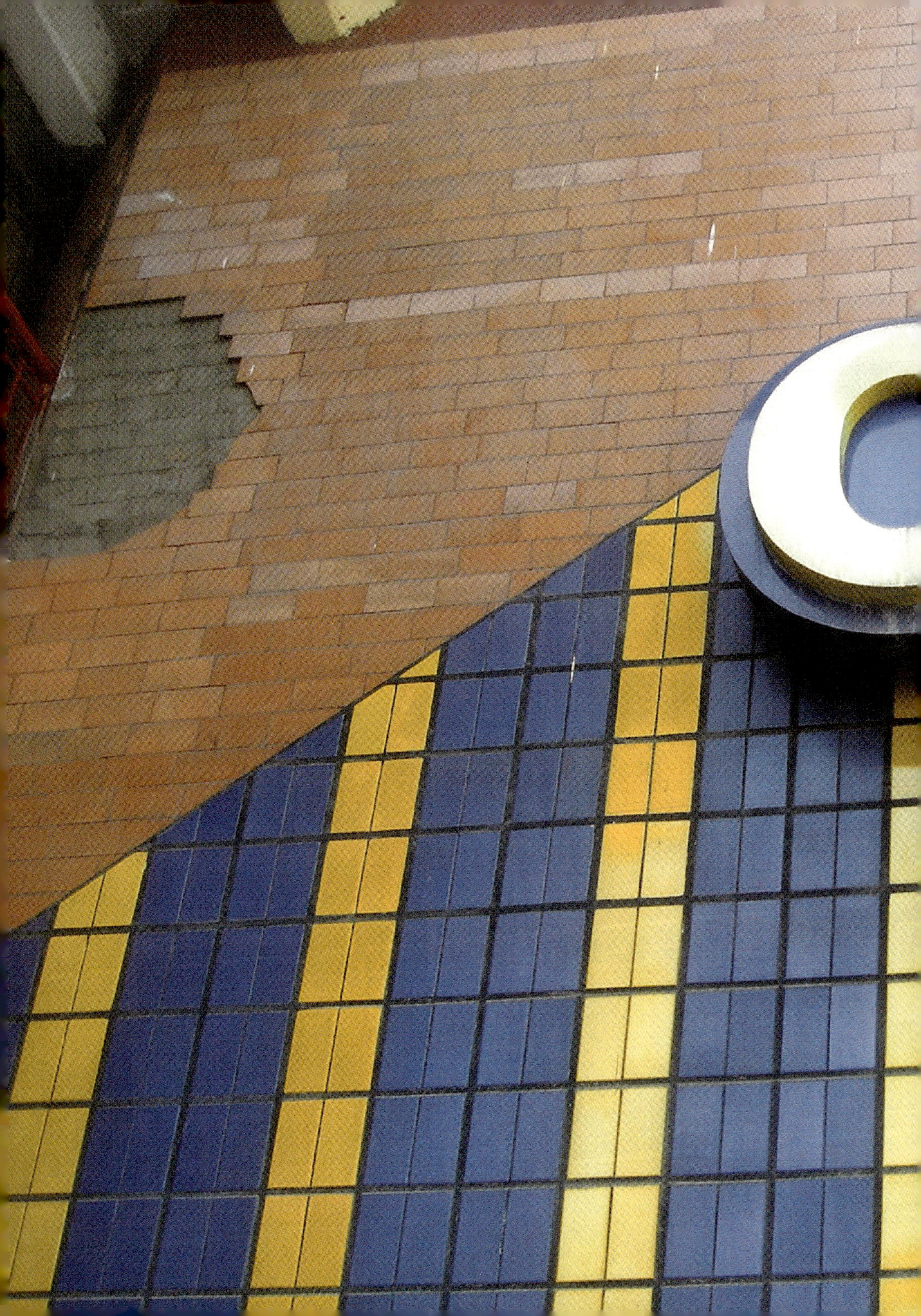

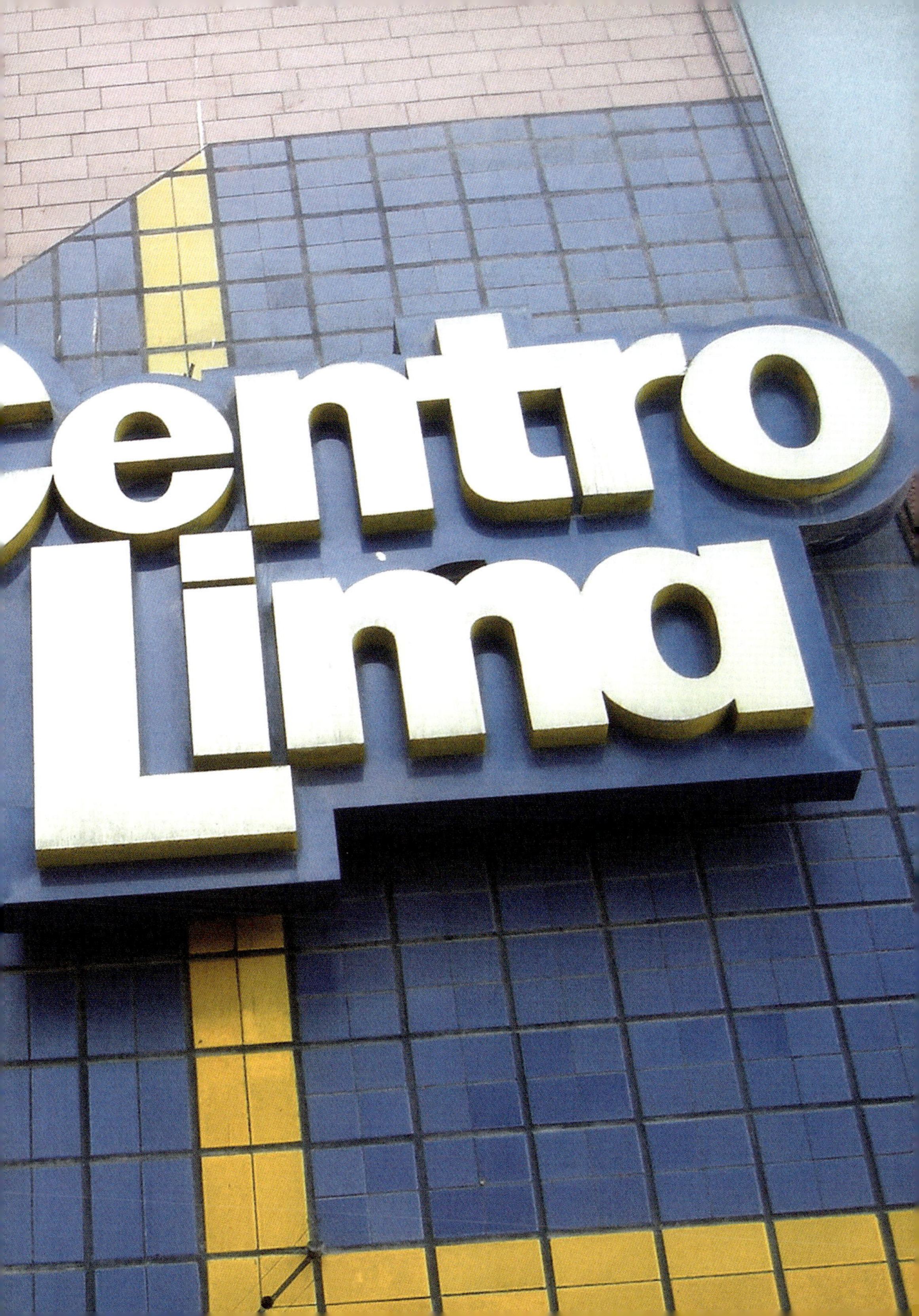

Centro
Lima

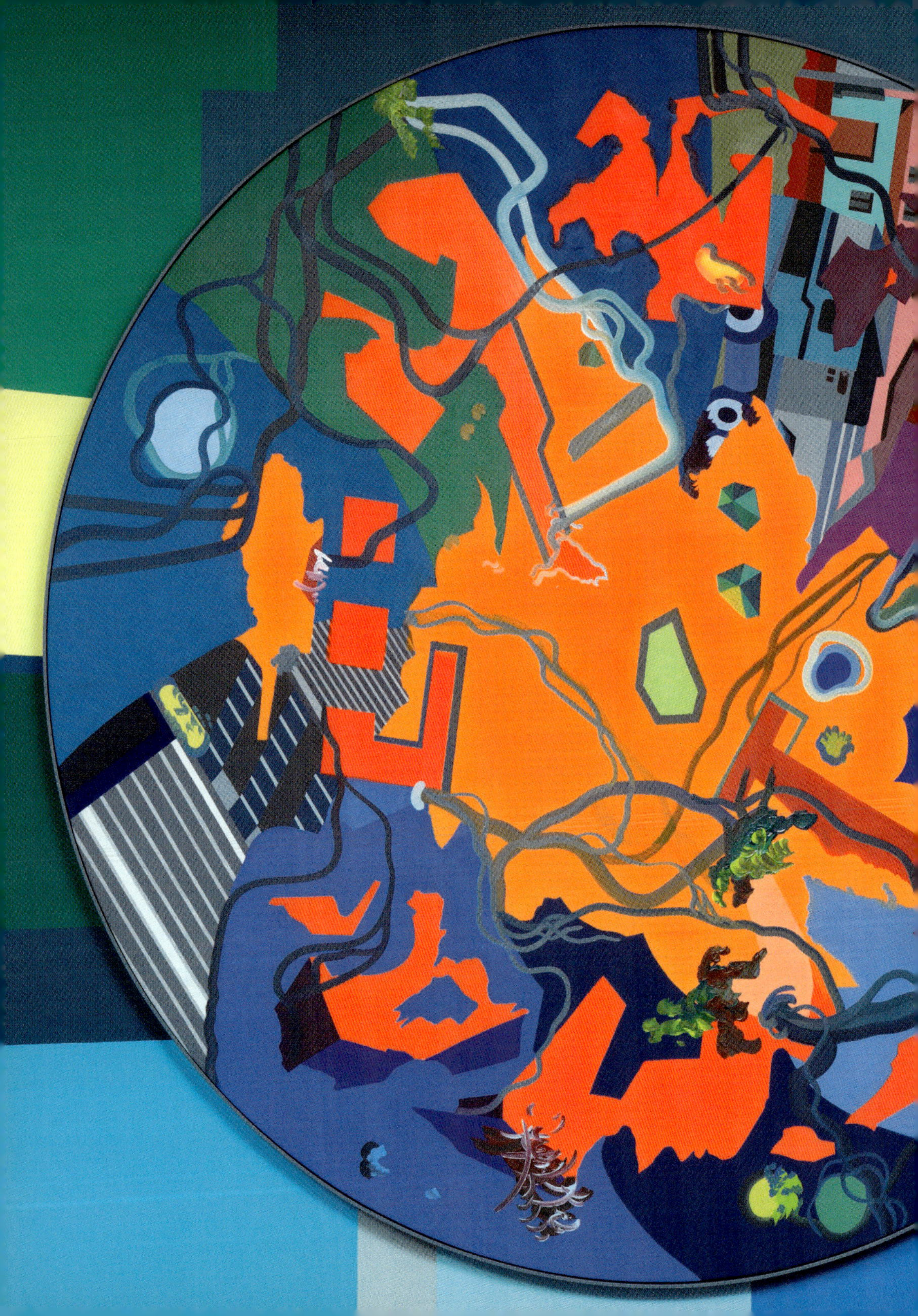

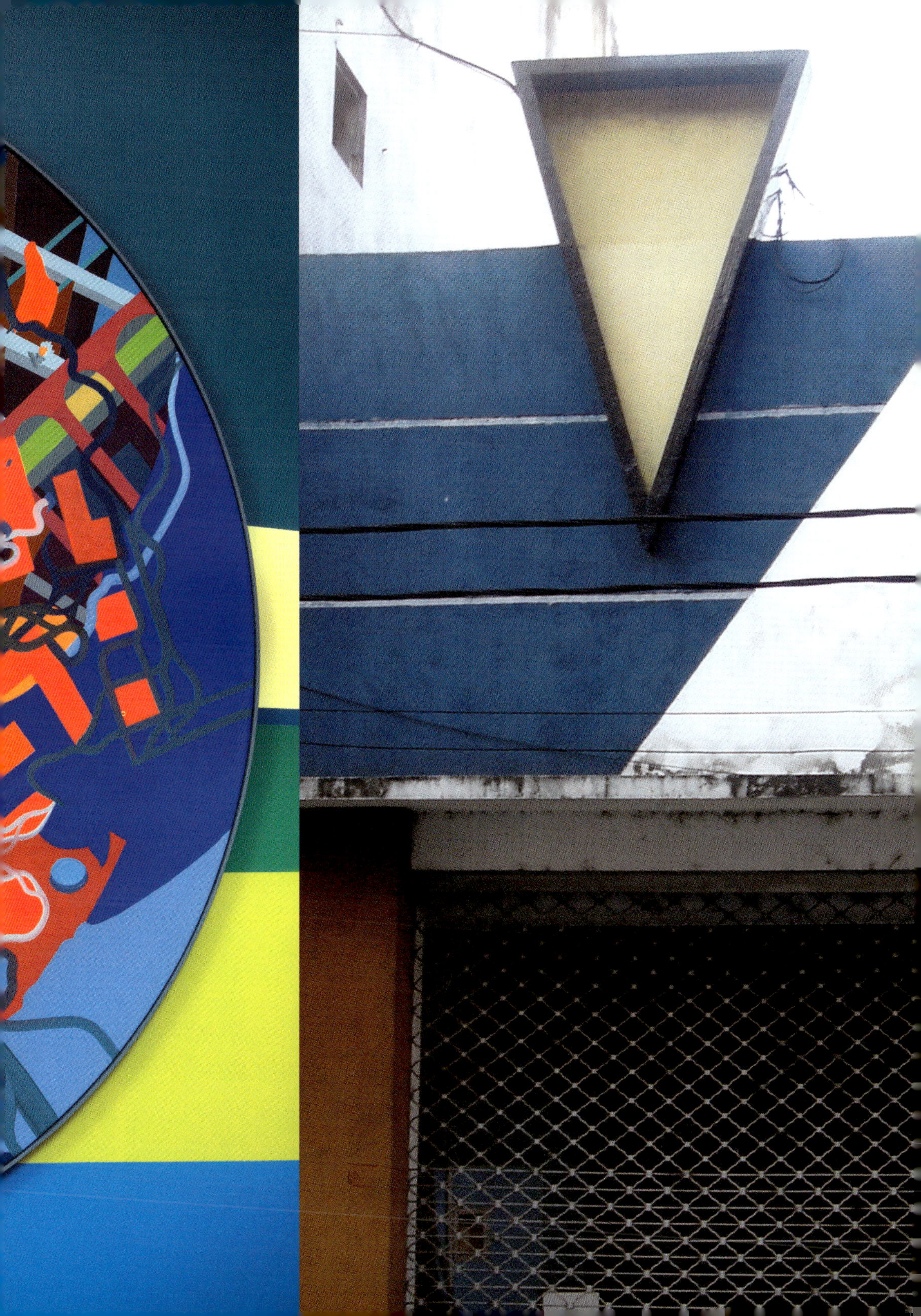

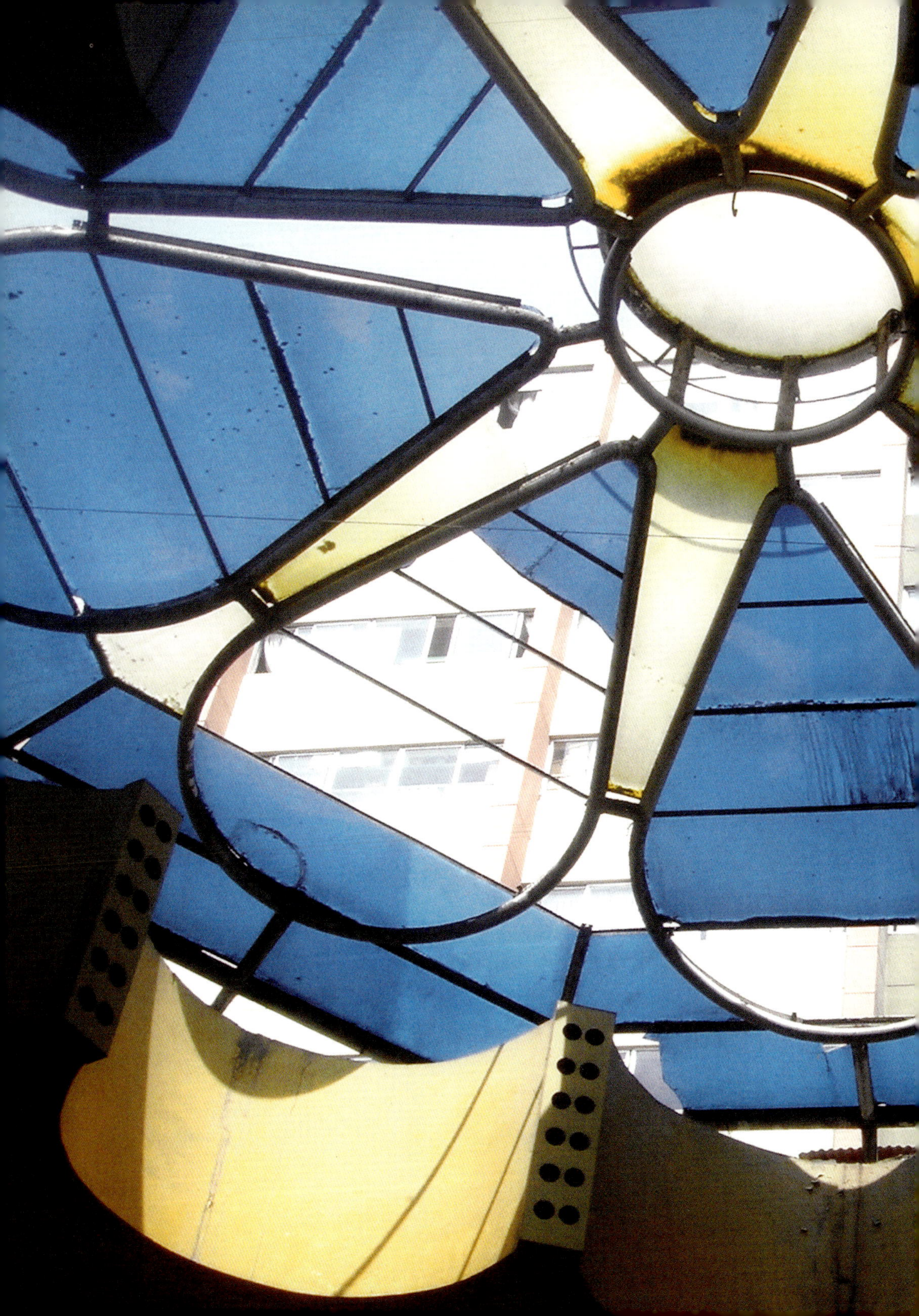

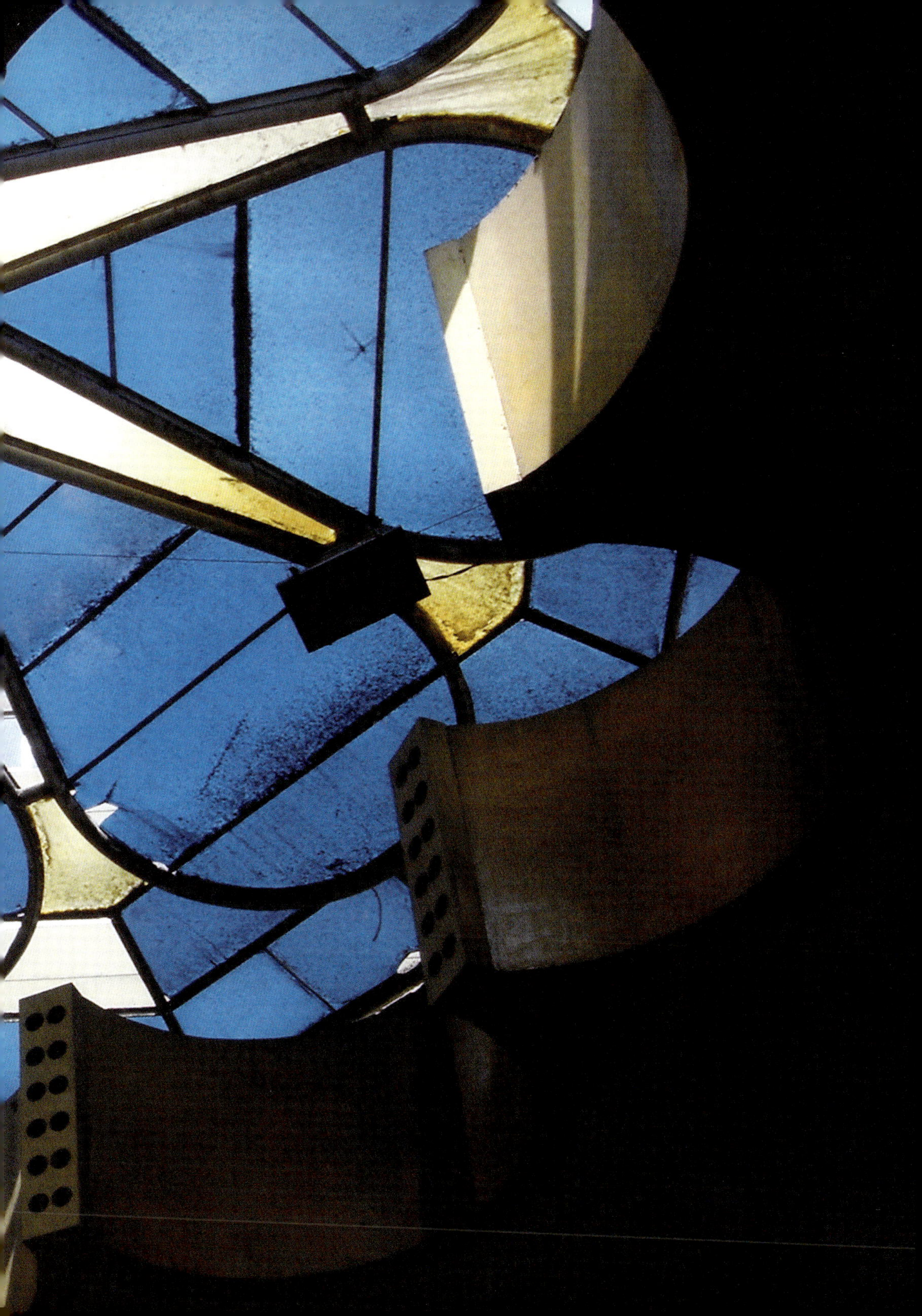

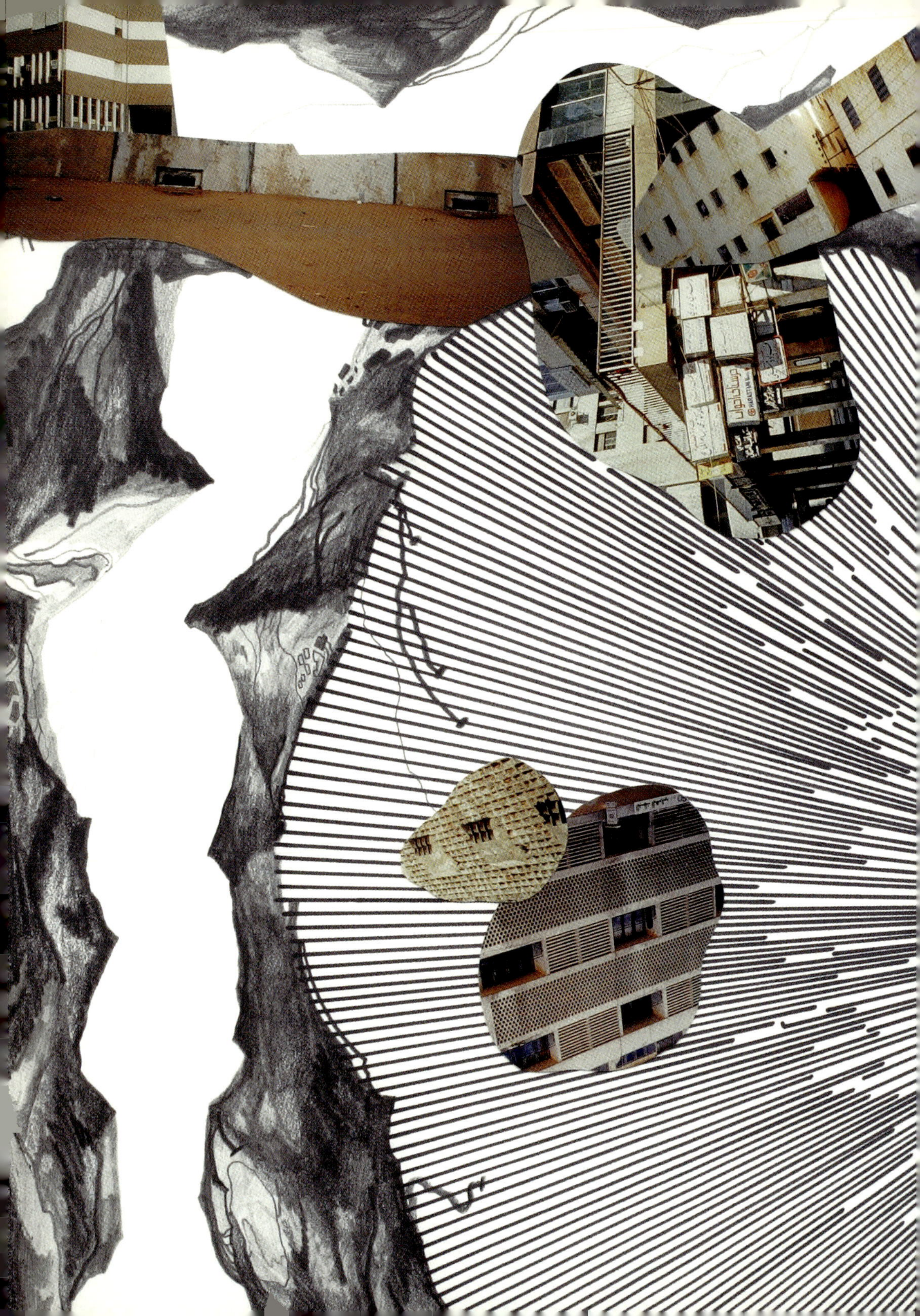

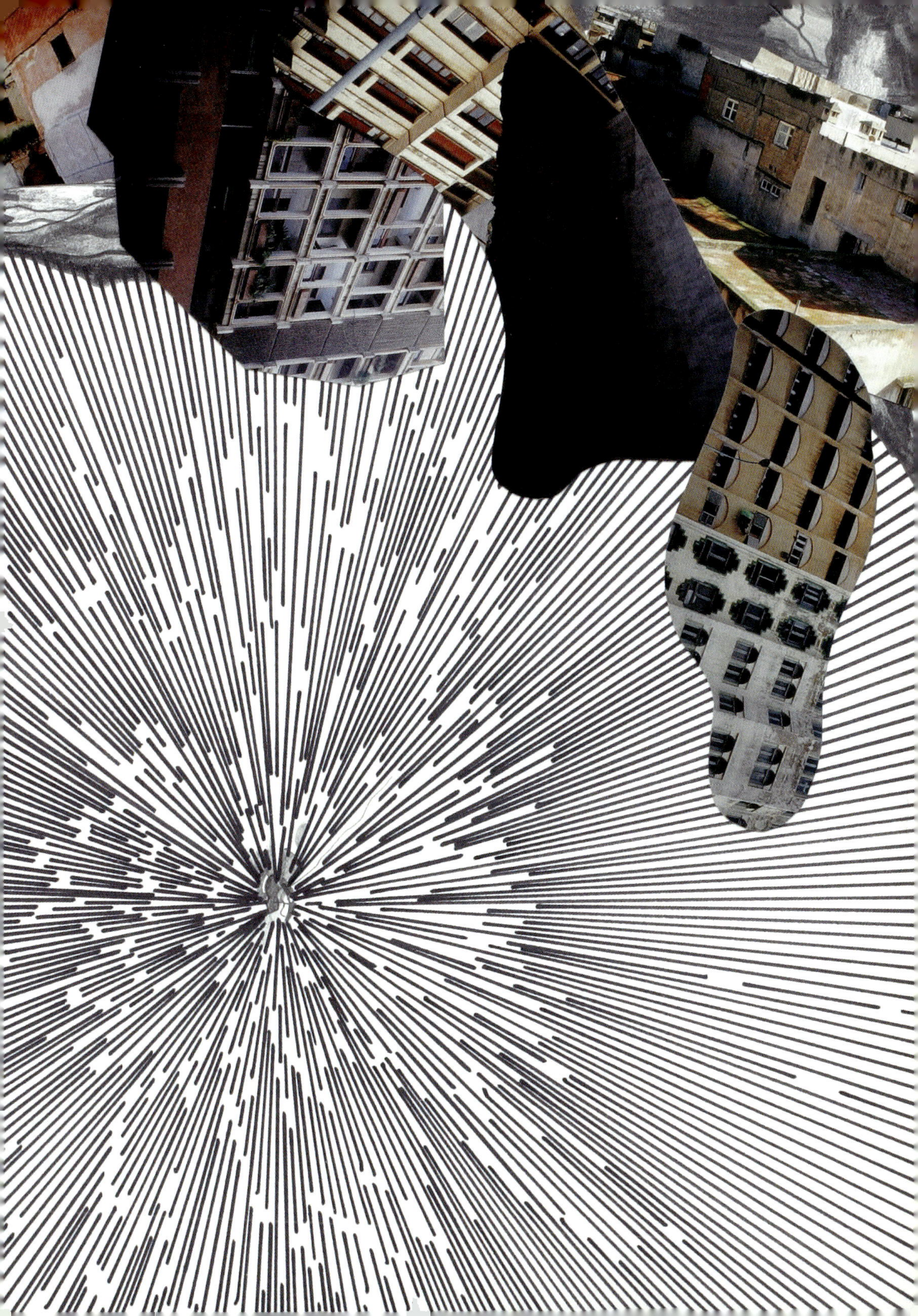

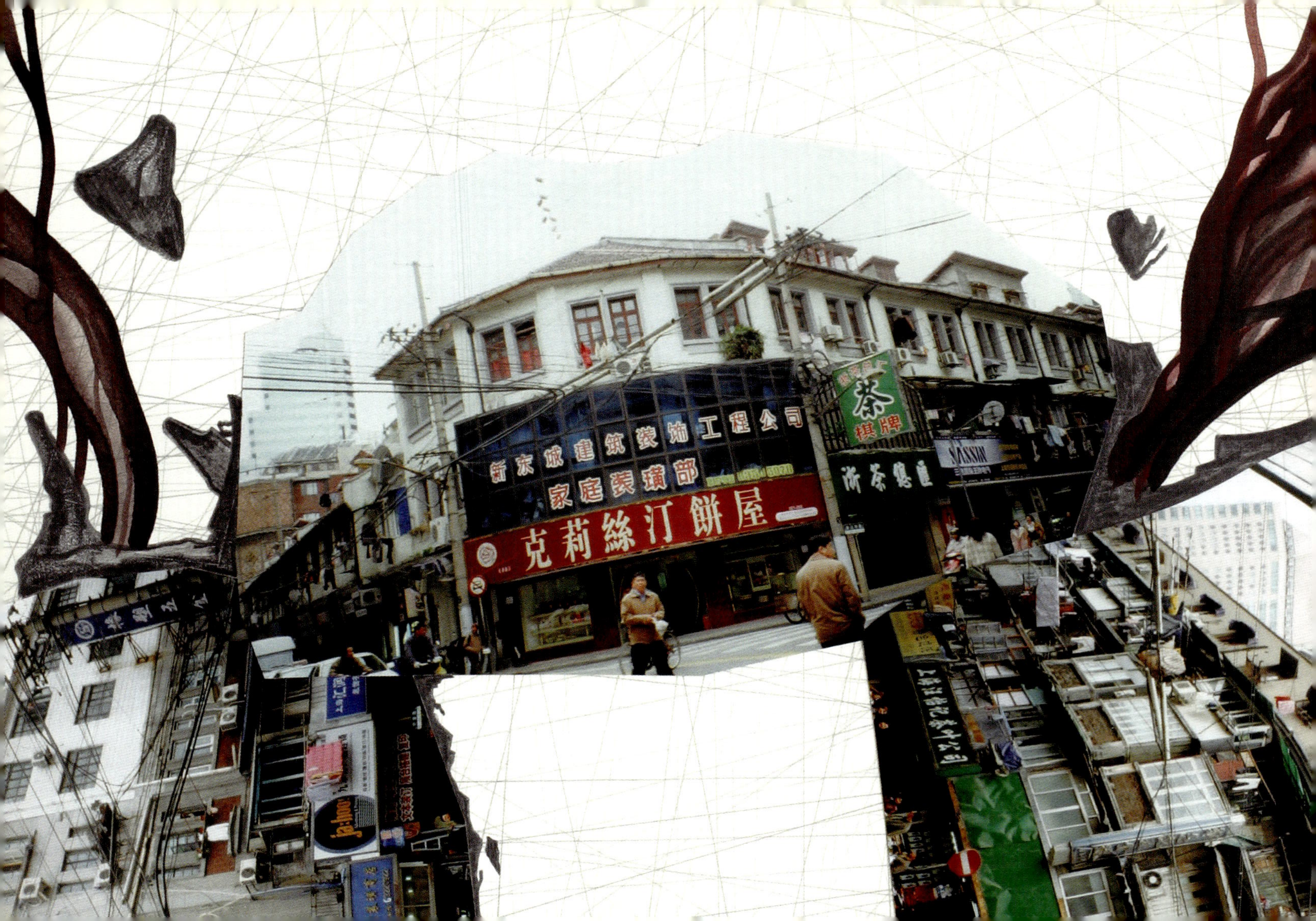
新东城建筑装饰工程公司
家庭装璜部
克莉絲汀餅屋
茶
棋牌
浙茶總匯
SASSIN

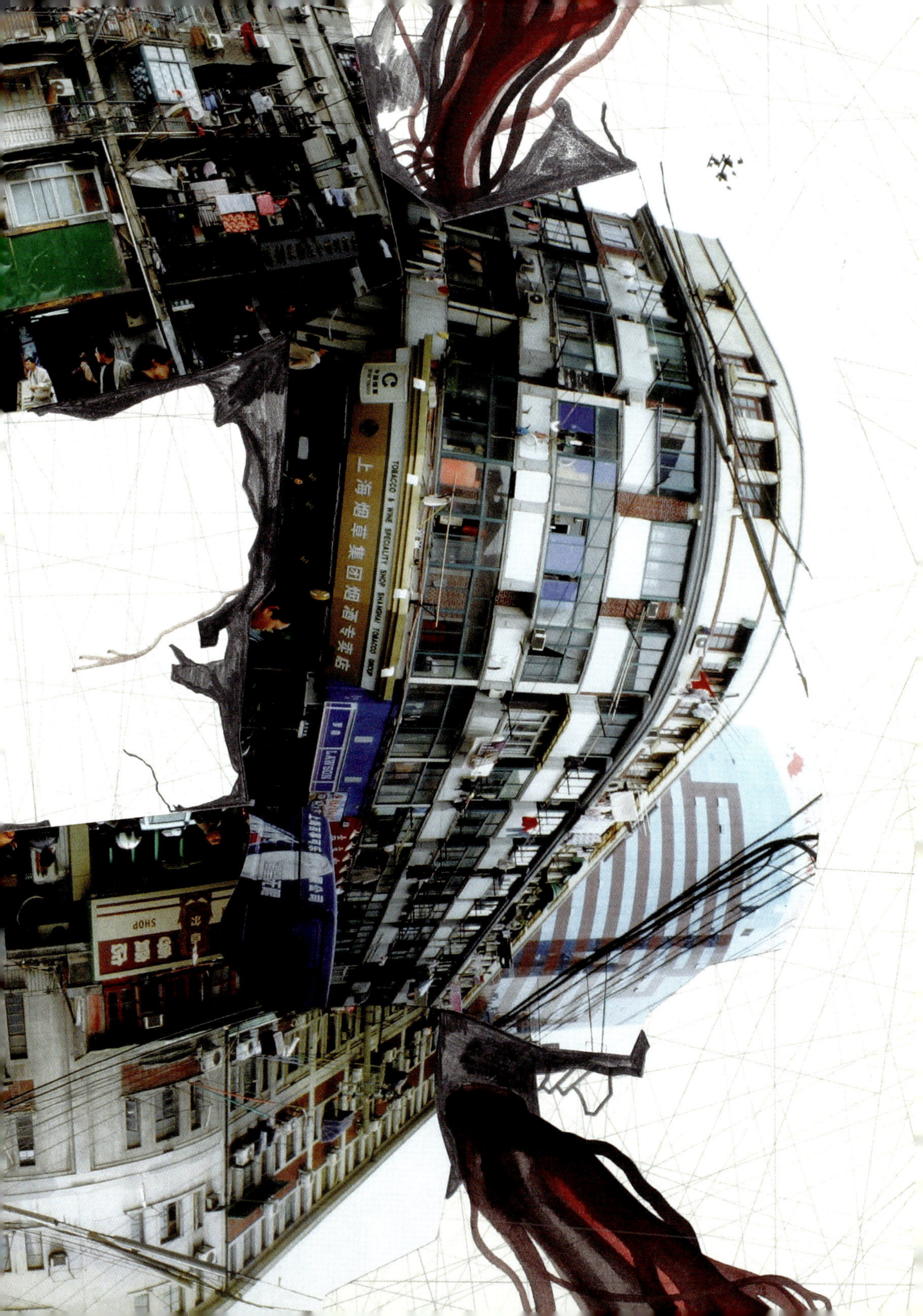

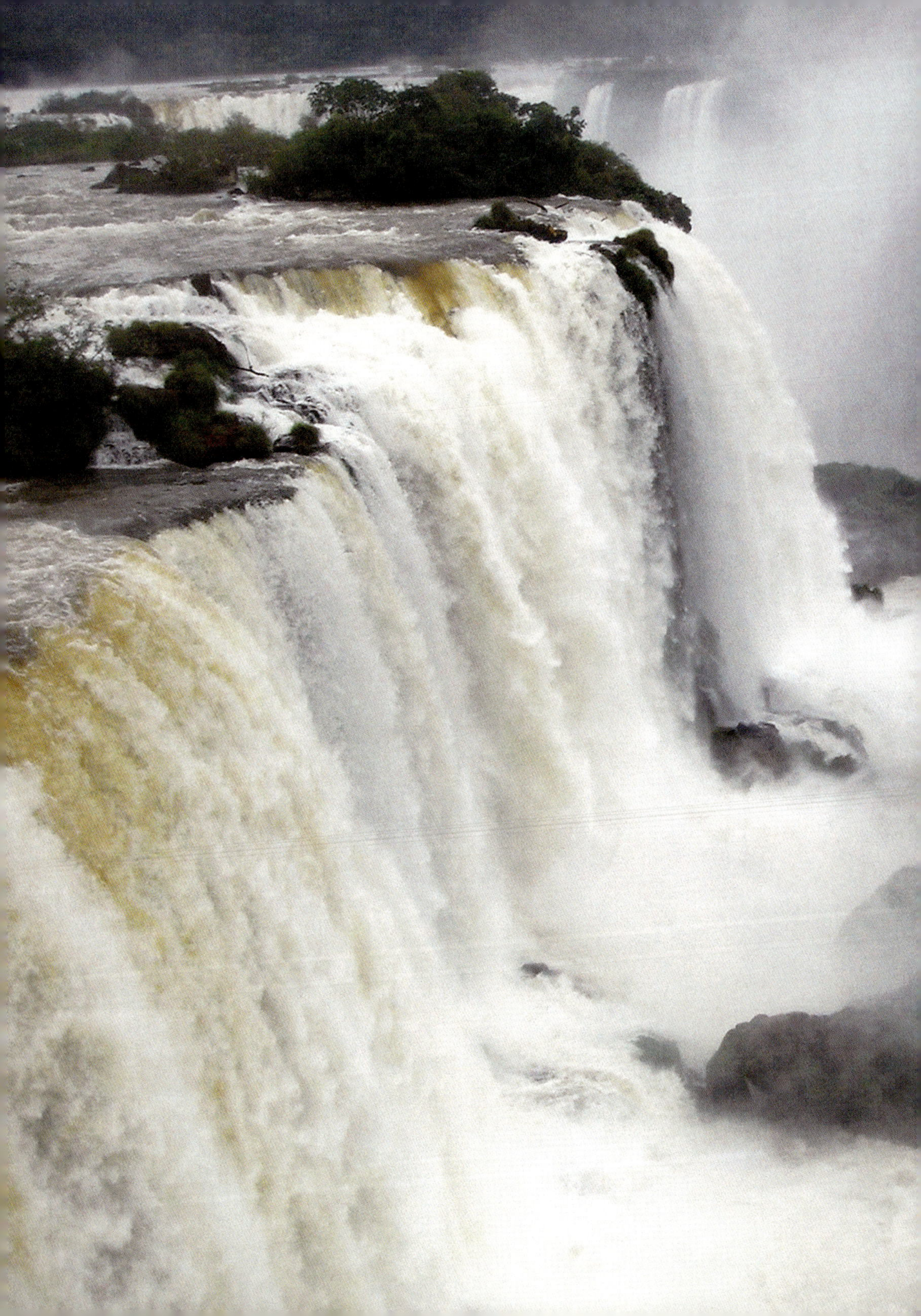

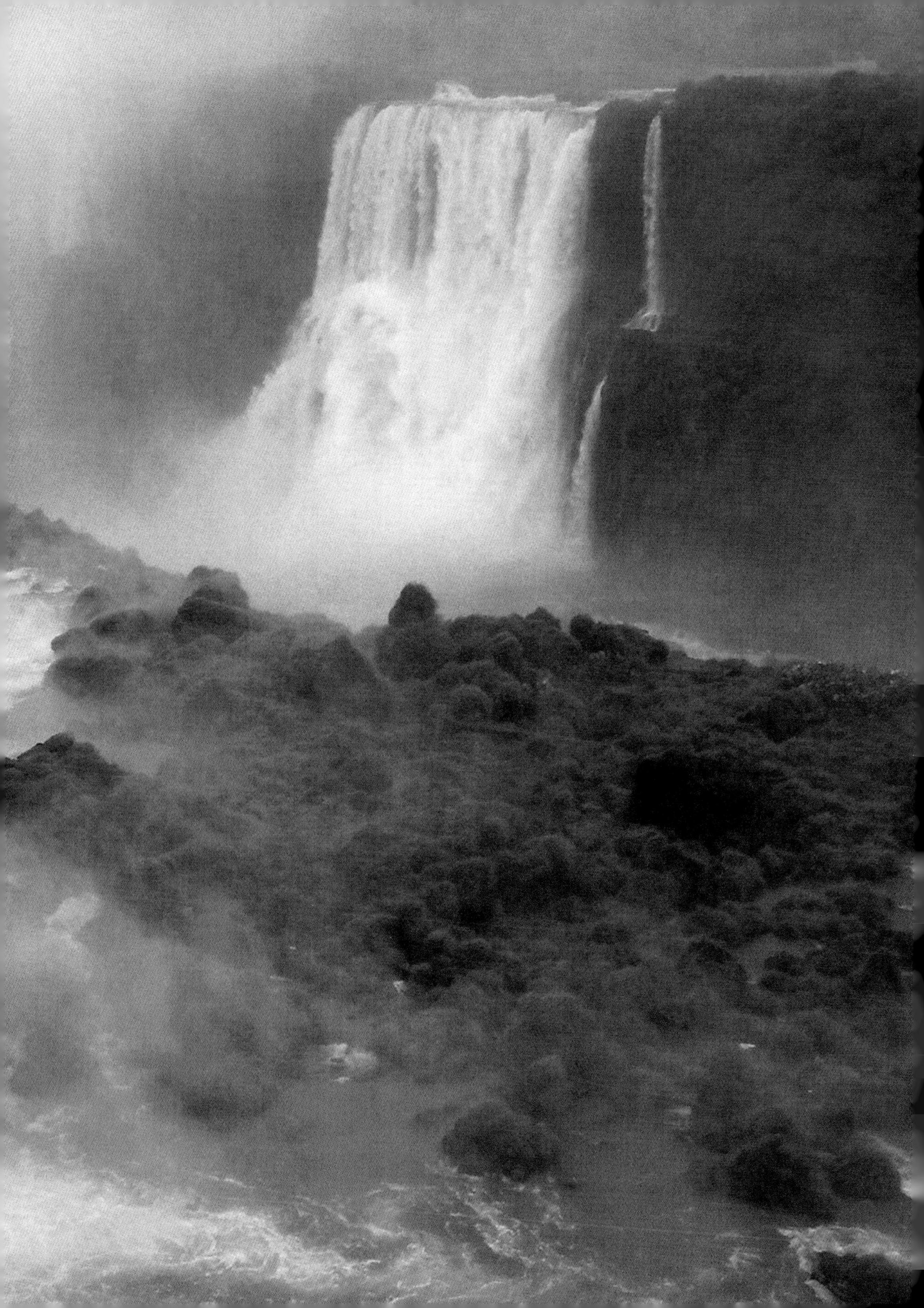

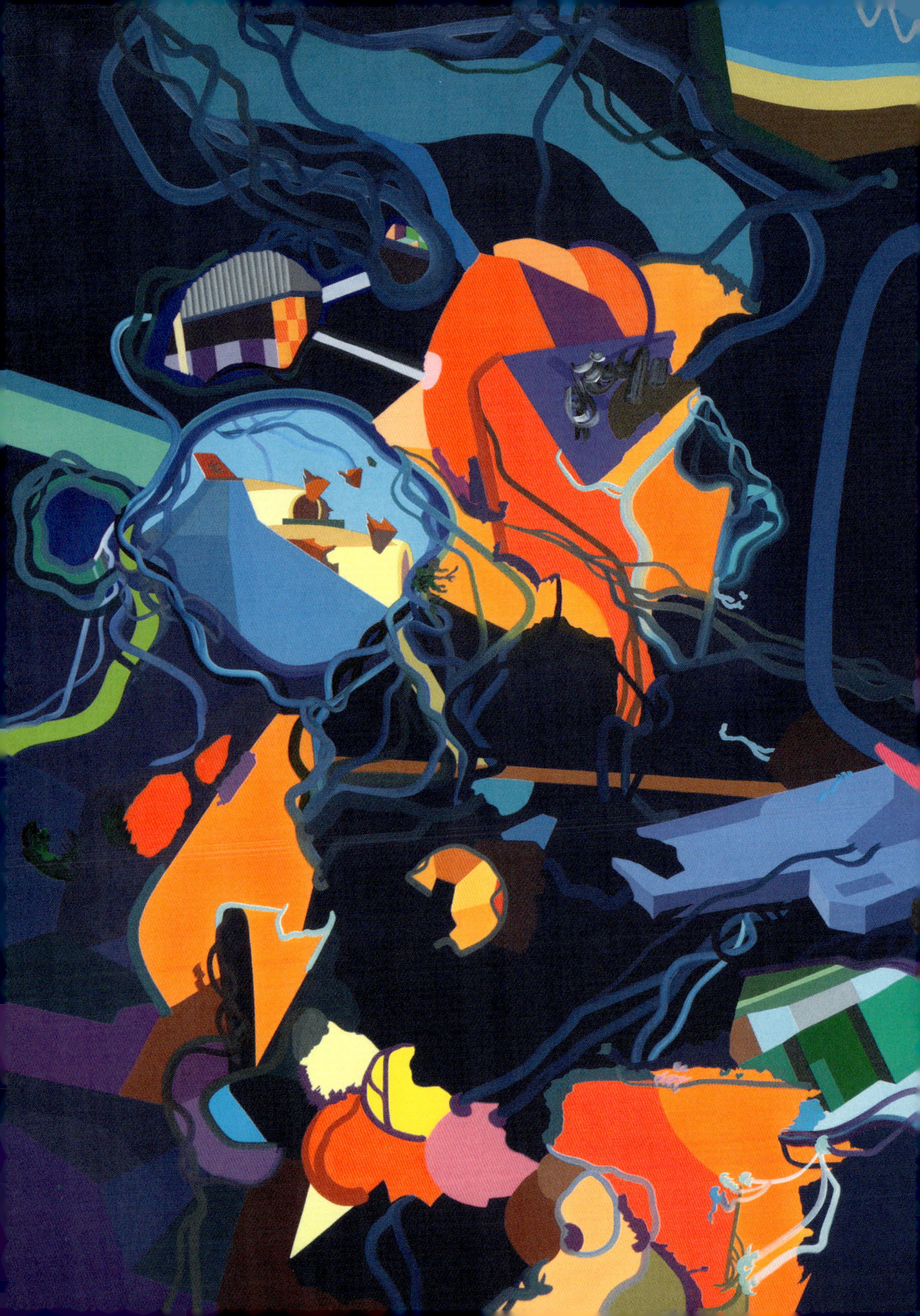

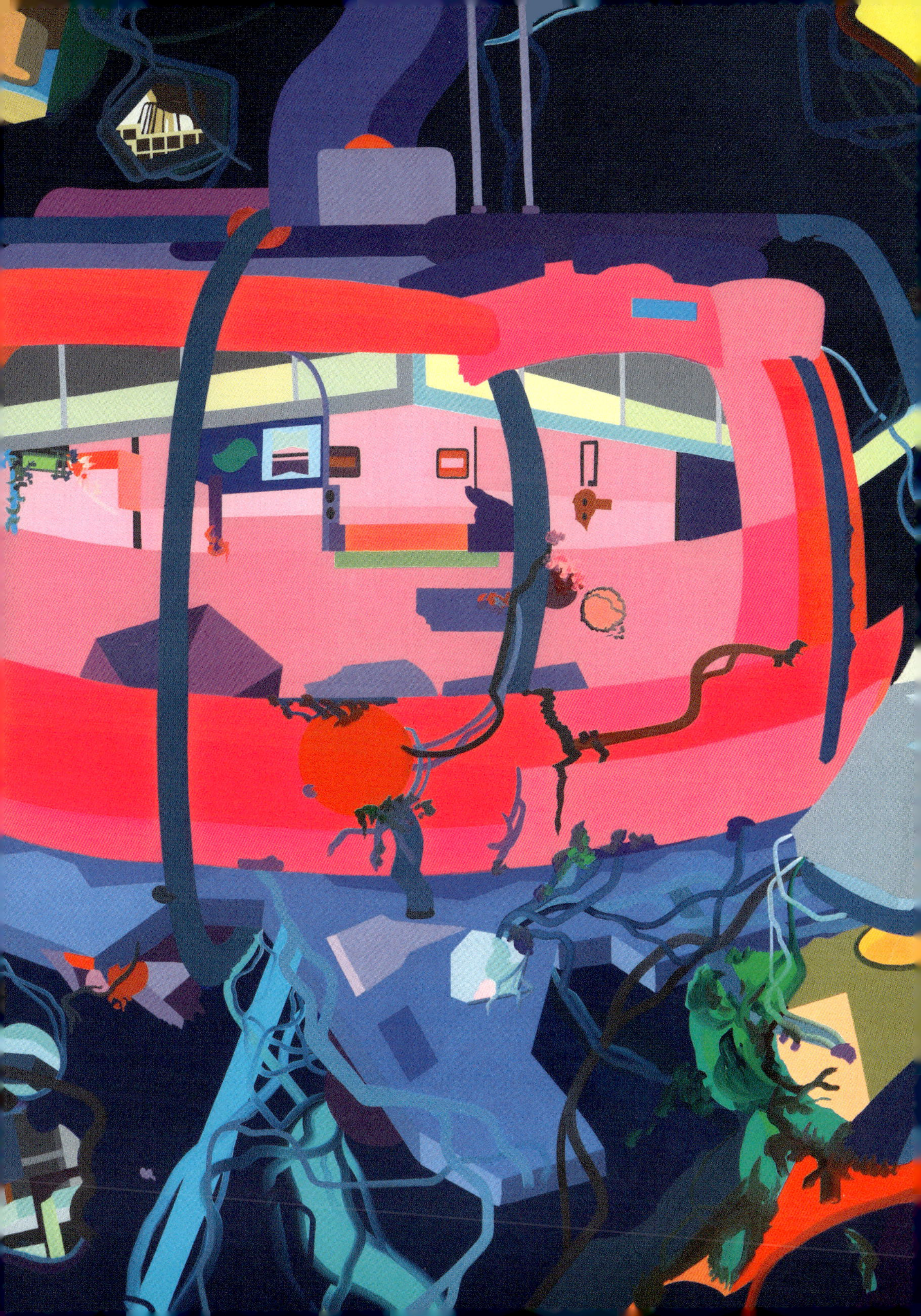

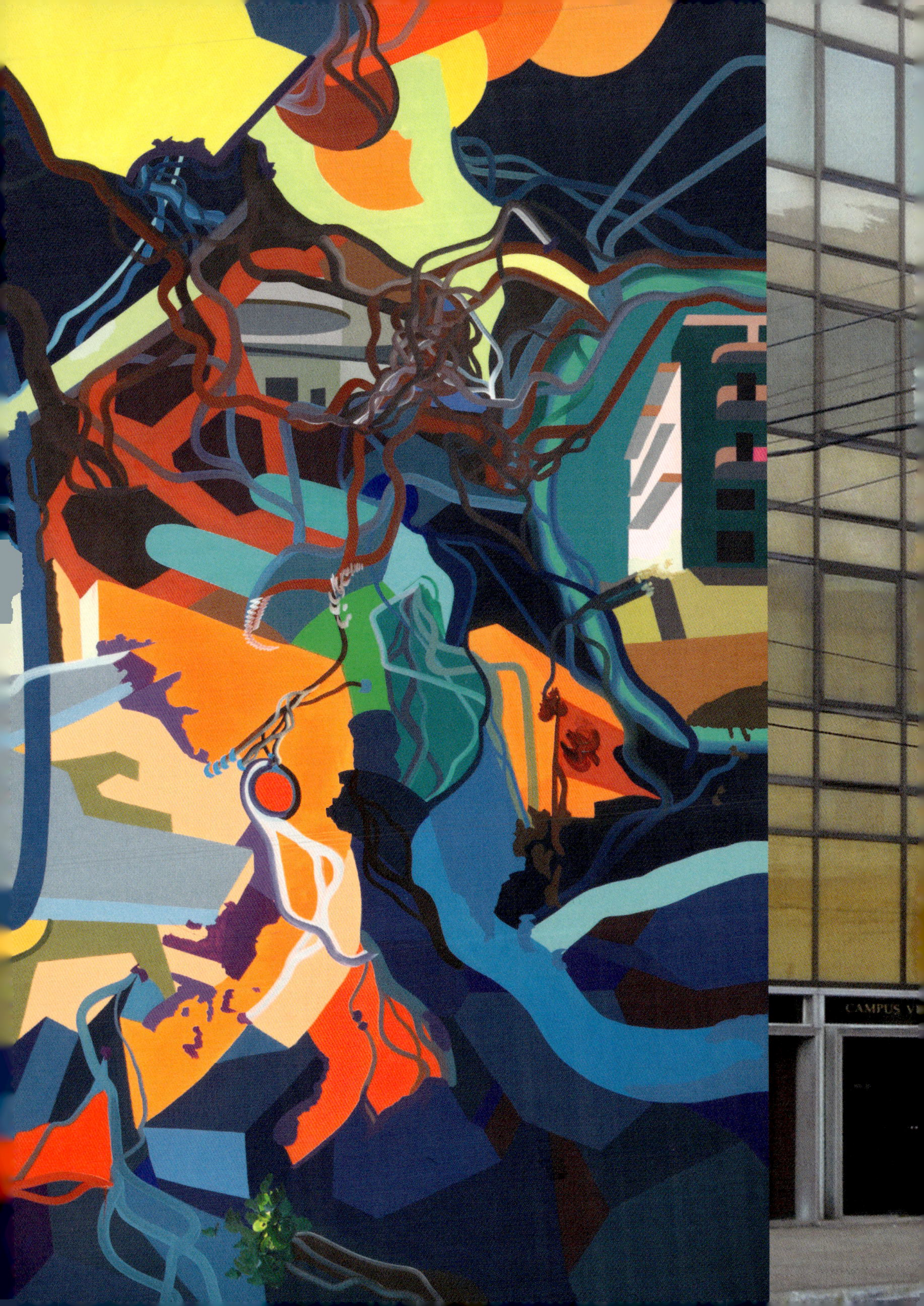
CAMPUS V

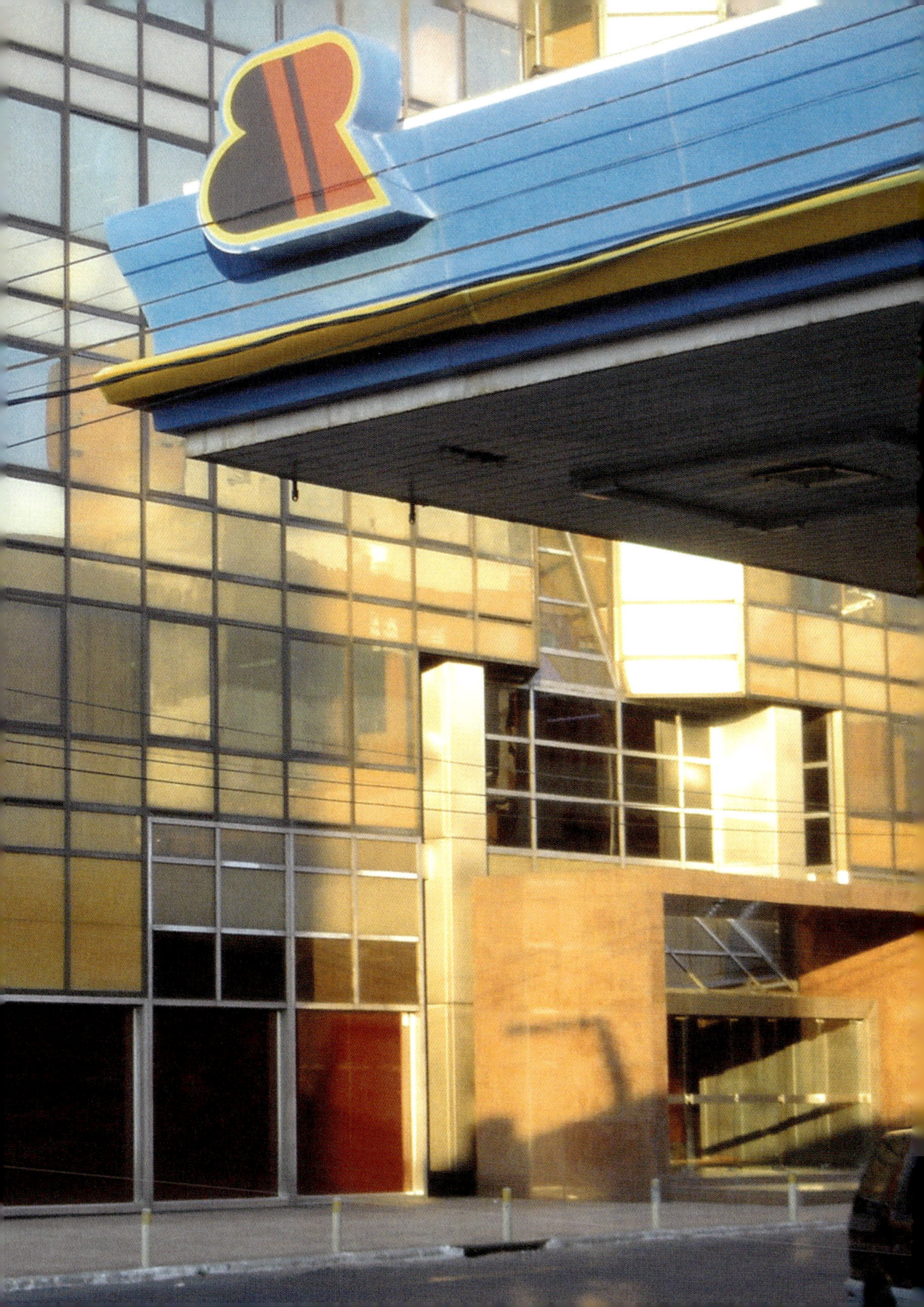

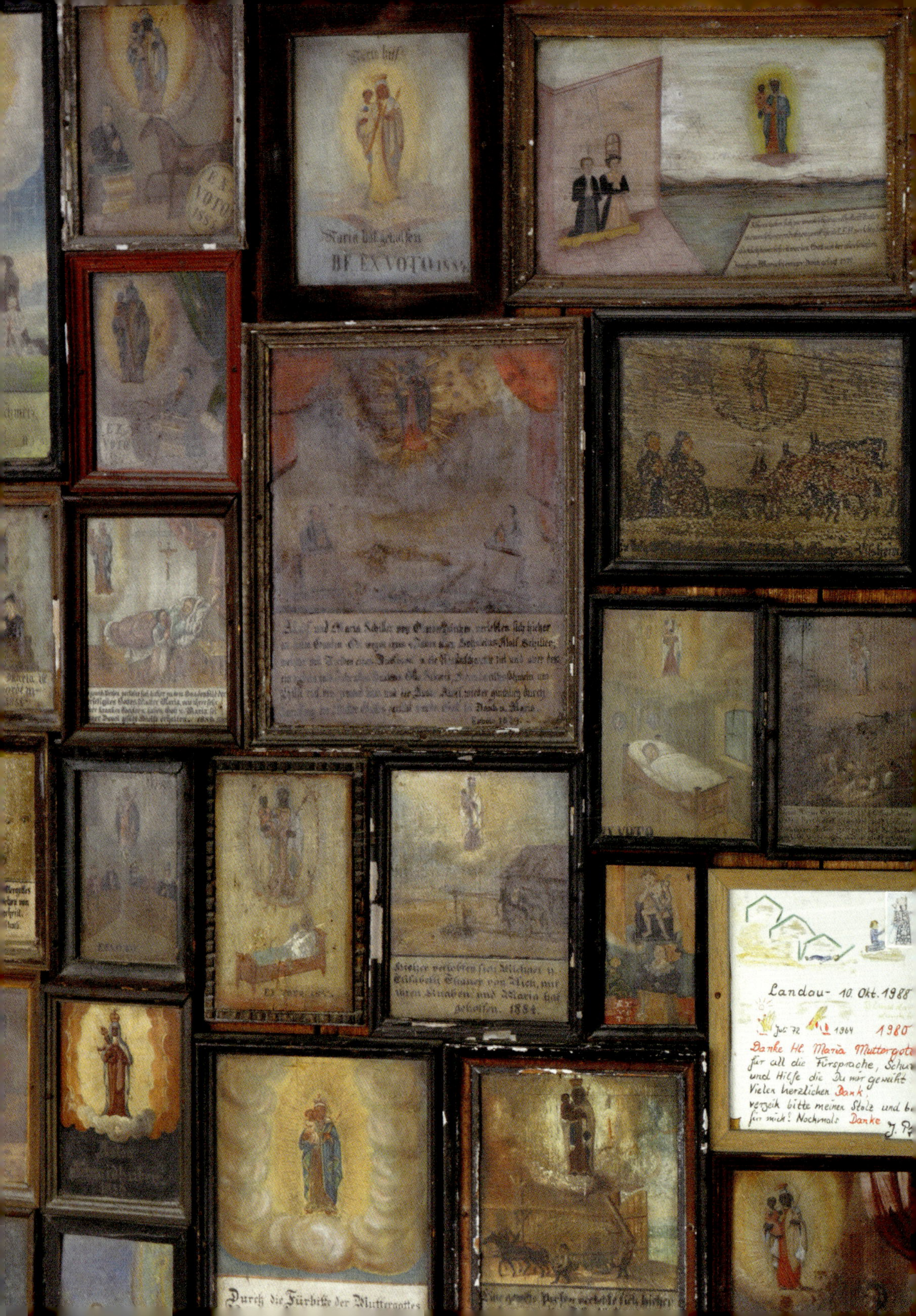

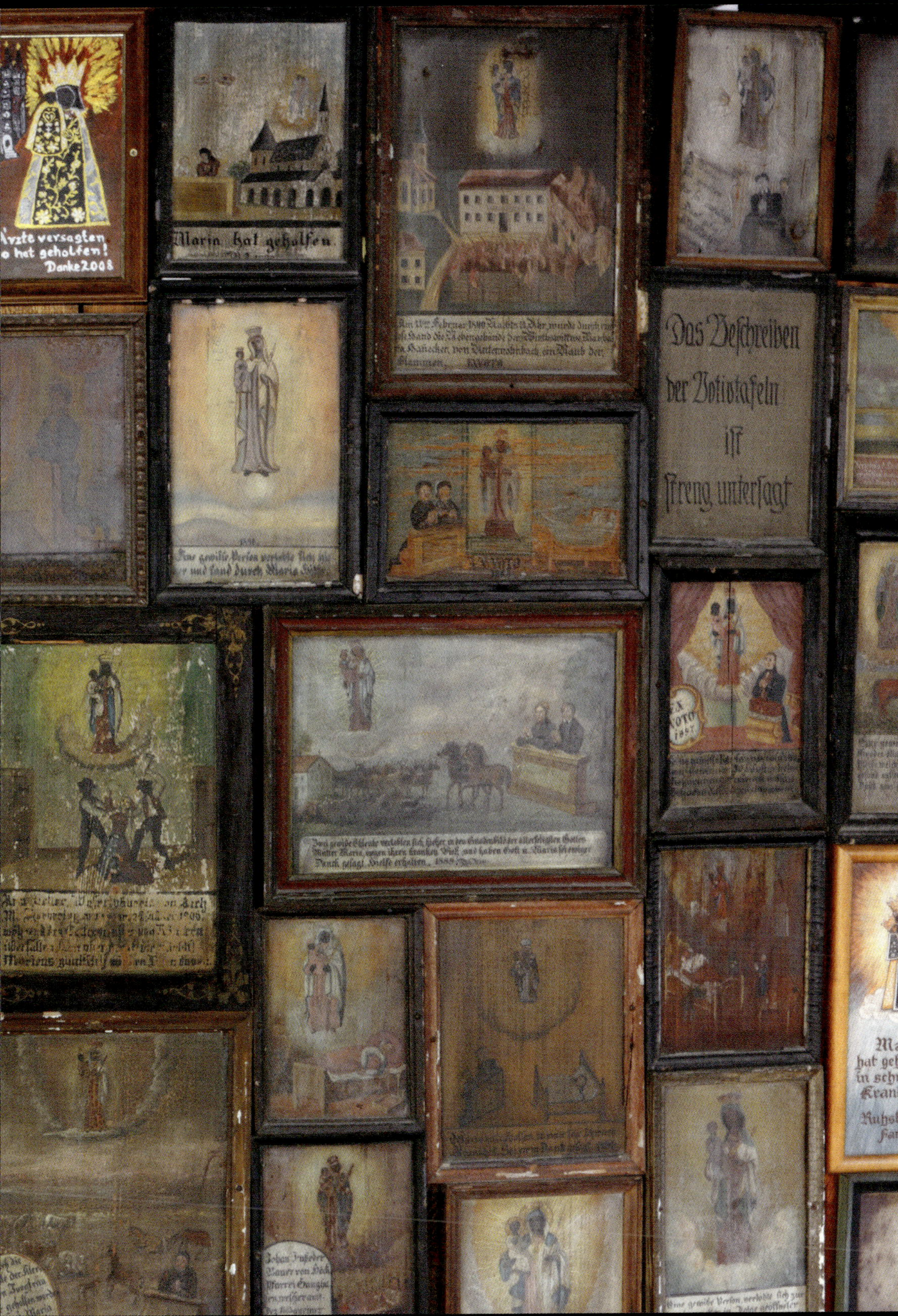

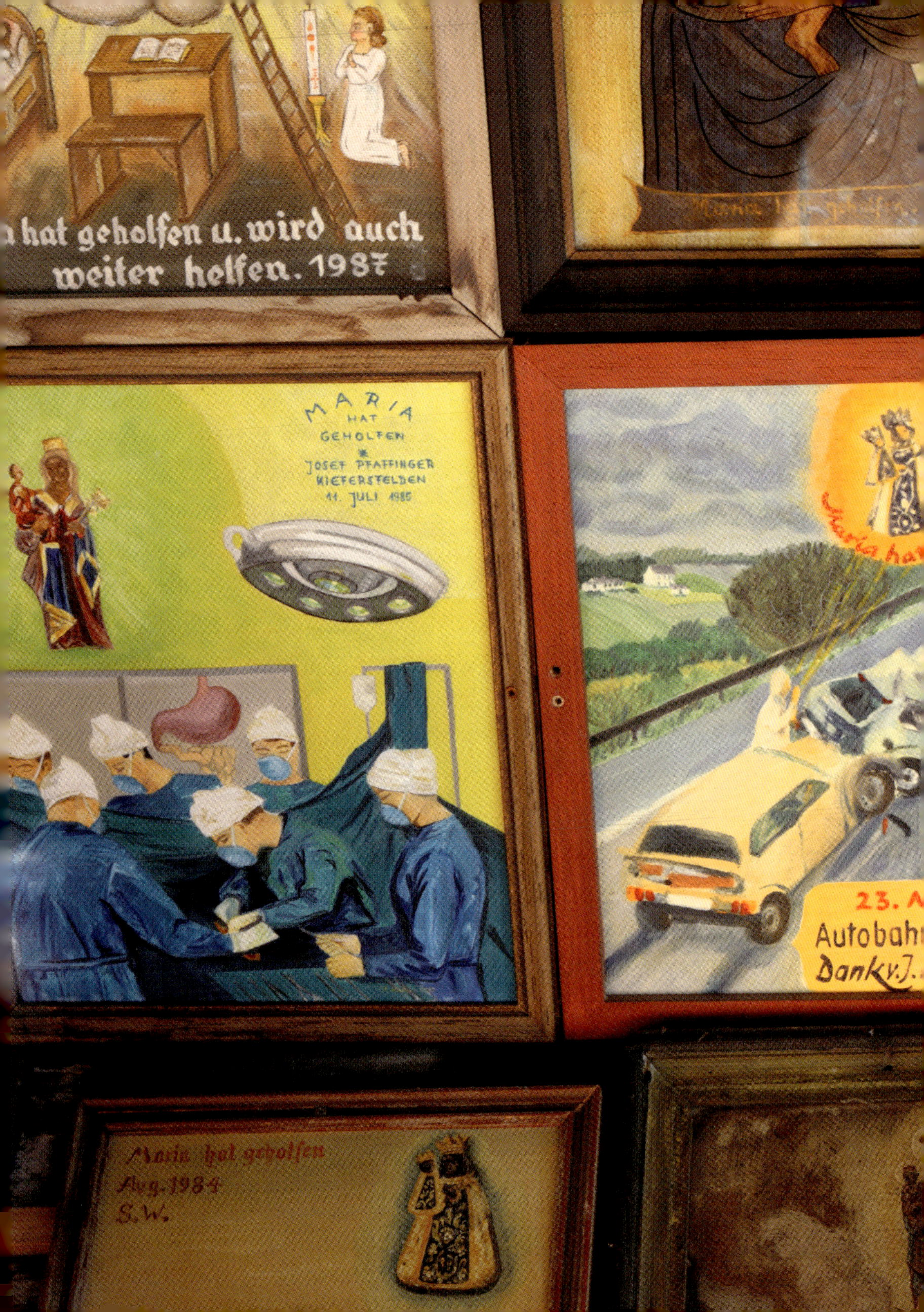
...a hat geholfen u. wird auch
weiter helfen. 1987
Maria hat geholfen
MARIA
HAT
GEHOLFEN
*
JOSEF PFAFFINGER
KIEFERSFELDEN
11. JULI 1985
Maria ha...
23. ...
Autobahn
Dank v. J...
Maria hat geholfen
Aug. 1984
S.W.

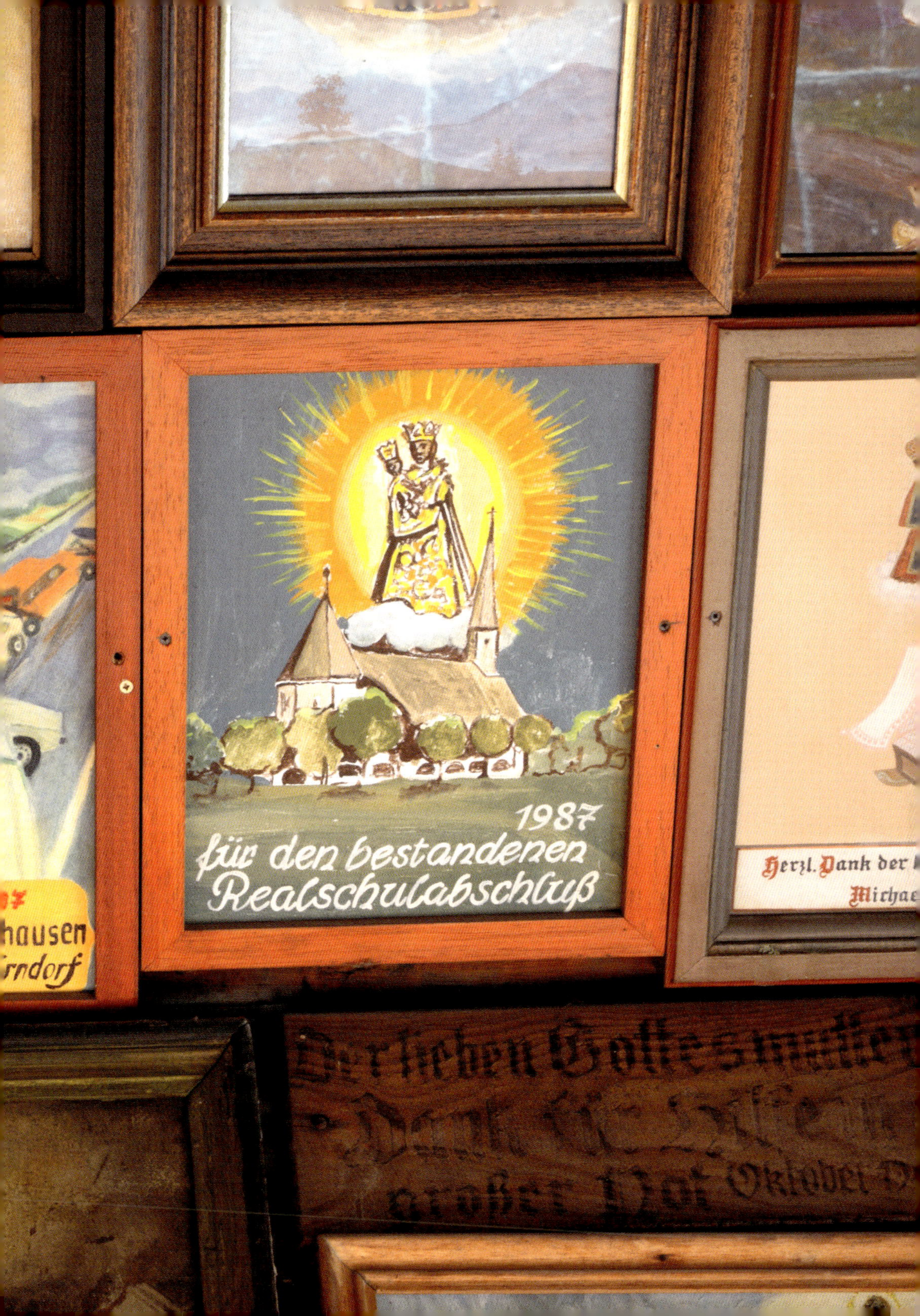

1987
für den bestandenen
Realschulabschluß
hausen
rndorf
Herzl. Dank der
Michae
Der lieben Gottesmutter
Dank für
großer Not Oktober

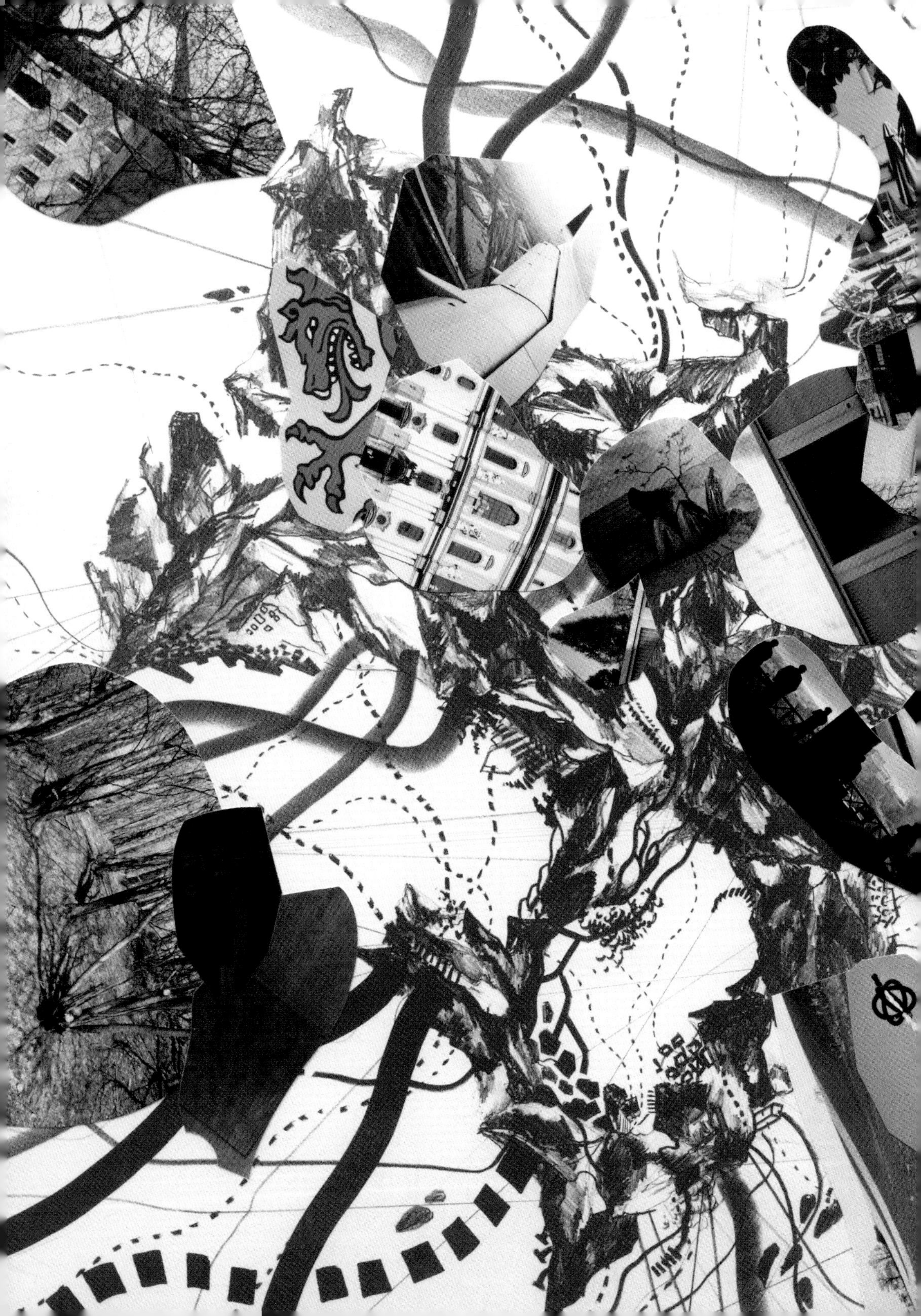

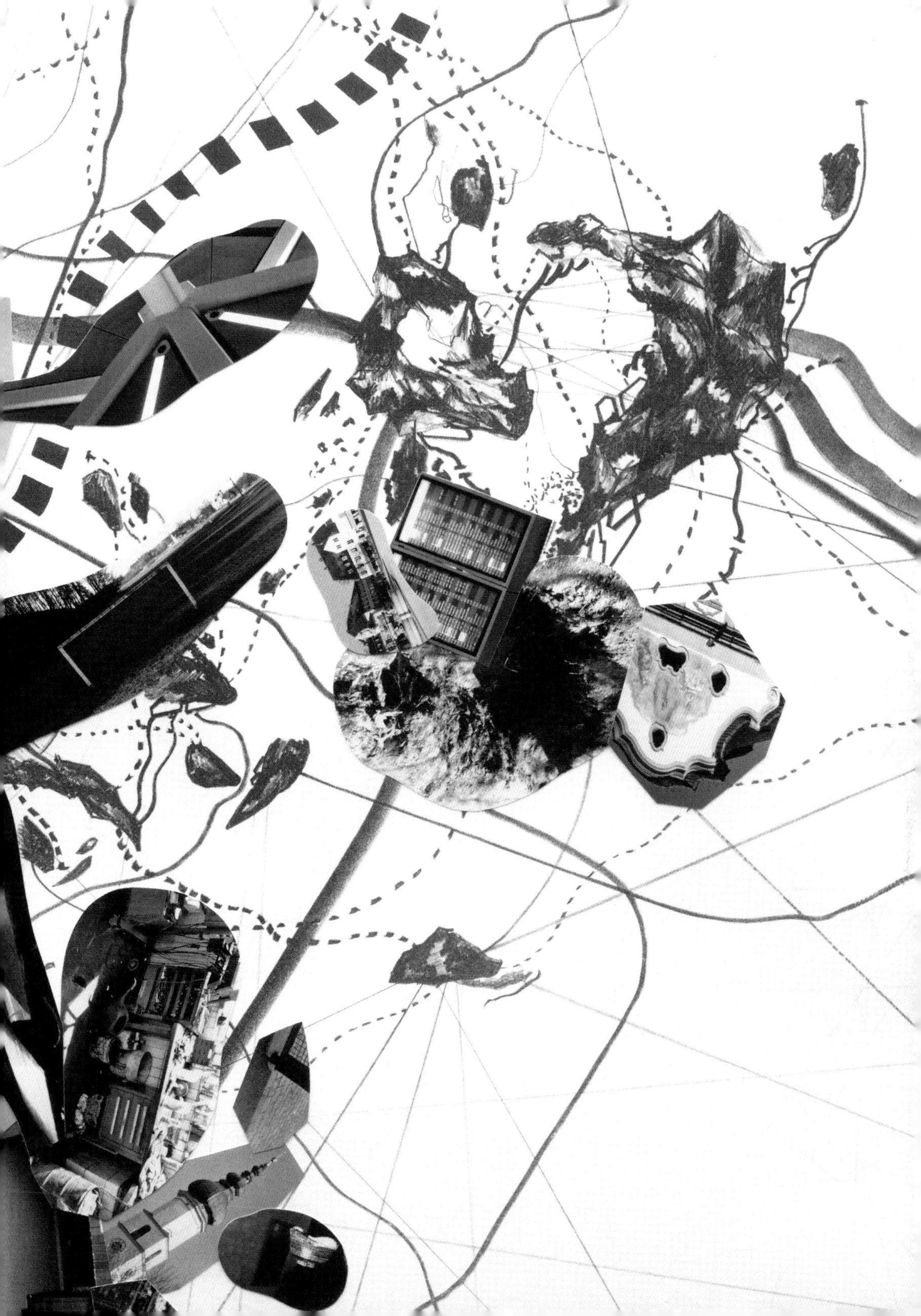

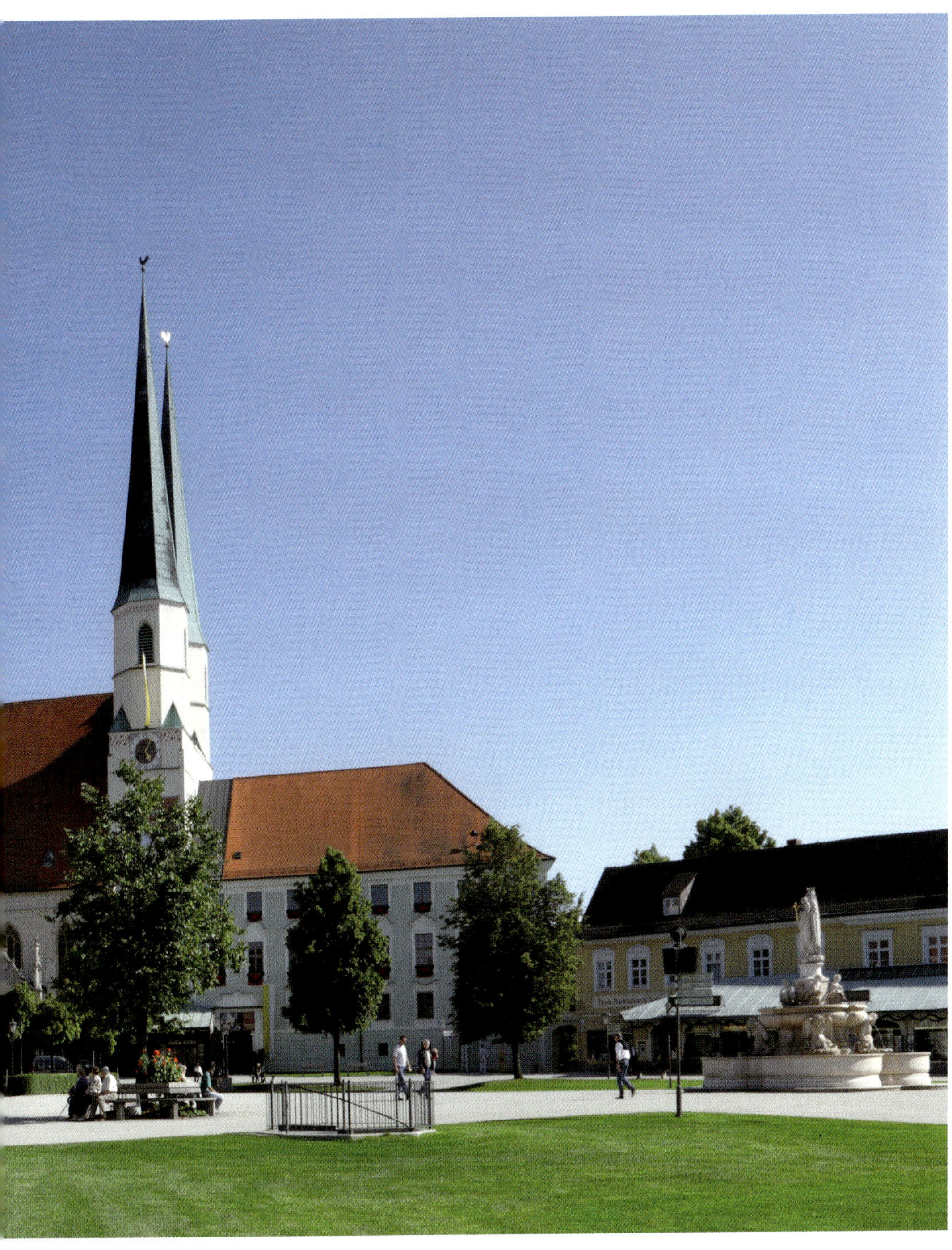

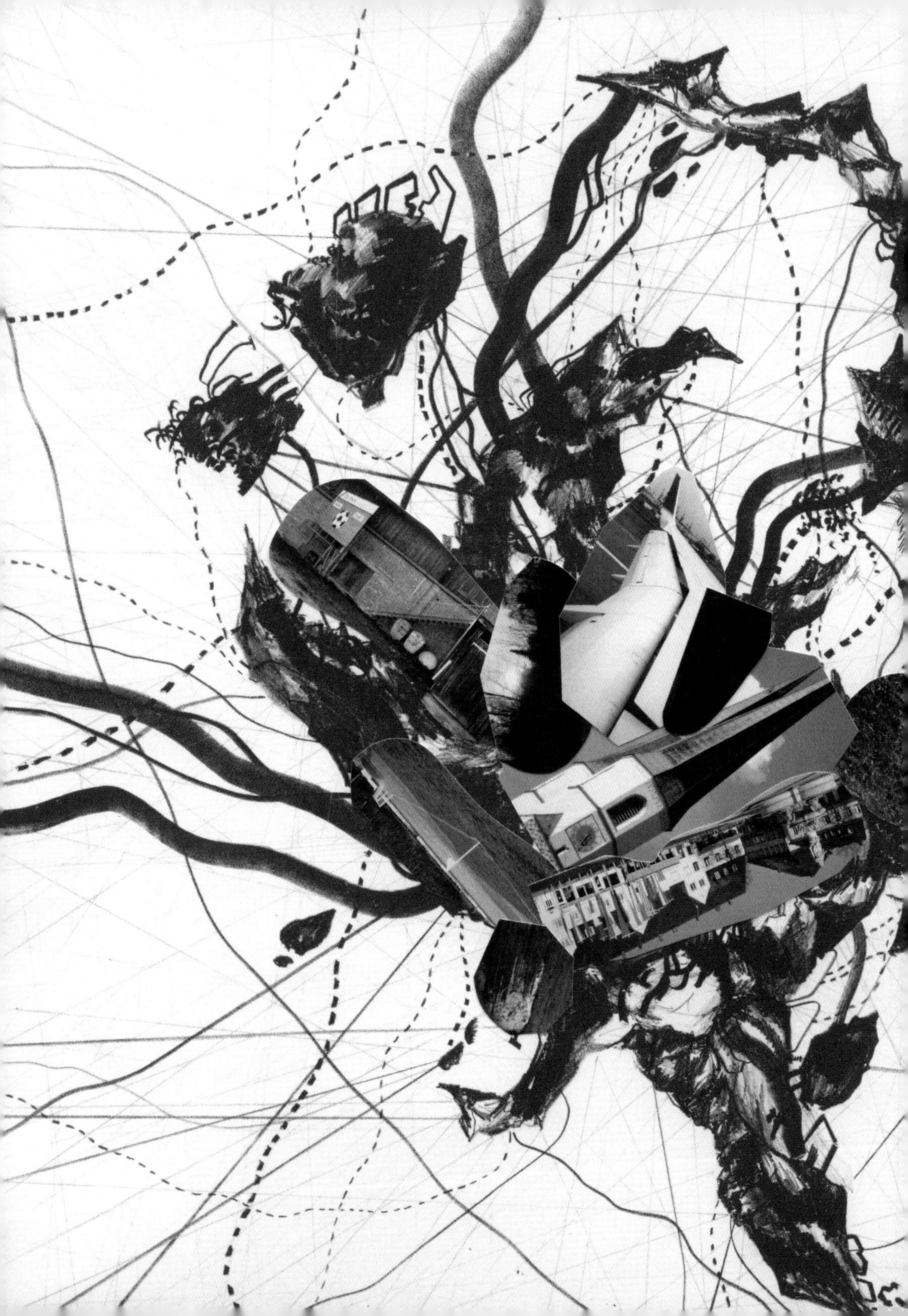

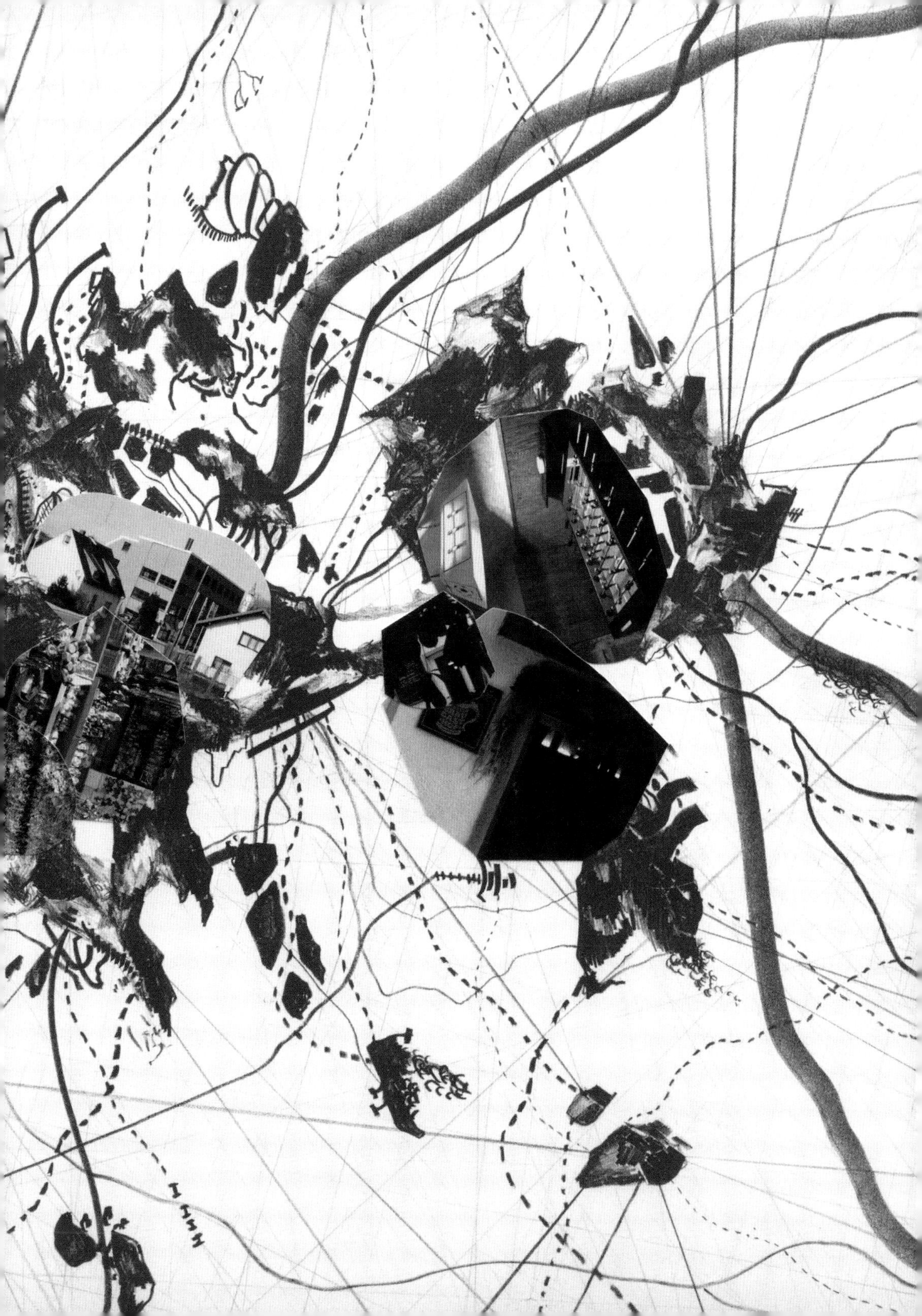

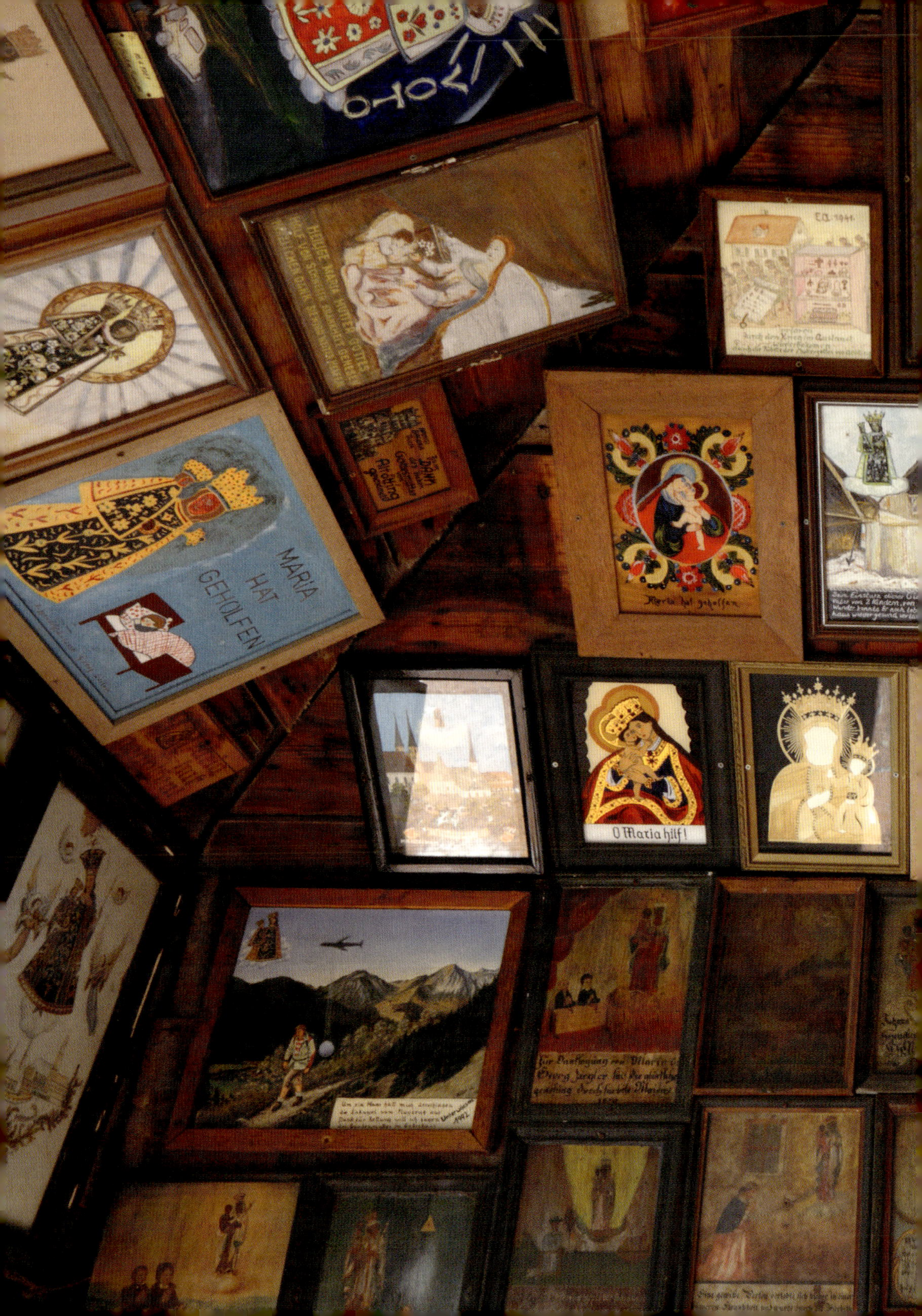

MARIA HAT GEHOLFEN
O Maria hilf!

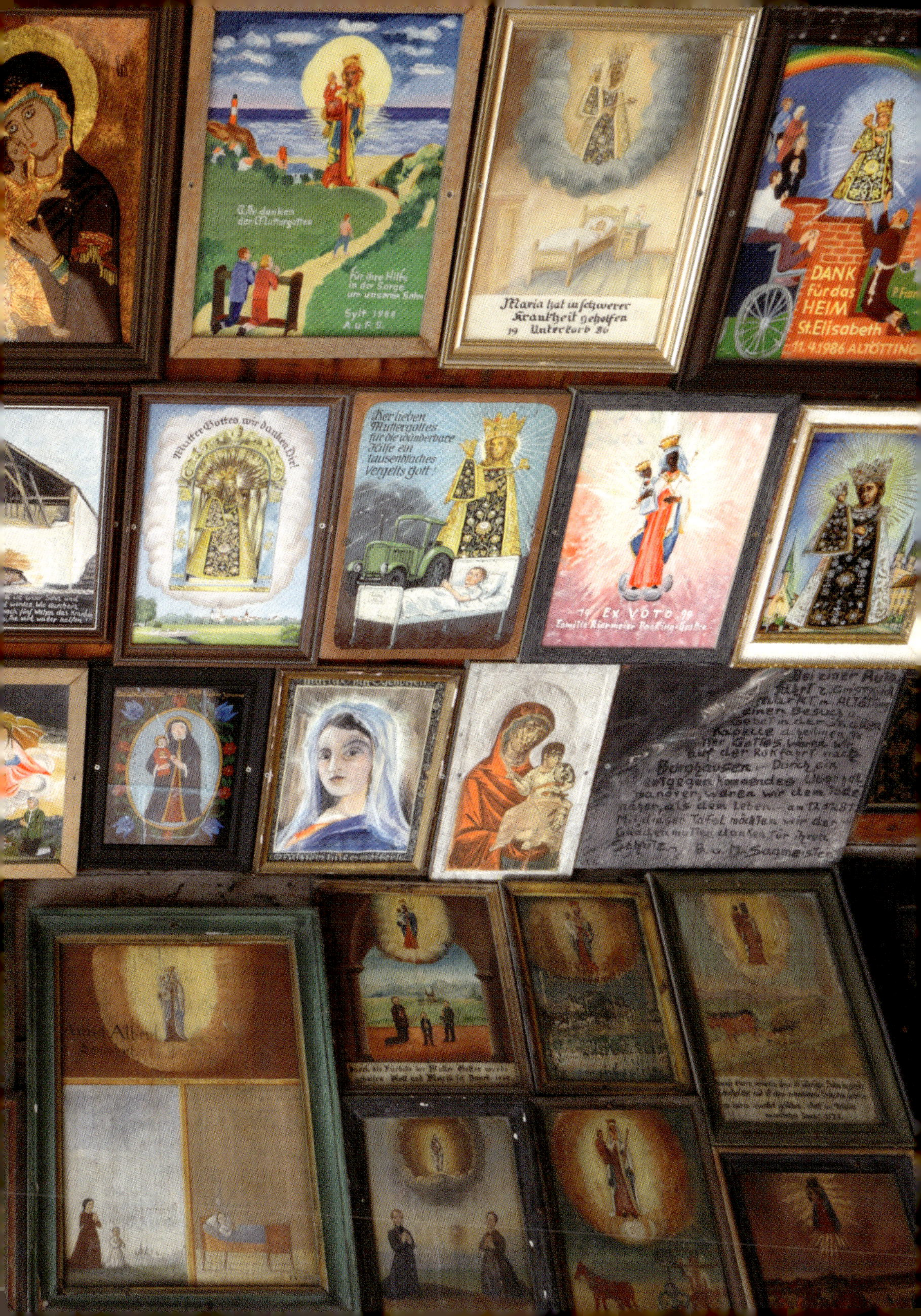

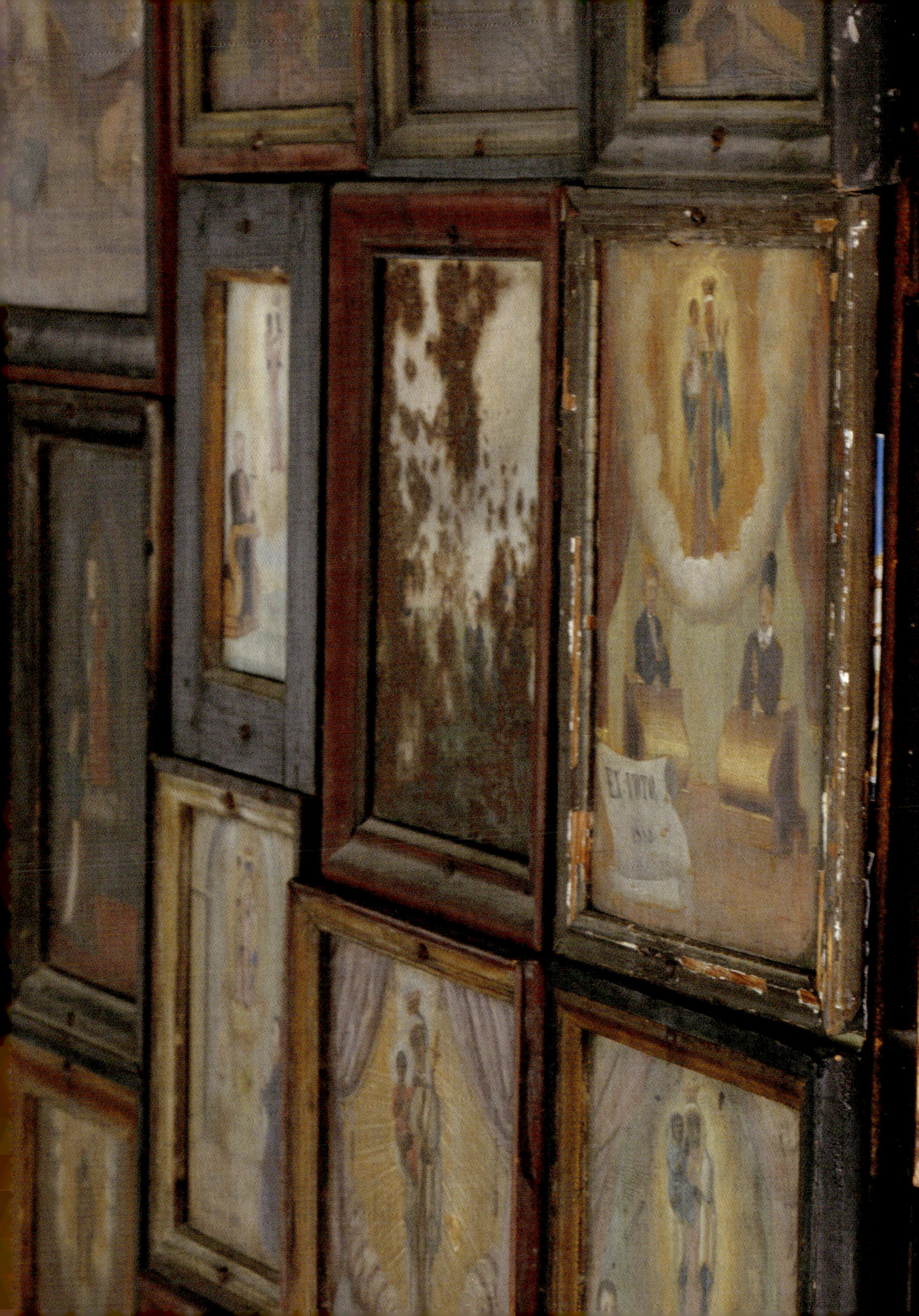

...ne gewisse Familie verlobte
... hieher, und fand Maria
sei Dank Hilfe.
1880

Wir haben ein
große Vertrau[en]
zu dir Jesus
o Maria
bitt für uns
1845.

Johañ und Barbara Wesmaier
Zehetmaier Eheleute v. Högling.
Landg. Aibling verlobten sich hie[her]

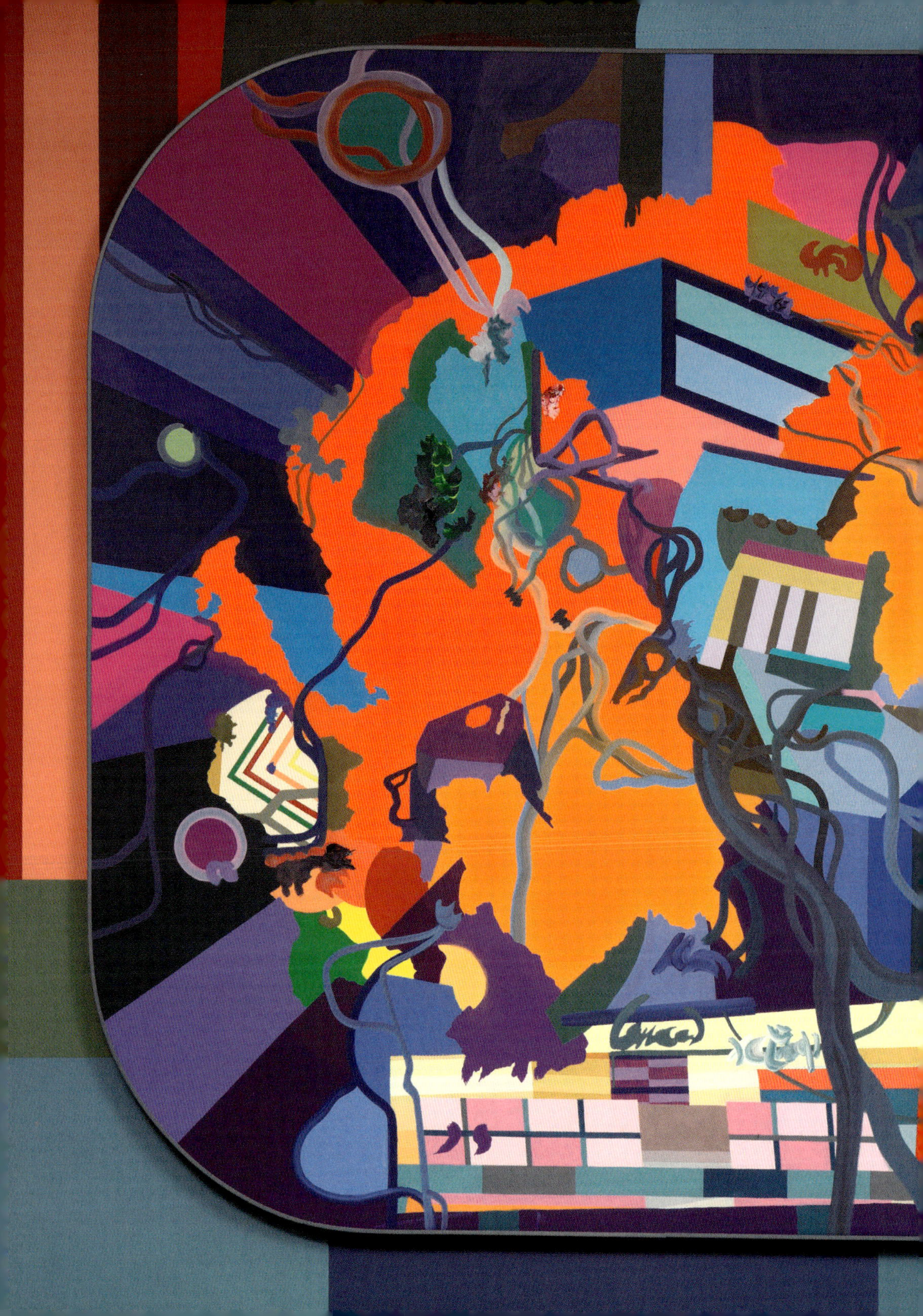

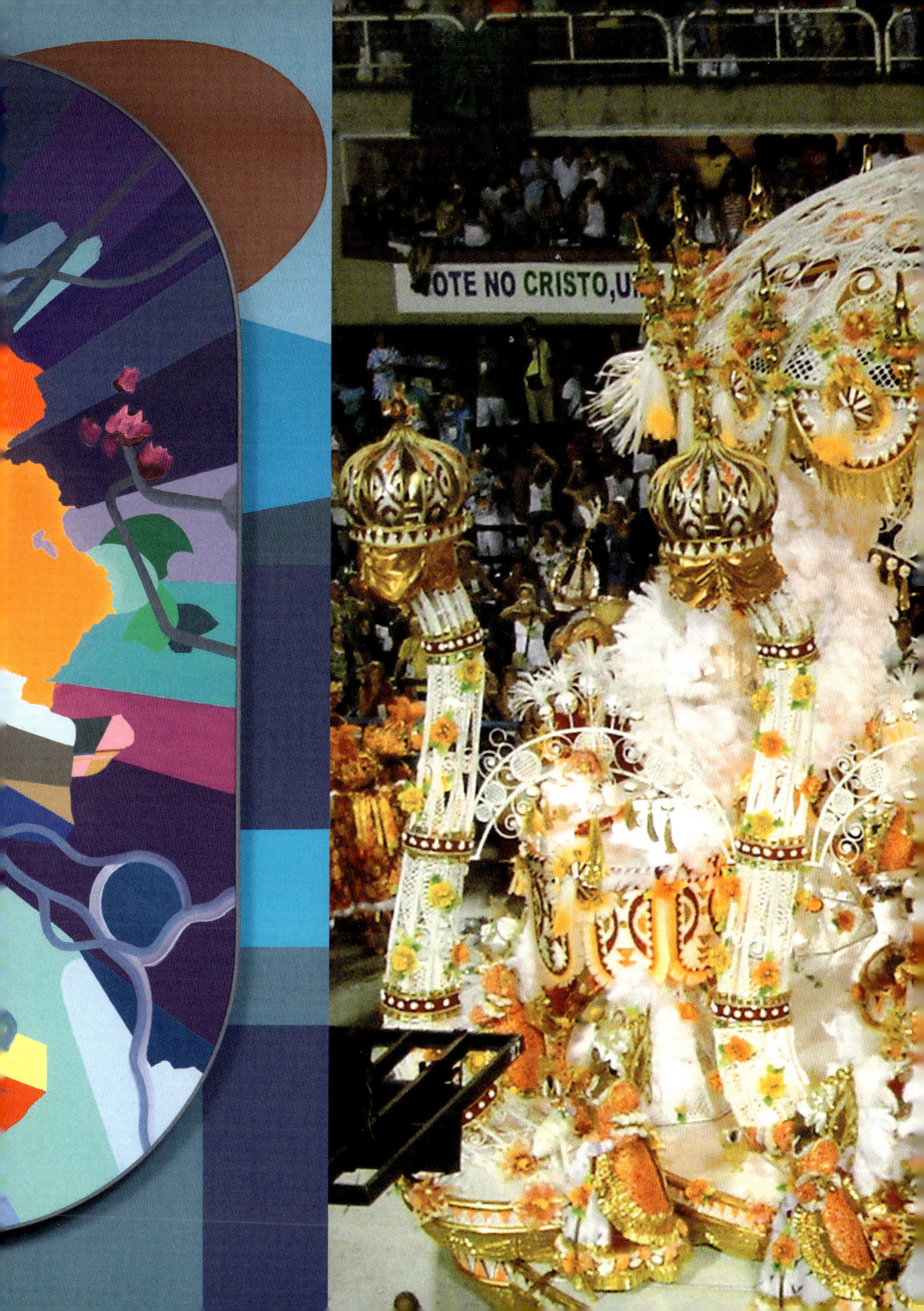
OTE NO CRISTO,U

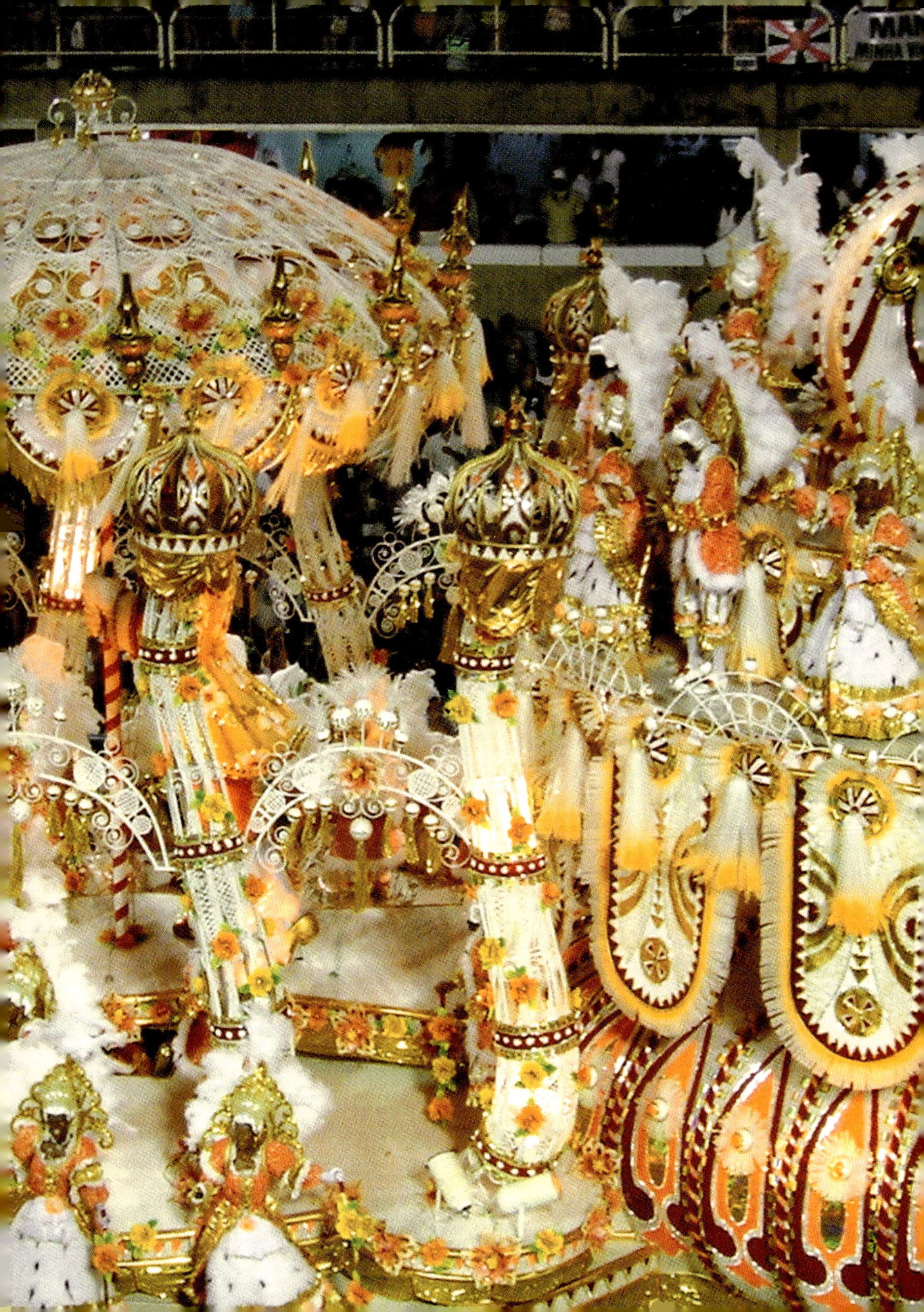

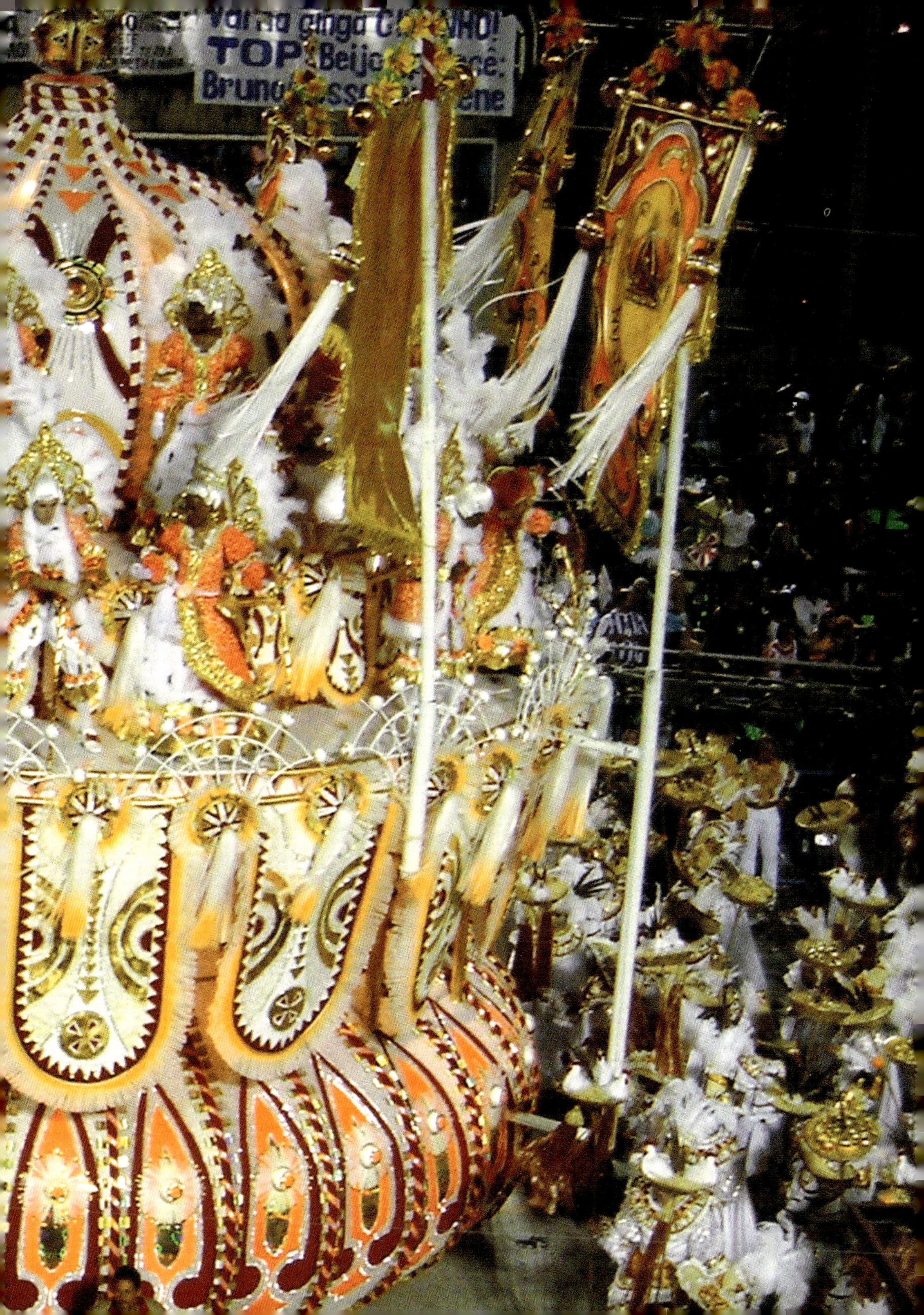

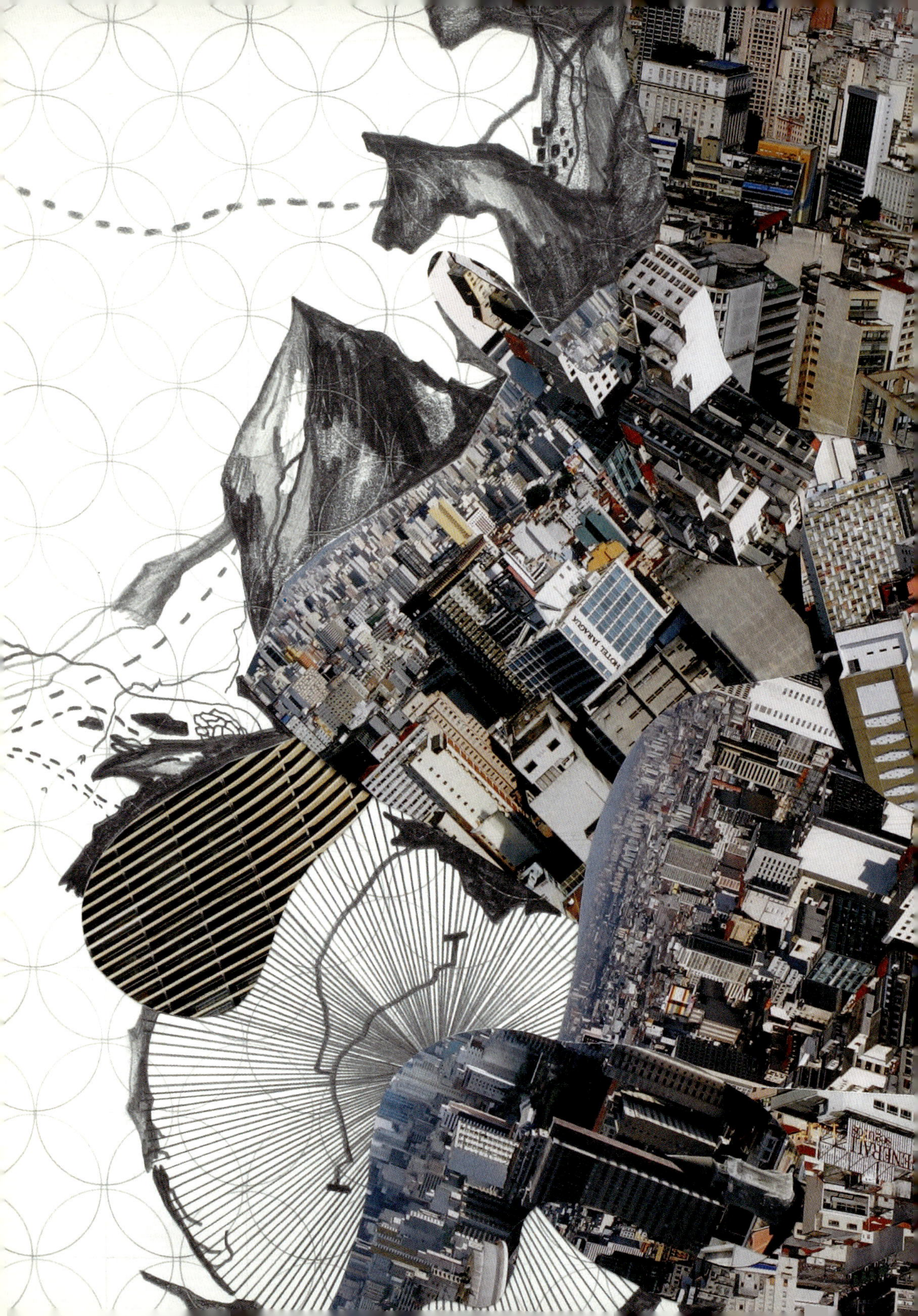

HOTEL JARAGUÁ

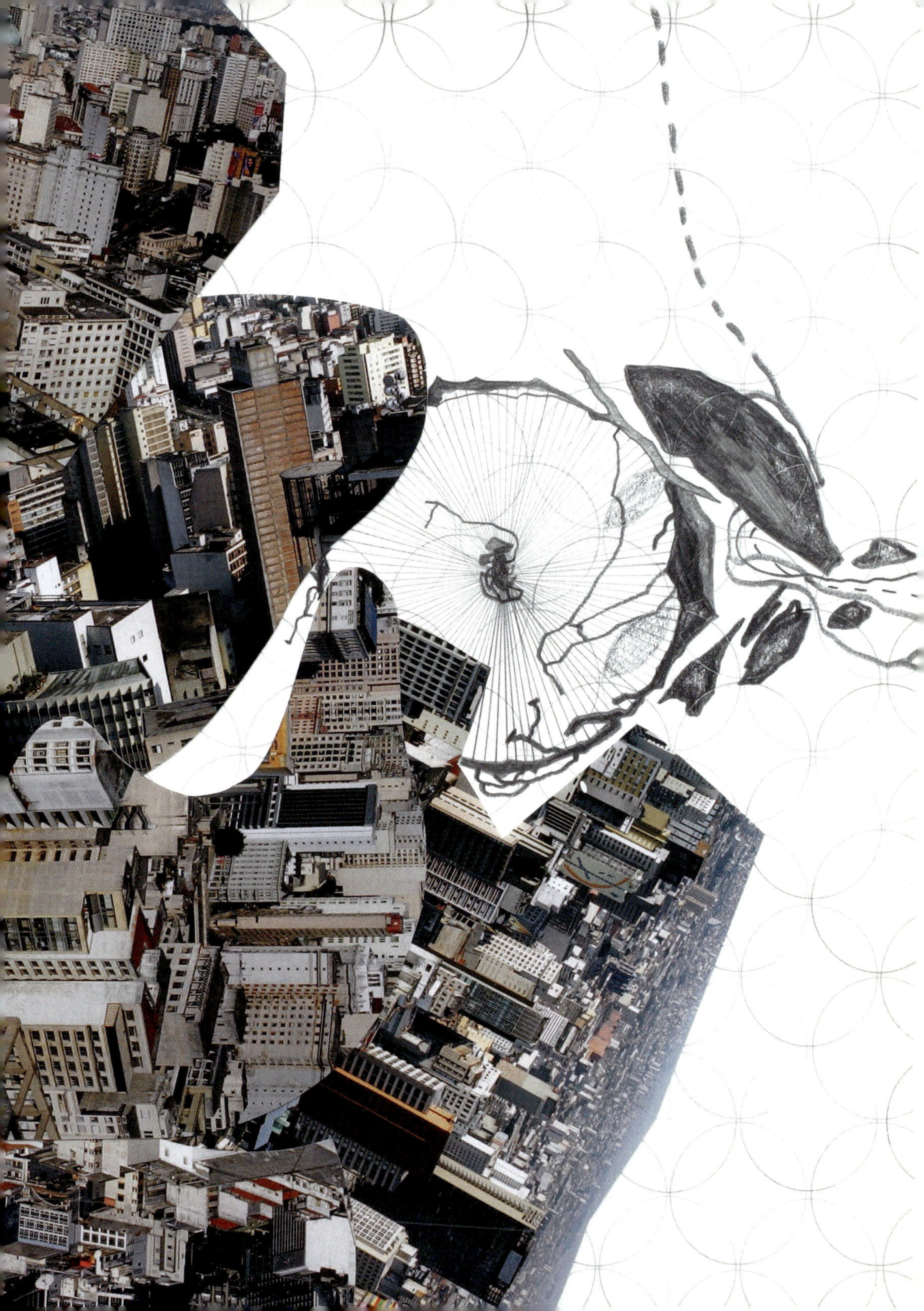

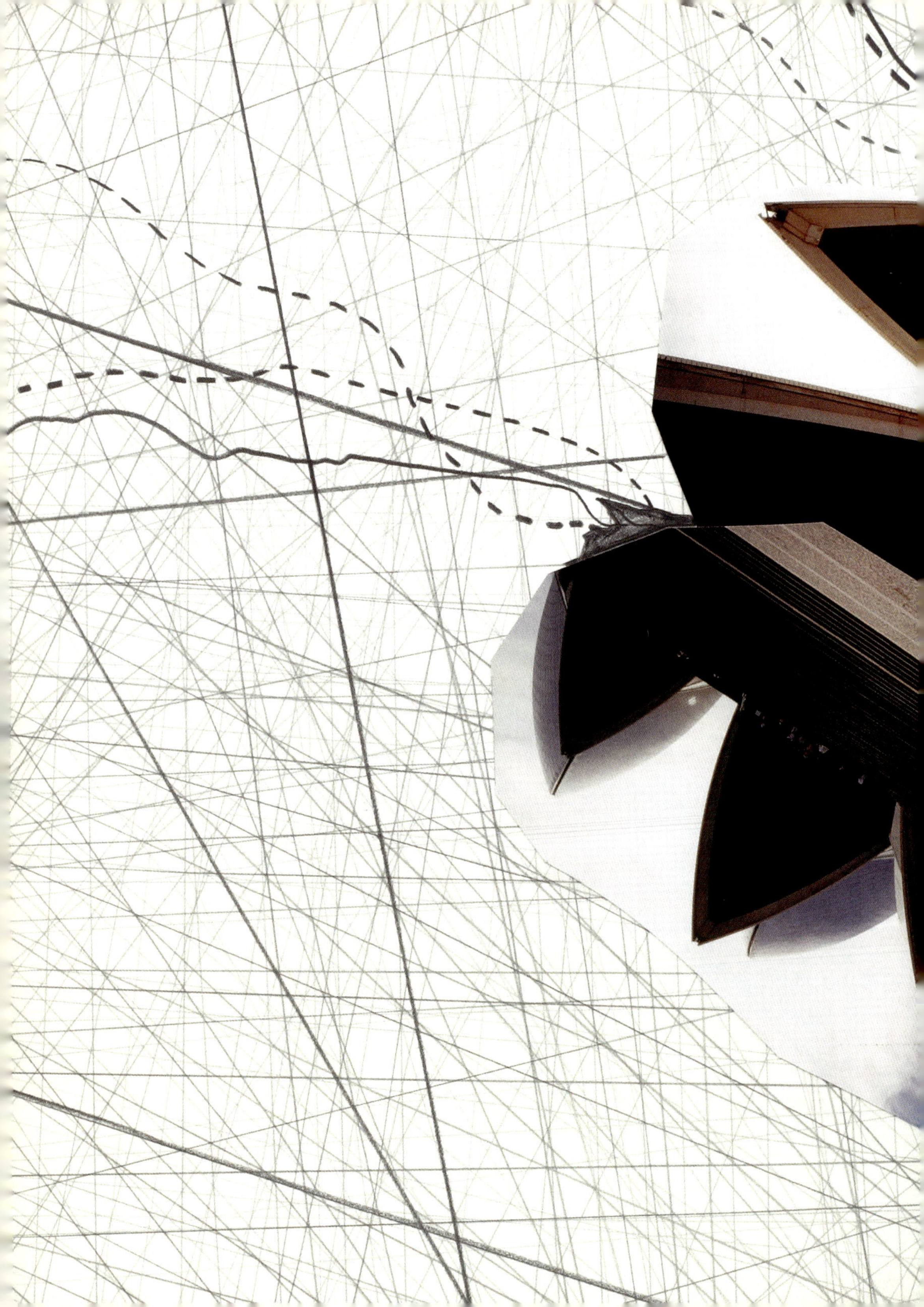

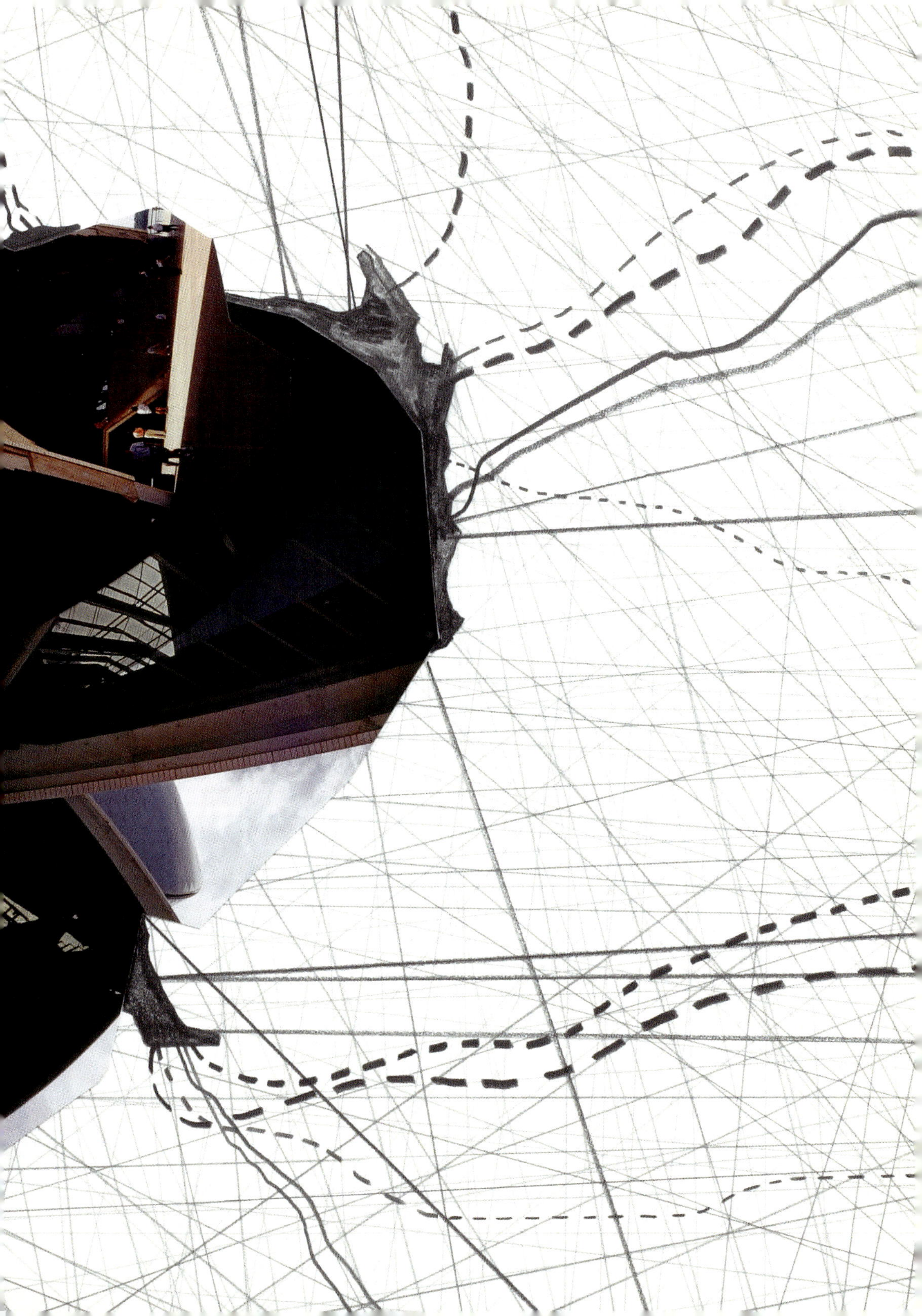

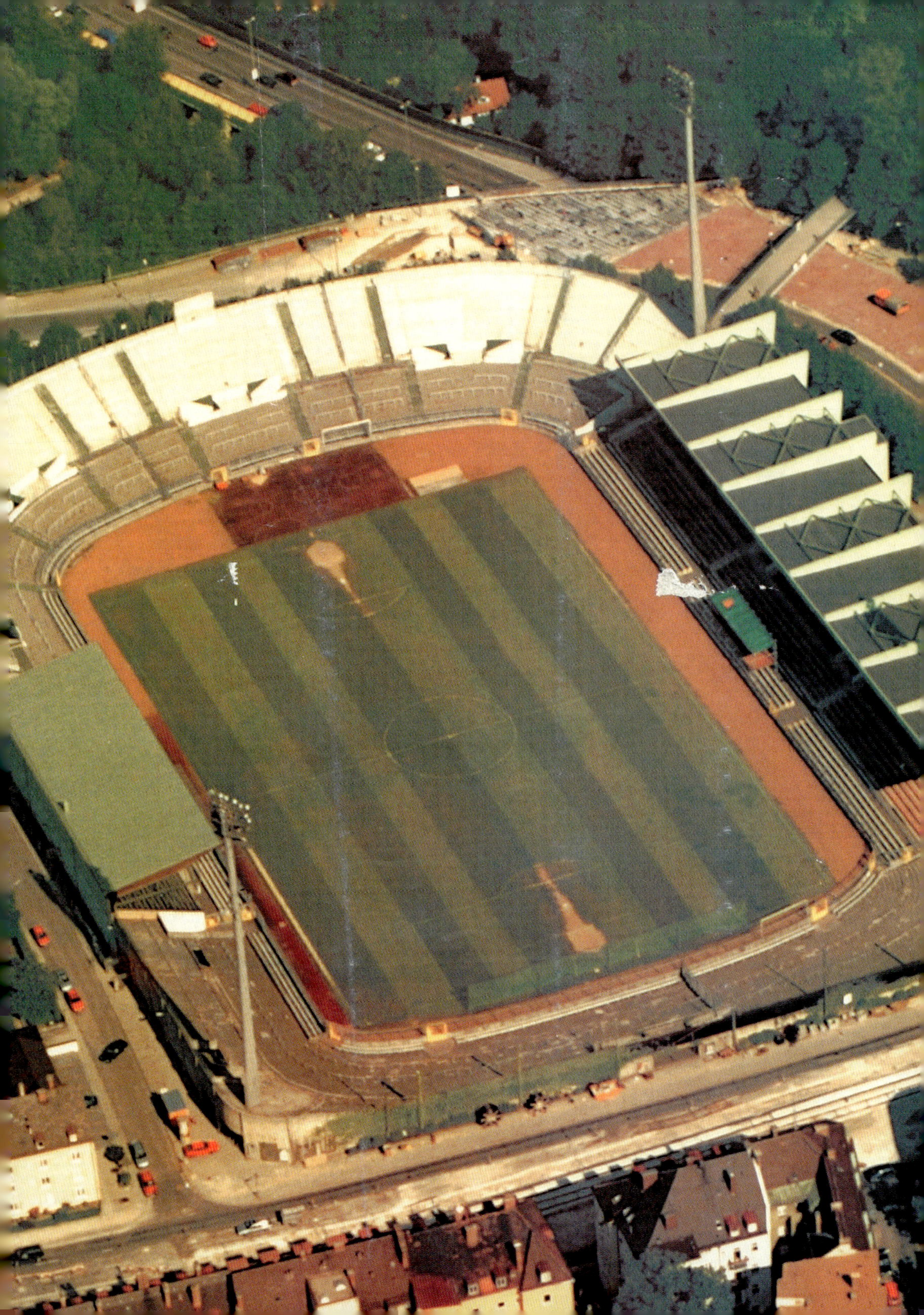

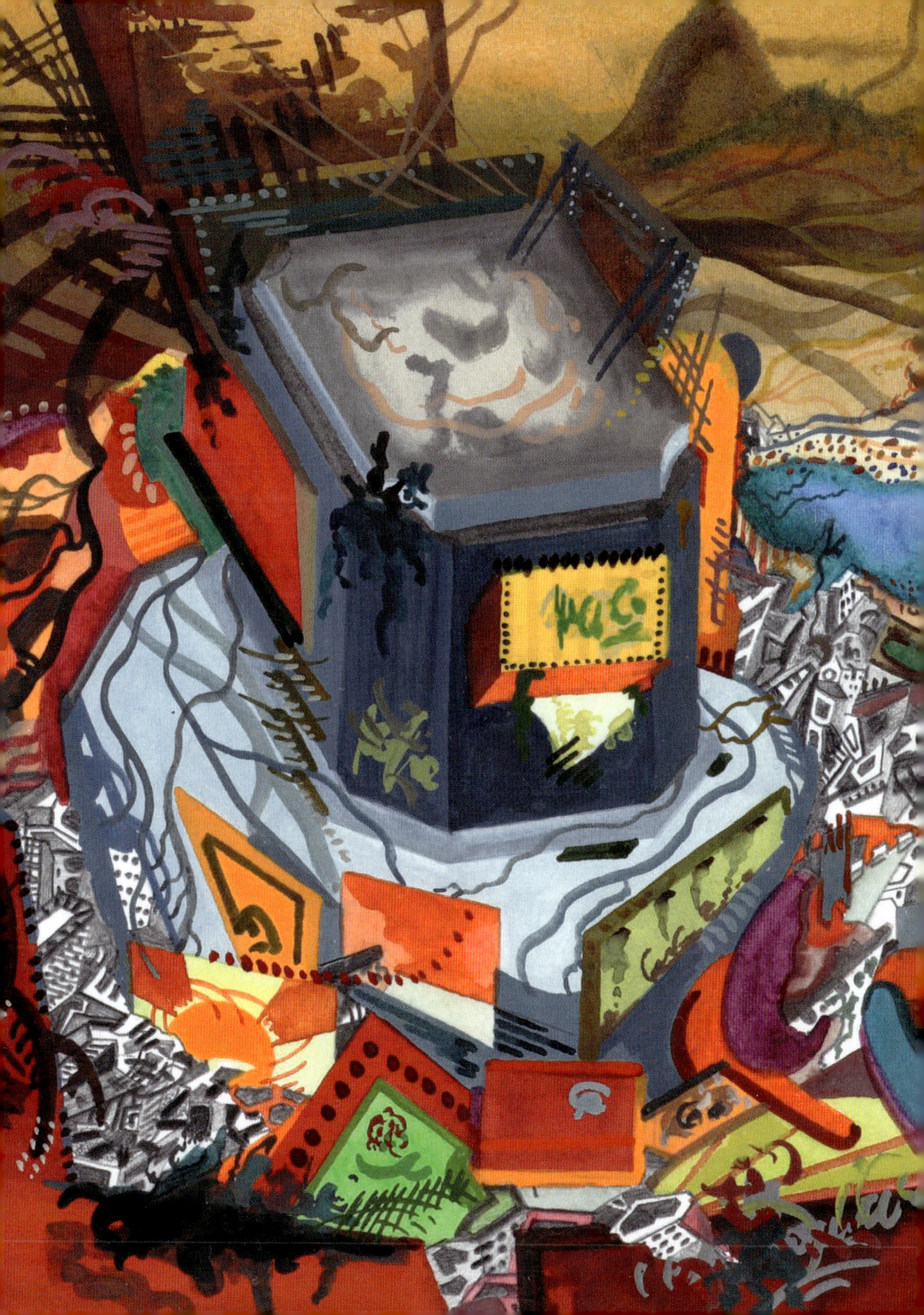

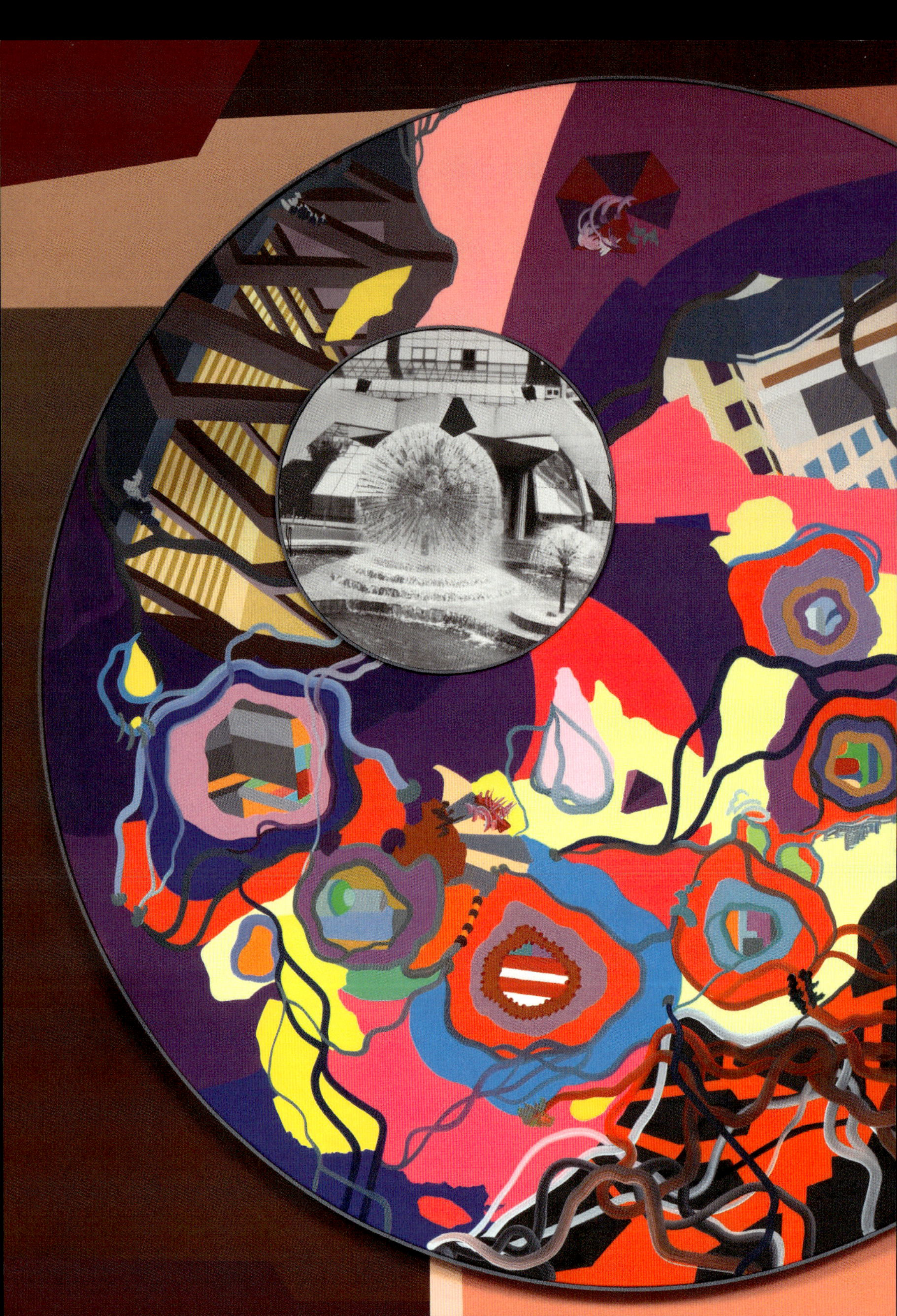

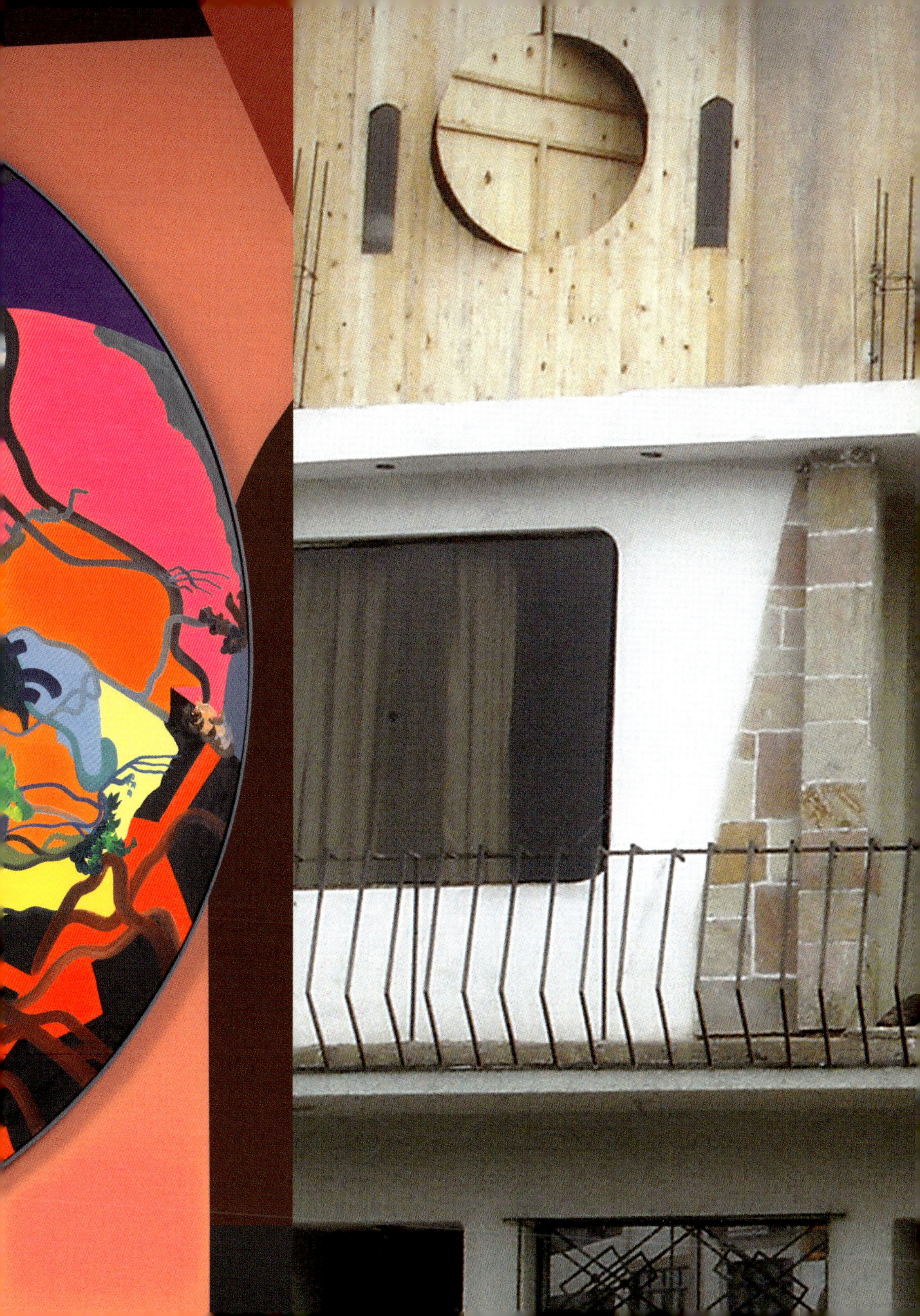

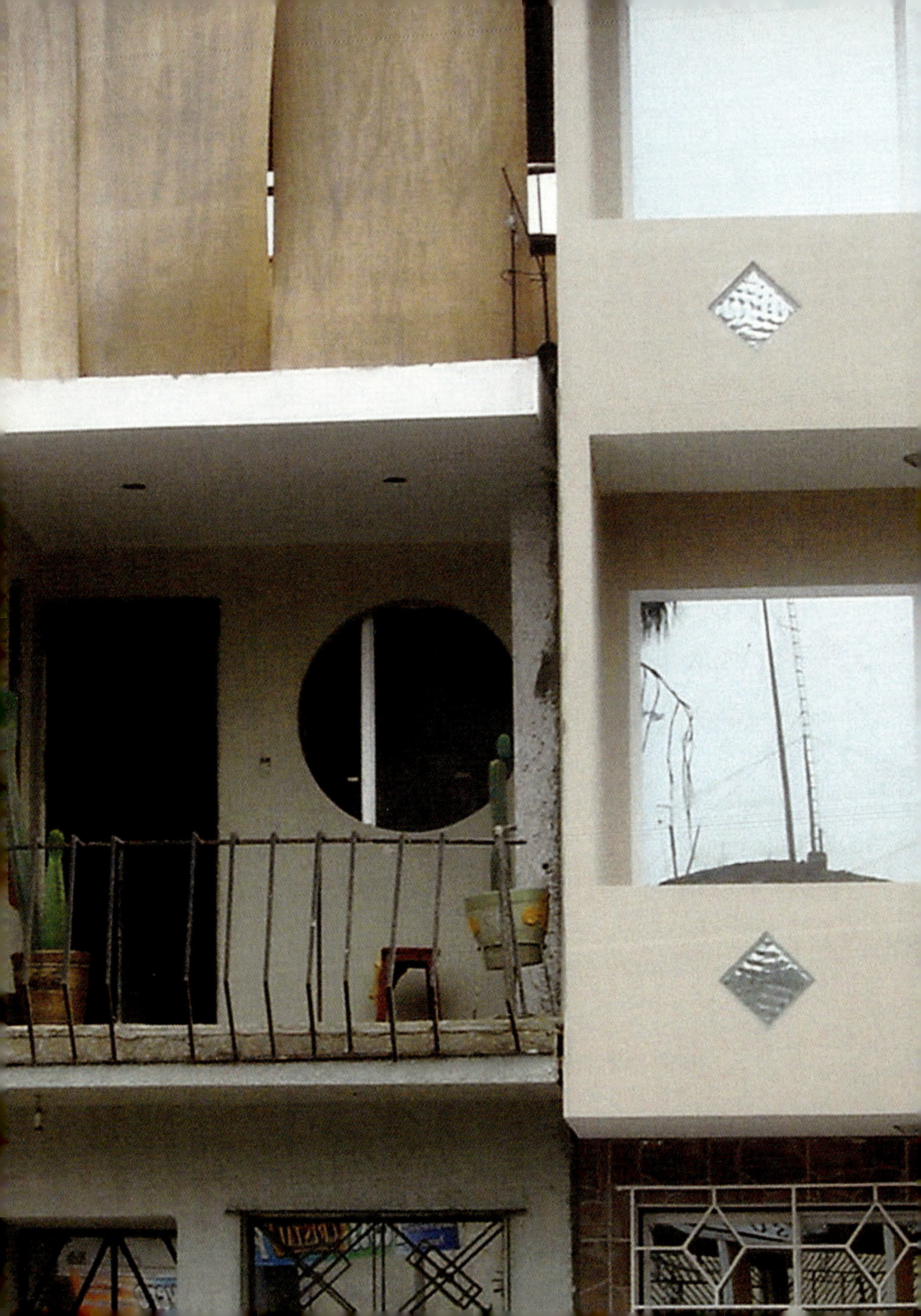

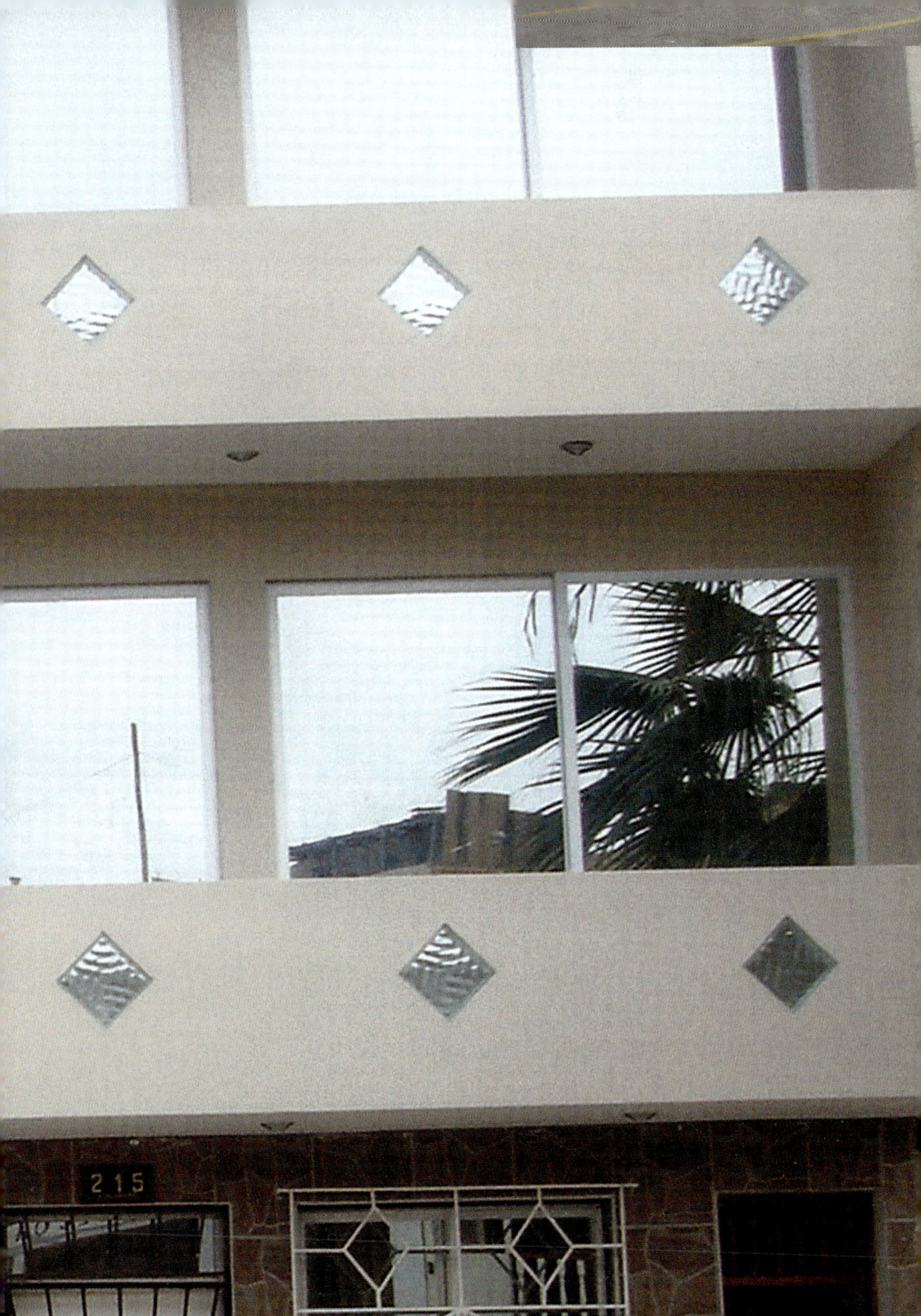

2 1 5

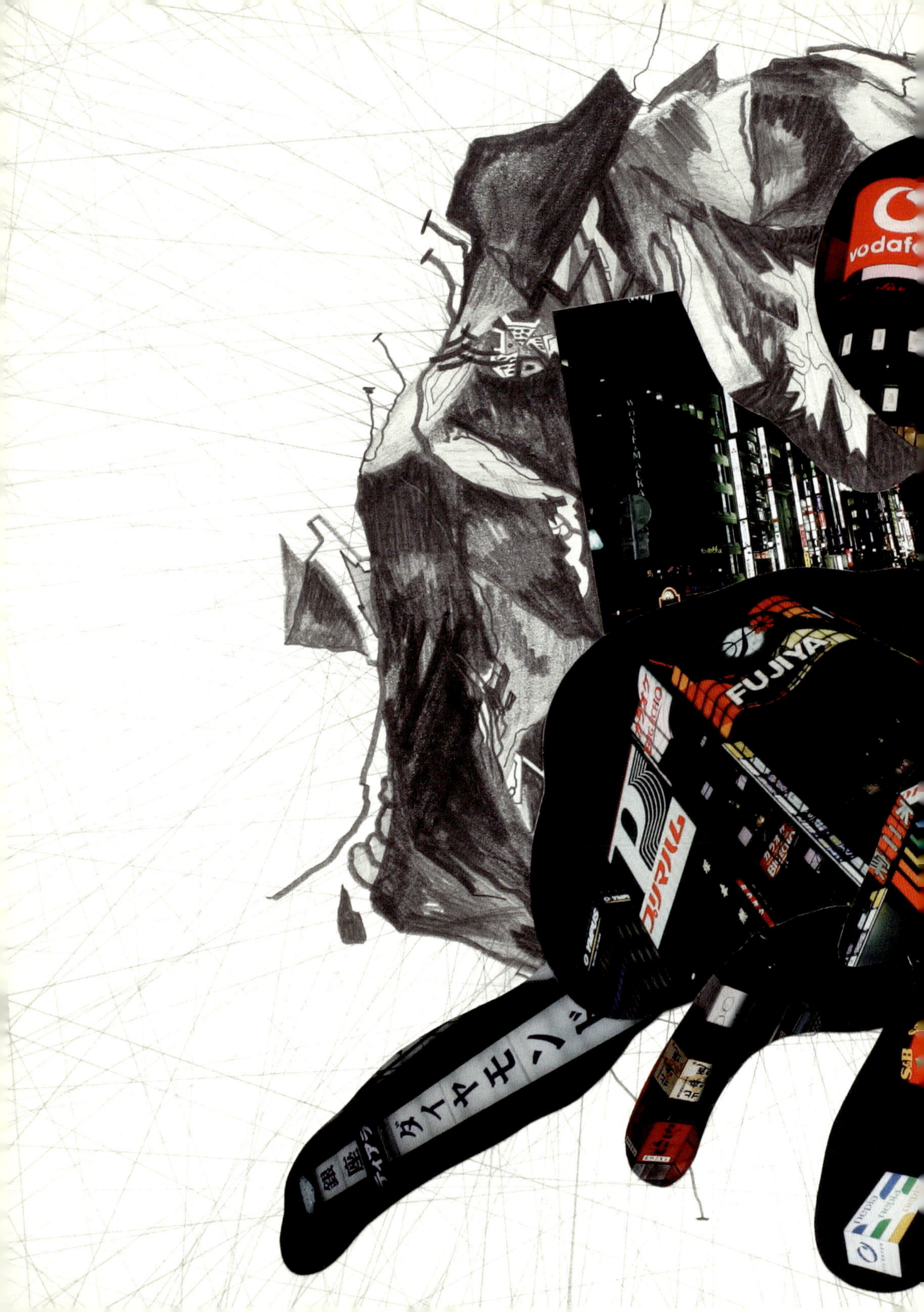

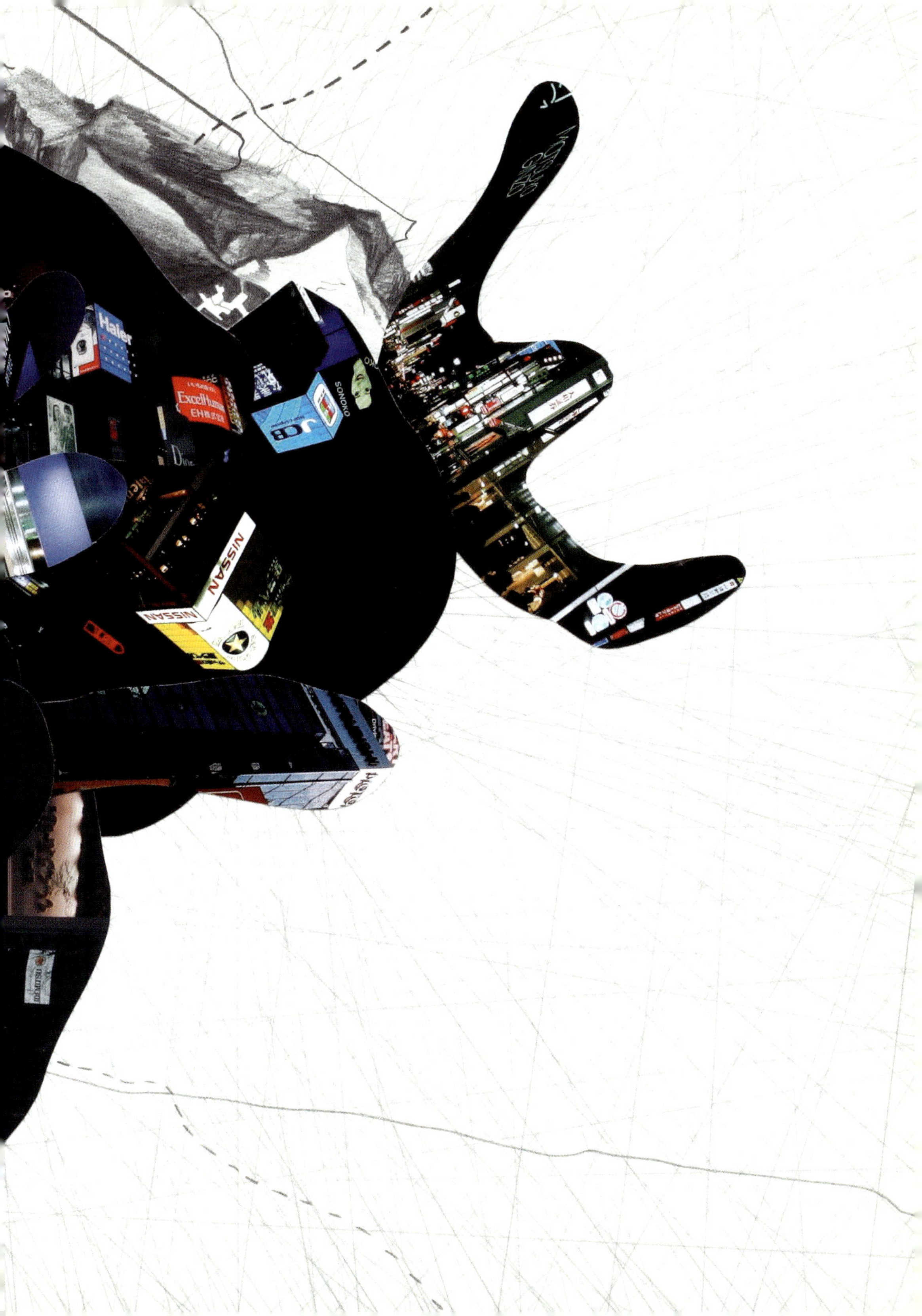

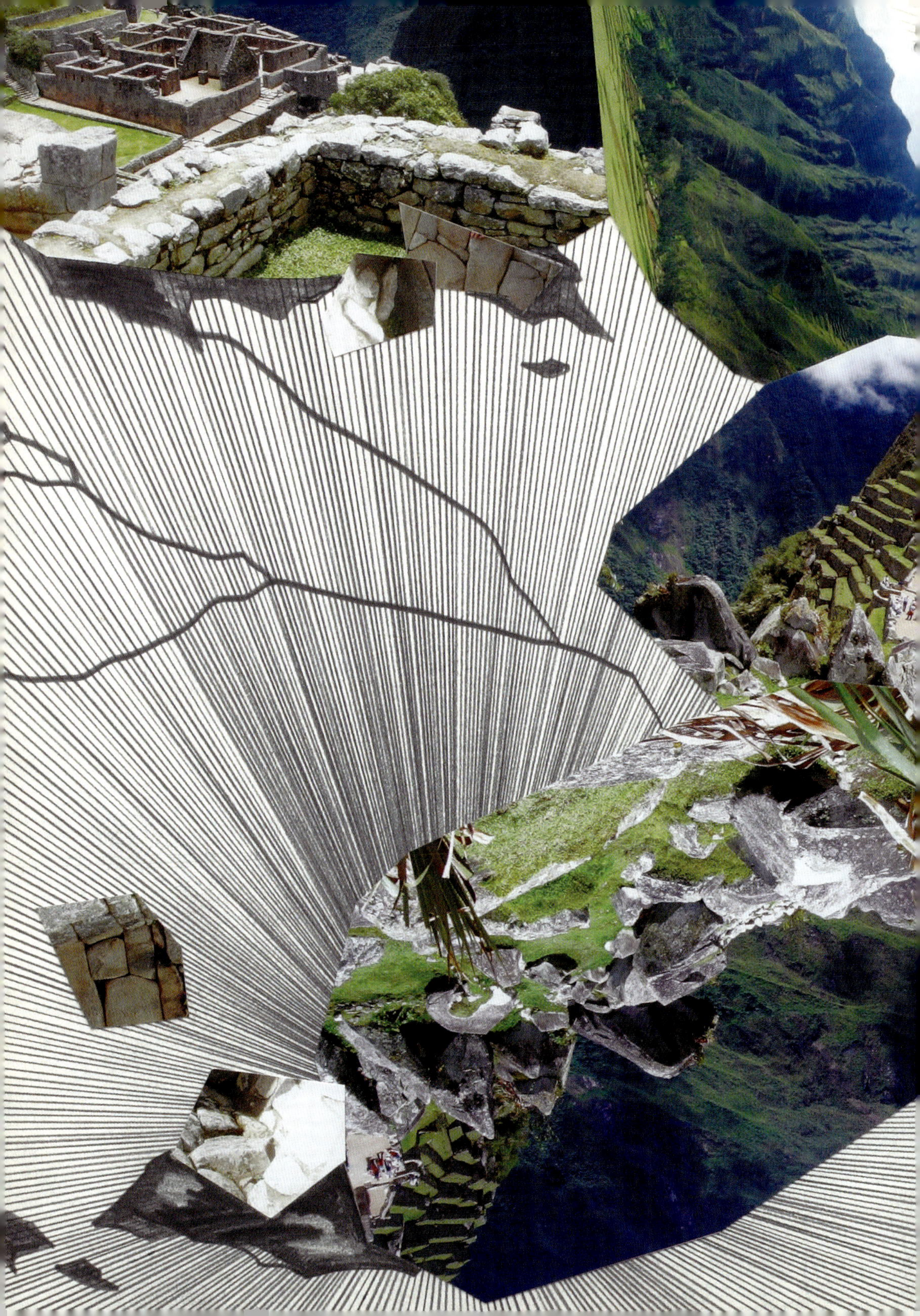

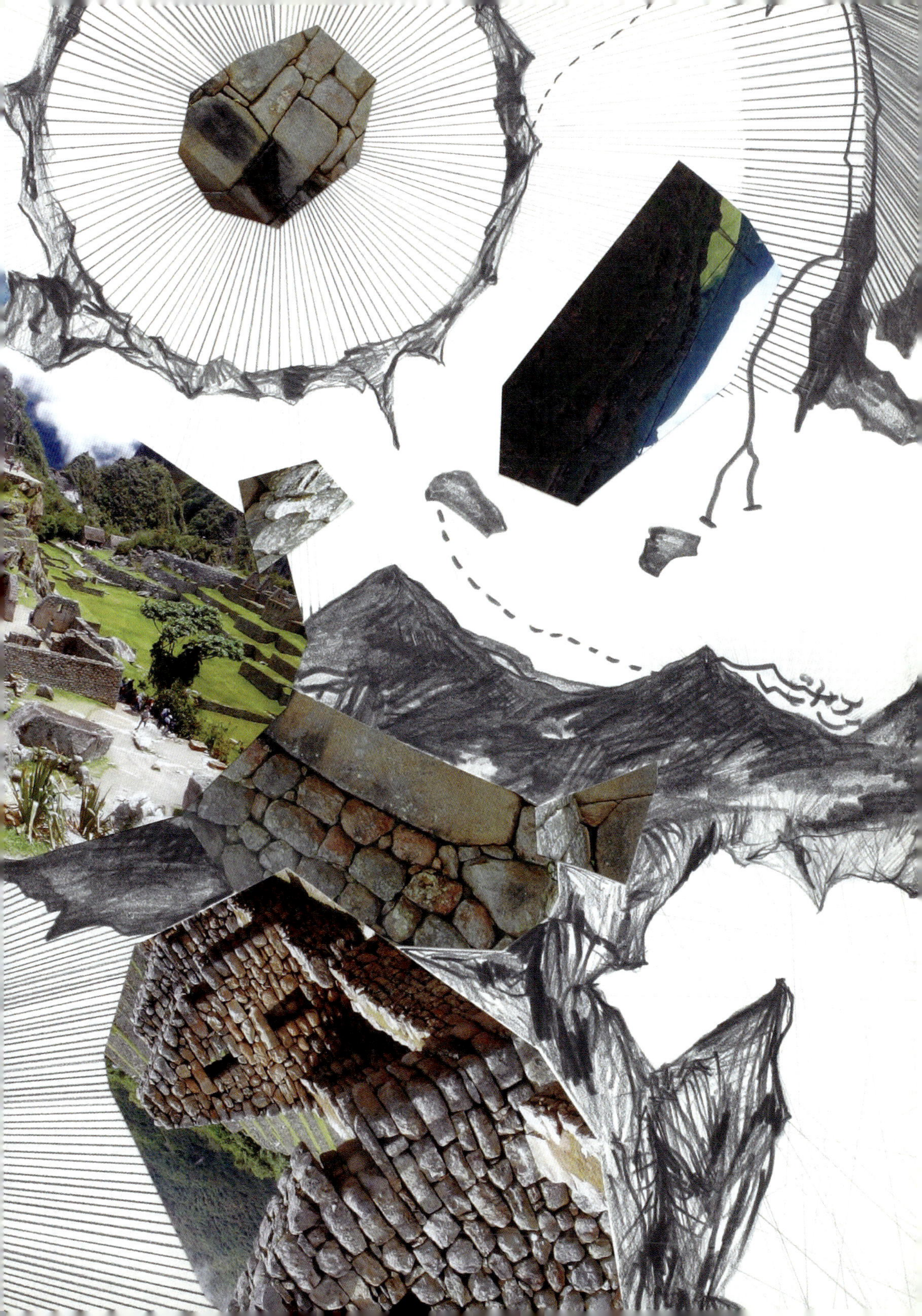

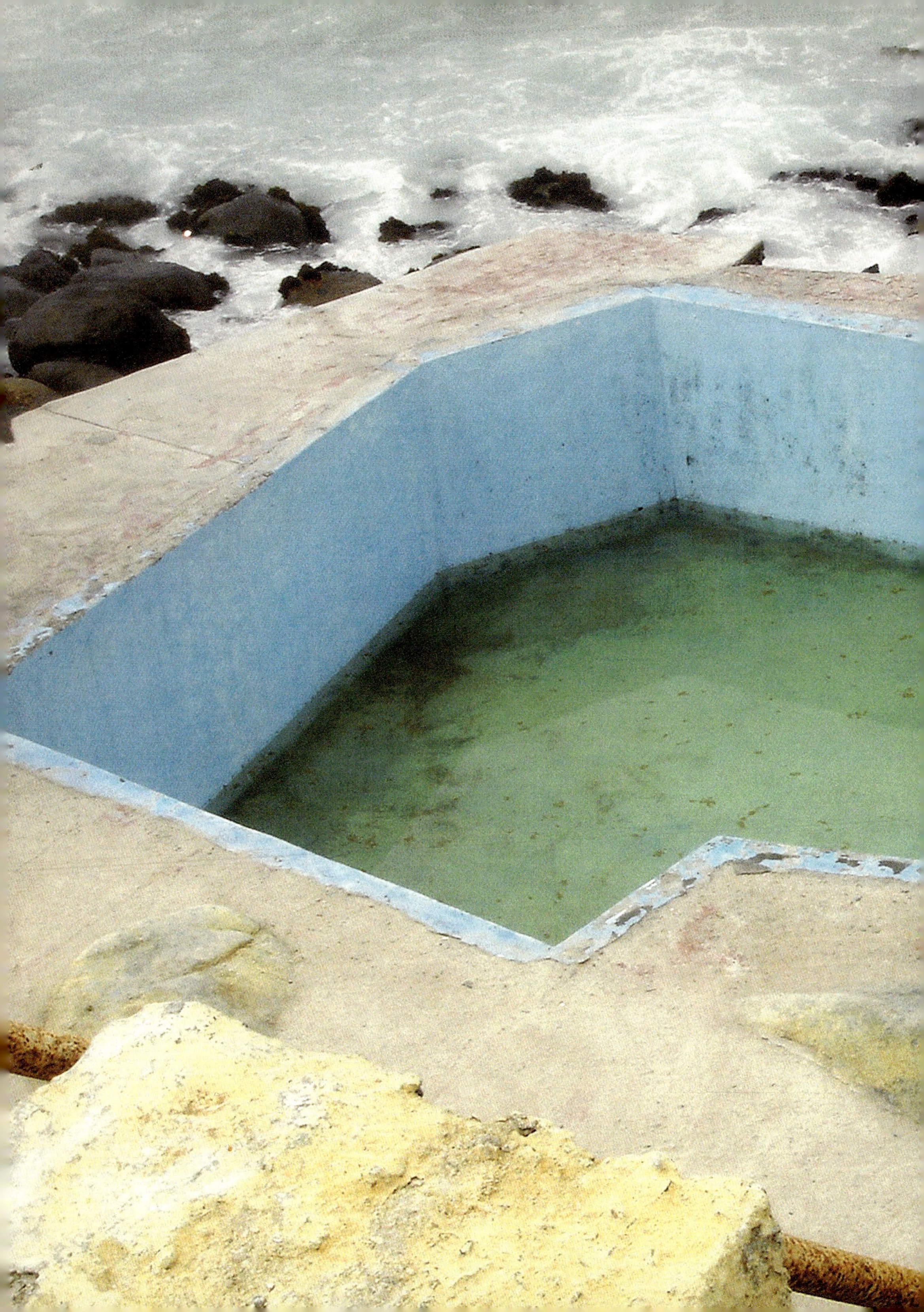

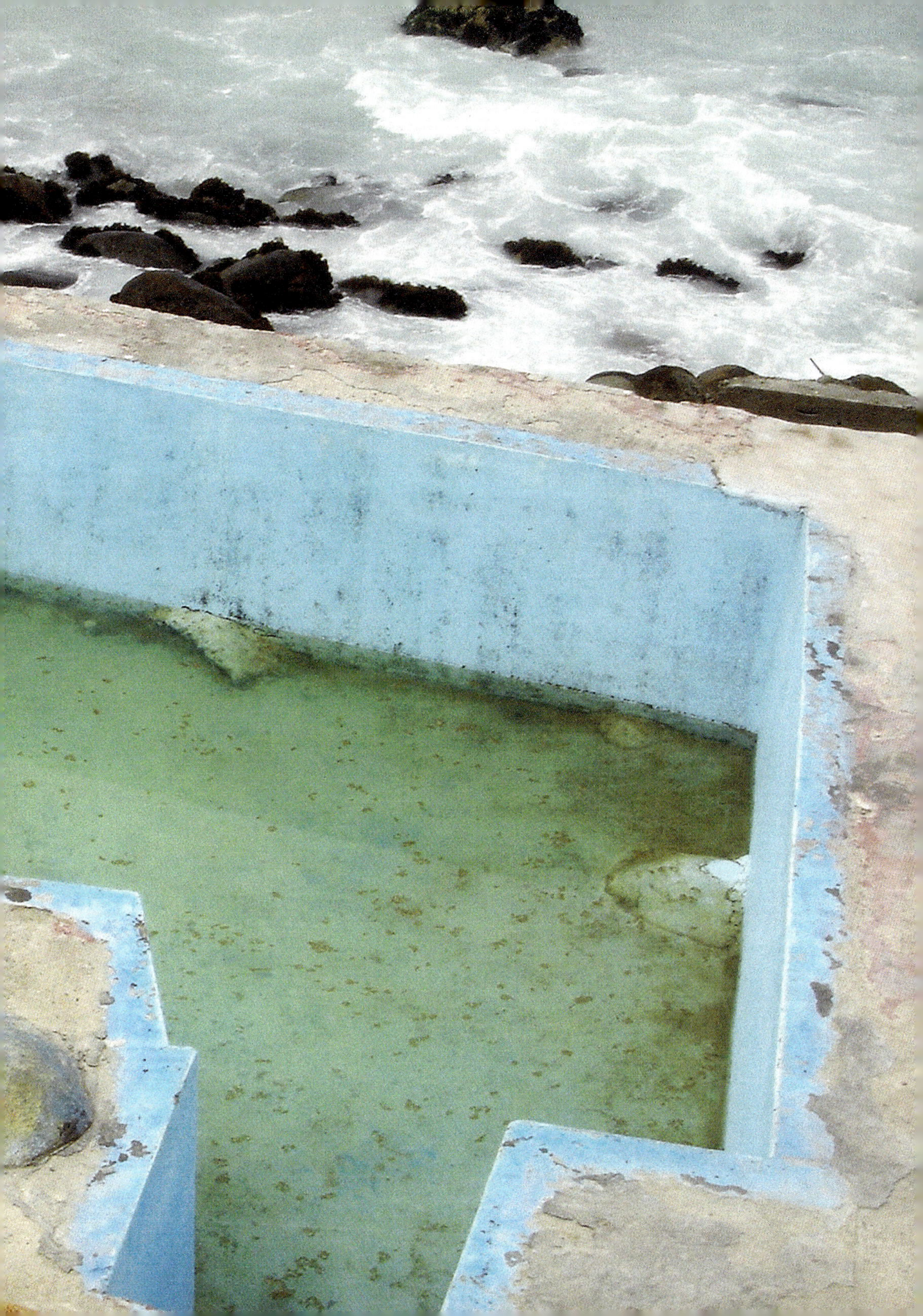

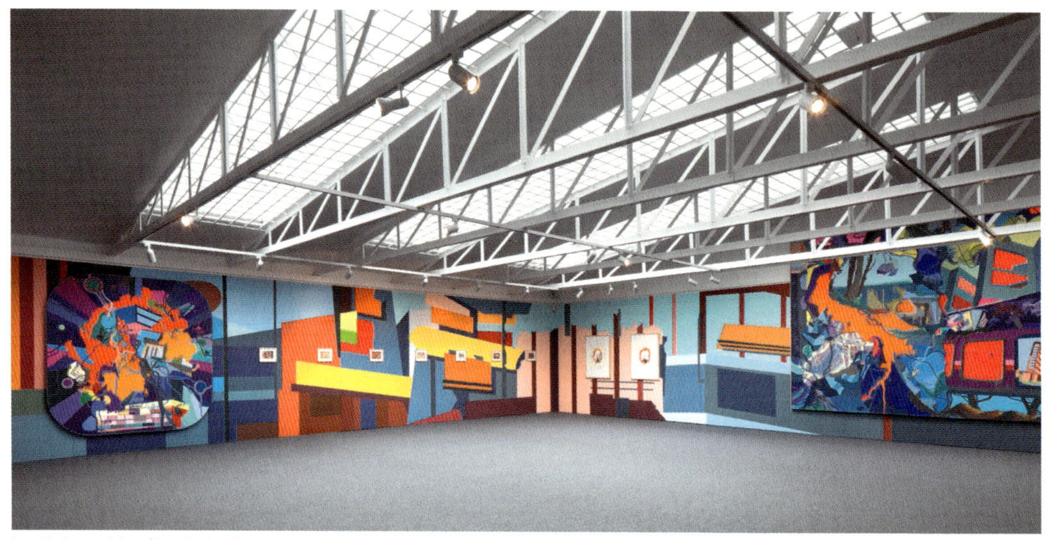

Installationsansichten | Installation Views

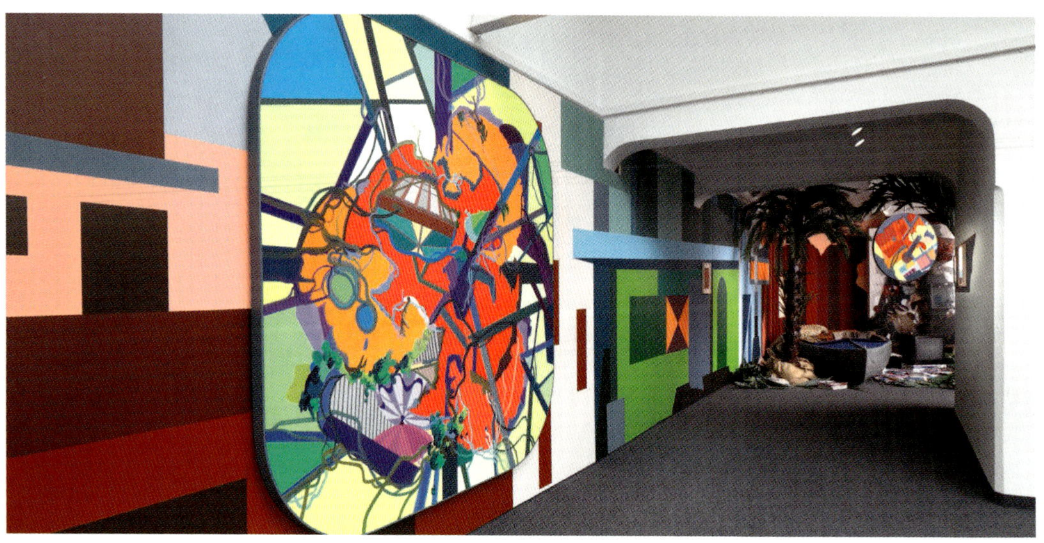

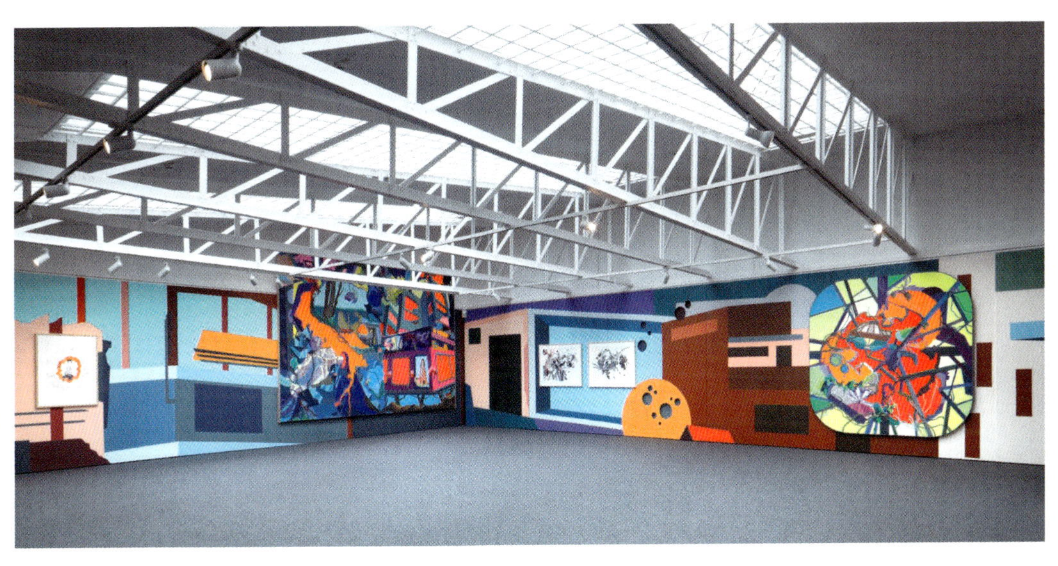

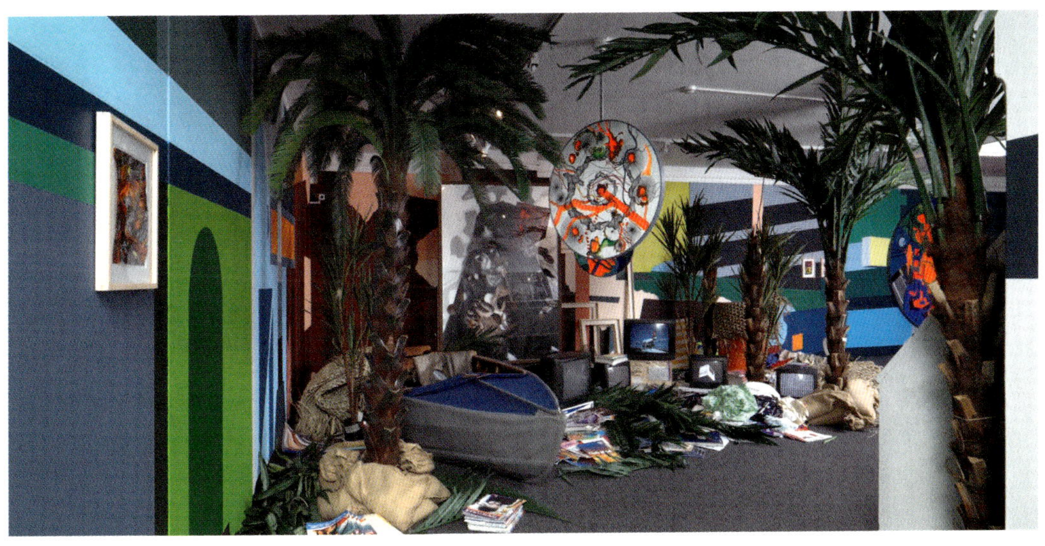

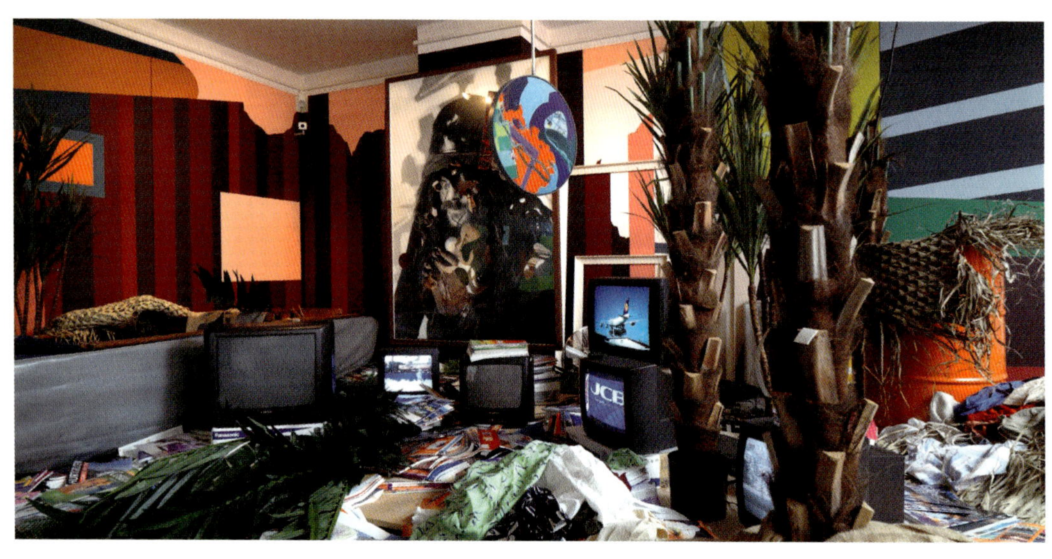

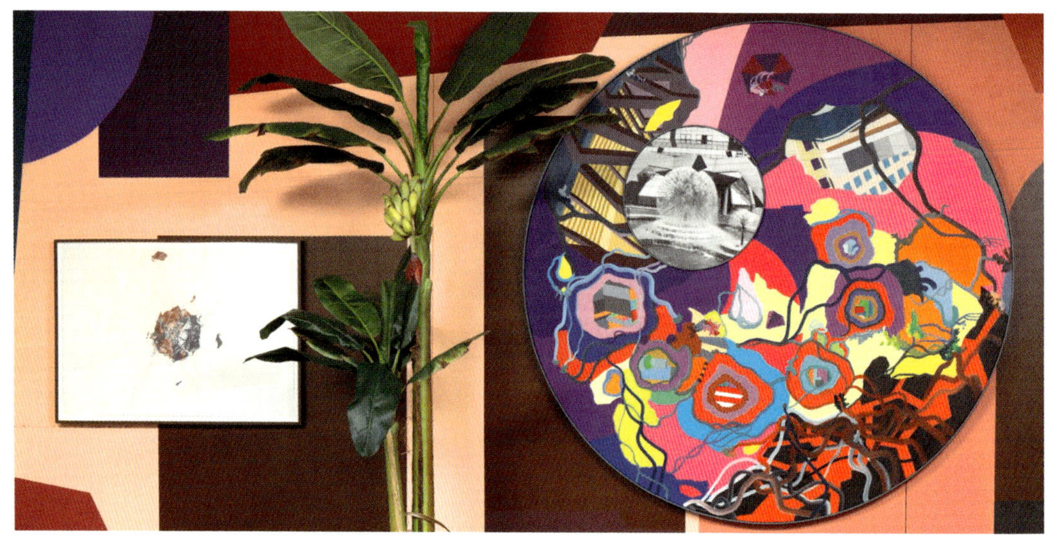

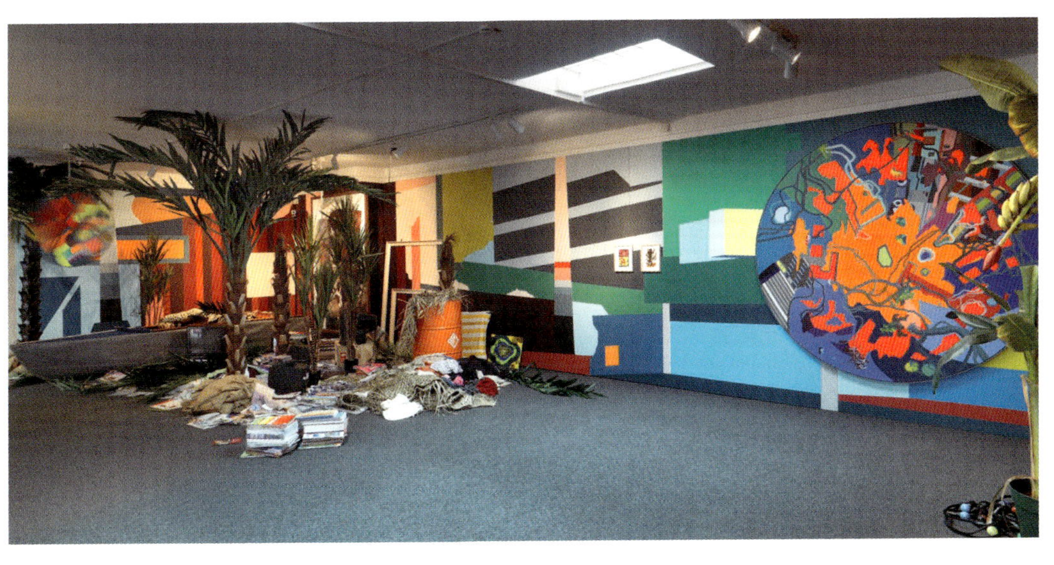

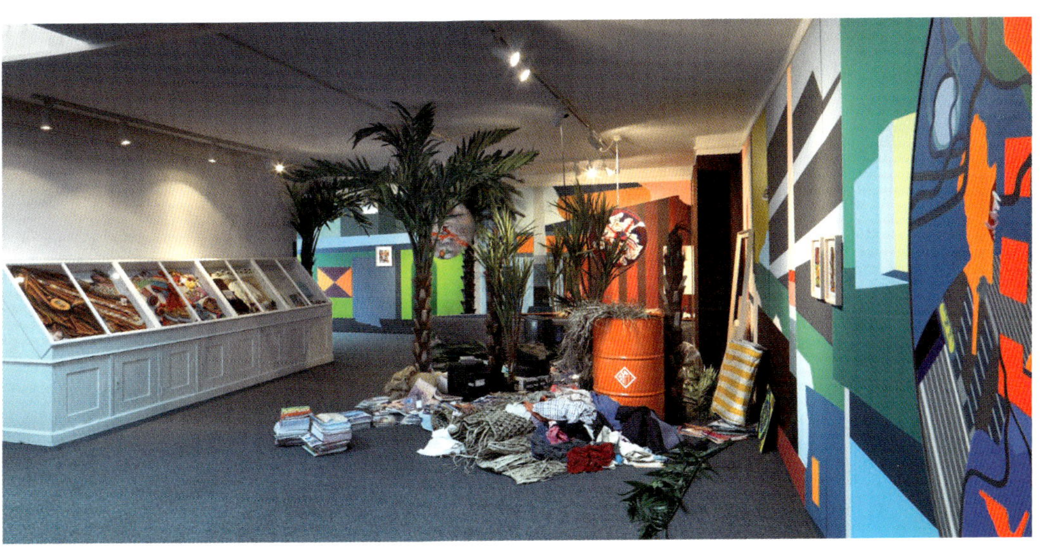

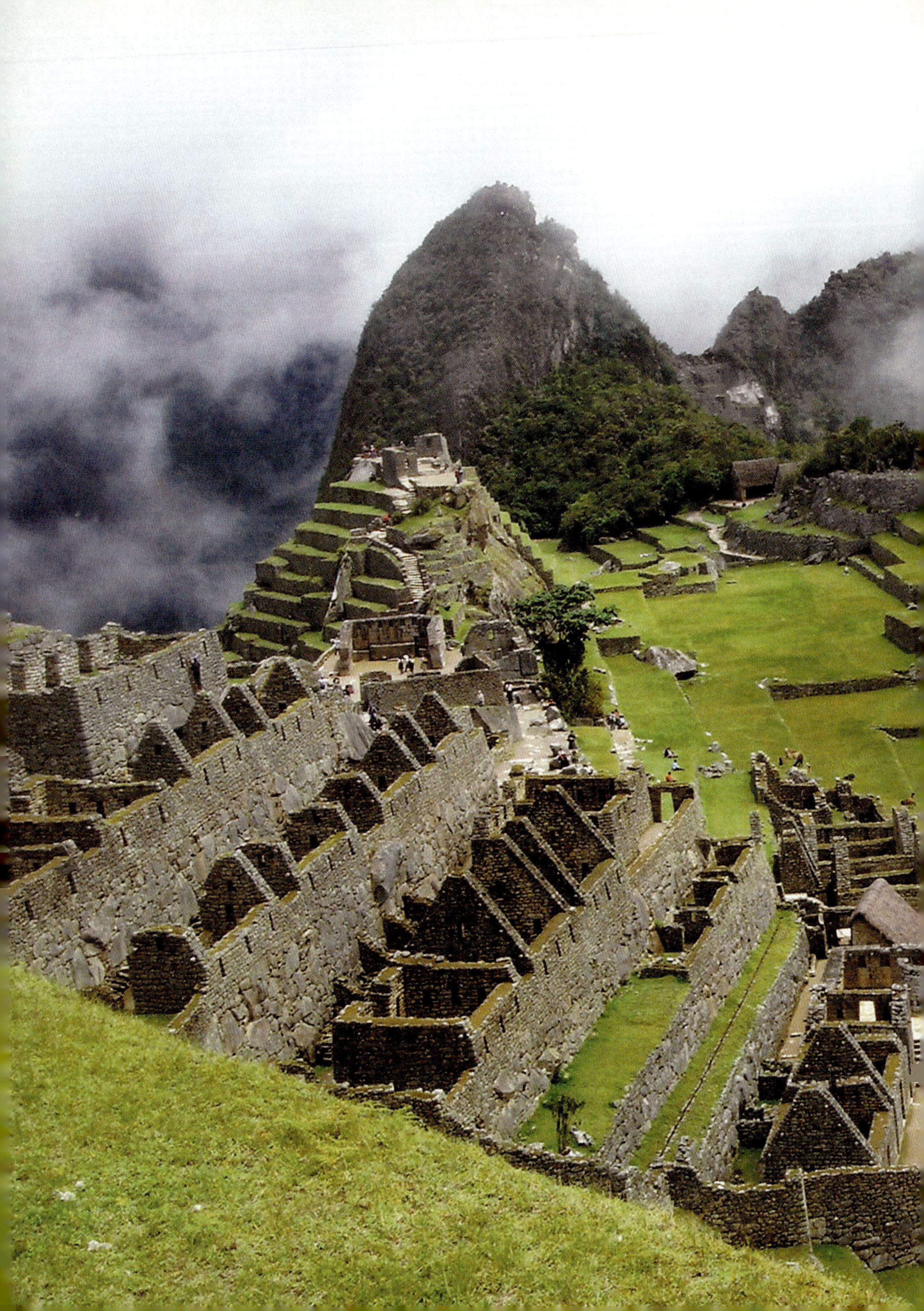

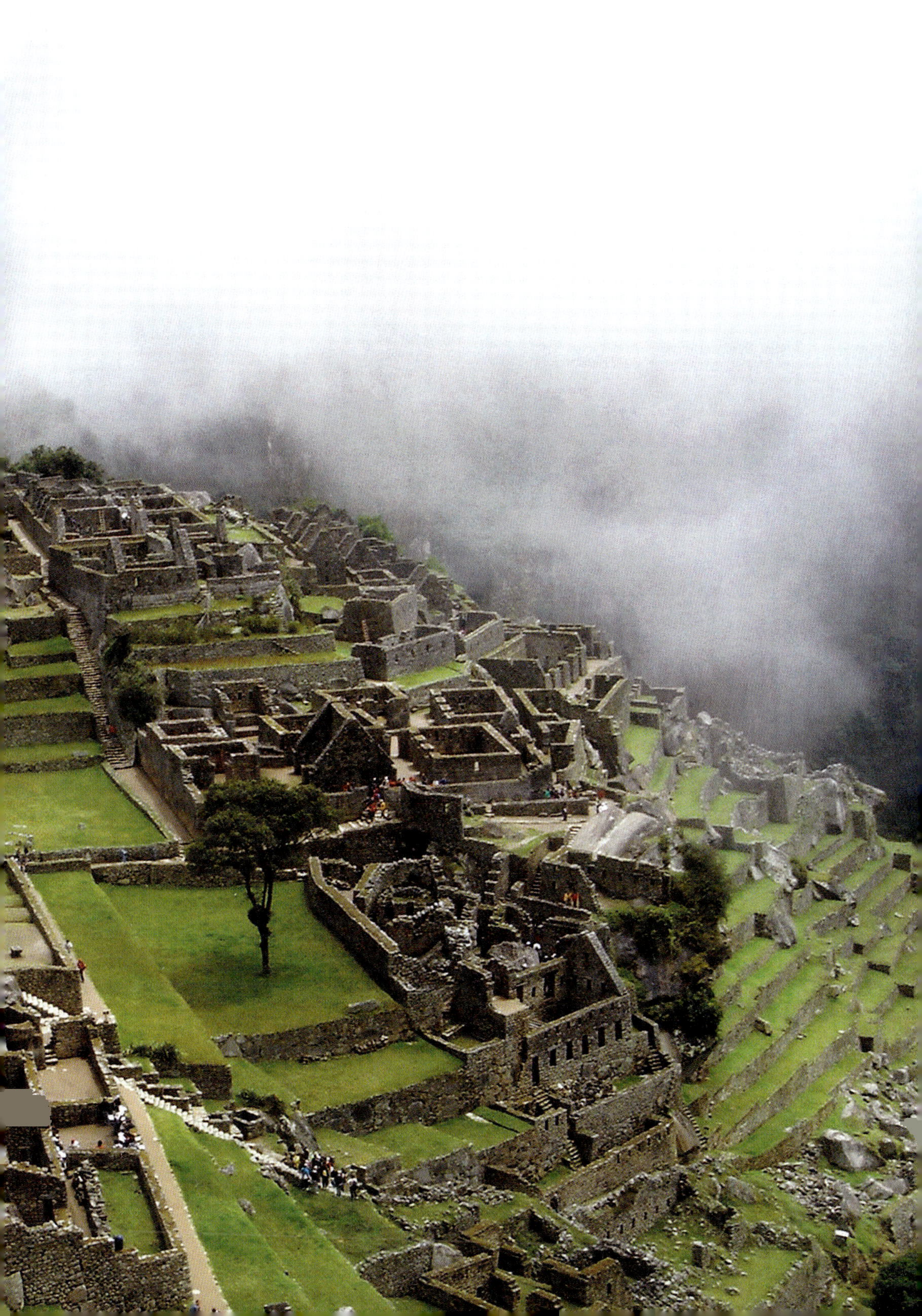

FRANZ ACKERMANN

*Neumarkt St. Veit, 1963
1984-88 Akademie der Bildenden Künste, München
1989-91 Hochschule für Bildende Kunst, Hamburg
DAAD, Hong Kong
lebt und arbeitet in Berlin und Karlsruhe

EINZELAUSSTELLUNGEN | SOLO EXHIBITIONS

2009
- Lima,   Altötting, Stadtgalerie Altötting, Altötting, D

2008
- Franz Ackermann, Kunstmuseum St. Gallen, St. Gallen, CH (Kat.)
- Franz Ackermann, Mai 36, Zürich, CH
- Terminal, Meyer Riegger Galerie, Karlsruhe, D

2007
- no direction home, Galeria Fortes Vilaça, São Paulo, BR
- Gió Marconi, Mailand, I
- from eden to lima, neugerriemschneider, Berlin
- home, home again, DA2 Domus Artium 2002, Salamanca, SP

2006
- home, home again / 23 Gespenster, kestnergesellschaft, Hannover, D (Kat.)
- Kunstparterre, München, D
- Home, home again, White Cube, London, G
- Árvores Douradas, Centro Cultural Banco do Brasil, Rio de Janeiro, BR

2005
- Cosmic Dancer, Galeria Fortes Vilaça, São Paulo, BR
- IMMA Irish Museum of Modern Art, Dublin, IR (Kat.)
- FRAC, Champagne-Ardenne, Reims, F (Kat.)
- Tomio Koyama Gallery, Tokyo, J

2004
- nonstop with the hhc, Gavin Brown's enterprise, New York, USA
- tourist, Städtische Galerie im Lenbachhaus und Kunstbau, München, D
- travelantitravel, neugerriemschneider, Berlin, D

2003
- Naherholungsgebiet, Kunstmuseum Wolfsburg, Wolfsburg, D (Kat.)
- Eine Nacht in den Tropen, Kunsthalle Nürnberg, Nürnberg, D (Kat.)

2002
- Basel Public, Wandinstallation Nordtangente, Basel CH
- The Waterfall, Museum of Contemporary Art, Chicago, USA
- Seasons in the sun, Stedelijk Museum, Amsterdam, NL (Kat.)
- Transatlantic, mit Rupprecht Geiger; Städtische Galerie im Lenbachhaus und Kunstbau, München
- Mai 36 Galerie, Zürich, CH
- Eine Nacht in den Tropen, Kunsthalle Basel, CH (Kat.)

2001
- Gavin Brown's enterprise, New York, USA
- Gió Marconi, Mailand, I

2000
- B.I.T., Castello di Rivoli, Torino, I
- Galeria Camargo Vilaça, São Paulo, BR
- welt 1 ... and no one else wanted to play, Meyer Riegger Galerie, Karlsruhe, D
- reisterrassen von basel, Wandmalerei, Rückwand der Kunsthalle Basel, CH

1999
- works on paper inc., Los Angeles, USA (Kat.)
- OFF, Kasseler Kunstverein, Kassel, D
- Trawler, Mai 36, Zürich, CH

1998
- neugerriemschneider, Berlin, D White Cube, London, GB
- Das Haus am Strand und wie man dorthin kommt, Meyer Riegger Galerie, Karlsruhe, D
- Pacific, White Cube, London, GB
- Songline, Neuer Aachener Kunstverein, Aachen, D

1997
- unexpected, Gavin Brown's enterprise, New York, USA
- unerwartet, Kunstpreis der Stadt Nordhorn, 1997 D (Kat.)
- Mai 36 Galerie, Zürich, CH
- Portikus, Frankfurt am Main, D (Kat.)
- Gió Marconi, Mailand, I

1996
- Das weiche Zimmer, kuratiert von Florian Waldvogel, Hann. Münden, D
- neugerriemschneider, Berlin, D

1995
- Thomas Solomon´s Garage, Los Angeles, USA
- Gavin Brown's enterprise, New York, USA

1994
- Ackermanns Wörterbuch der Tätigkeiten, Buchpublikation
- Dialo(o)g, Belgisches Haus, Köln, D (Kat.)
- condominium, neugerriemschneider, Berlin, D

1991
- Art Acker, Berlin, D

1990
- Galerie Fischer, Hamburg, D

1989
- Galerie Komat, Braunschweig, D

2009
- Altermodern, Tate Triennial, Tate Britain, London, GB

2008
- Die Tropen Ansichten von der Mitte der Weltkugel, Martin Gropius Bau, Berlin, D (Kat.)
- Vertrautes Terrain Aktuelle Kunst in & über Deutschland, ZKM, Karlsruhe, D
- All-Inclusive, die Welt des Tourismus, Schirn Kunsthalle, Frankfurt, D
- A Room of One´s Own, Castello di Rivoli, Turin, I

2007
- Paul Thek Werkschau im Kontext zeitgenössischer Kunst, ZKM, Karlsruhe, D
- Imagery play, PKM gallery, Beijing, CHINA; Seoul, KOREA
- Blind date Istanbul. Deutsche Bank Collection and Sakip Sabanci Museum,
  Sabanci University Sakip Sabanci Museum, Istanbul, TR (Kat.)
- Reality Bites, Mildred Lane Kemper Art Museum, St. Louis, USA; Opelvillen, Rüsselsheim, D (Kat.)
- Temporäre Kunsthalle Berlin, Berlin, D
- Imagination becomes reality, ZKM, Karlsruhe, D
- Udomsak Krisanamis and a German Artist, Gavin Brown's enterprise, New York, USA

2006
- Casa aberta, INHOTIM centro de arte contemporanea, Minas Gerais, Brasil
- Idylle. Traum und Trugschluss, Sammlung Falckenberg, Hamburg, D
- Ellipse Foundation, Cascais, P
- FASTER! BIGGER! BETTER!, ZKM, Karlsruhe, D (Kat.)
- Der Blaue Reiter im 21. Jahrhundert, Ackermann/Marc, Demand/Macke, Eliasson/Kandinsky,
  Grosse/Jawlensky, Lenbchhaus, München, S

2006
- Public Image, Painting The City, Fundament Foundation, Tilburg, NL (Kat.)
- Anstoss Berlin, Haus am Waldsee, Berlin, D
- RADAR:Selections from the Collection of Vicki and Kent Logan, Denver Art Museum, Denver, USA
- Goethe Abwärts, Werke aus der Sammlung Falckenberg, Mönchehaus-Museum für moderne Kunst, Goslar
- Infinite Painting, Villa Manin, Codroipo (Udine), I (Kat.)
- location shots, Galerie Erna Hécey, Brüssel, B
- Archipeinture, Le Plateau, Paris, F; Camden Arts Centre, London, GB
- Dark Places, Santa Monica Museum of Art, Santa Monica, USA
- Baroque and Neobaroque, The Hell of the Beautiful, Domus Artium 2002, Salamanca, SP
- Berlin-Tokyo, Mori Art Museum, Tokyo, JAP; Neue Nationalgalerie, Berlin, D (Kat)

2005
- 36 x 27 x 10, White Cube Berlin im ehemaligen Palast der Republik, Berlin
- Drive. Cars in Contemporary Art, Galleria D'Arte Moderna, Bologna, I (Kat.)
- Lichtkunst aus Kunstlicht, ZKM, Museum für Neue Kunst, Karlsruhe, D
- Ecstasy: in and about altered states, MOCA the Geffen Contemporary, Los Angeles, USA (Kat.)
- Styles und Stile – Aktuelle Malerei aus der Sammlung Scharpff, Sofia Art Gallery, Sofia, BG
- ackermann, bächli, balkenhol, kluge, slominski, Galeria Senda, Barcelona, SP Printemps de septembre, Toulouse, F (Kat.)
- Wittgenstein in New York, Kupferstichkabinett, Berlin, D
- Drawing from the Modern, 1975–2005, The Museum of Modern Art, New York, USA (Kat.)
- Biennale d'art contemporain de Lyon, Lyon, F
- Myslivska, Galleria Gentili, Montecatini, I
- Desired Constellations, Daniel Reich Gallery, New York, USA
- Imagination Becomes Reality, Part I: Expanded Paint Tools, Sammlung Goetz, München, D
- La nouvelle peinture allemande, Carré d'art Nîmes, Nîmes, F
- Remote Viewing (Invented Worlds in Recent Painting and Drawing), Whitney Museum of American Art, New York, USA
- Blumenstück Künstlers Glück, Museum Morsbroich, Leverkusen, D (Kat.)
- Works on Paper, Galerie Max Hetzler, Berlin, D
- Zur Vorstellung des Terrors: Die RAF Ausstellung, Kunst-Werke, Berlin (Kat.)
- Dosenhos: A-Z (Drawings: A-Z), Porta 33, Funchal, Ilha da Madira, P
- The Triumph of Painting Part II, Saatchi Gallery, London, GB (Kat.)
- Colors and Trips, Künstlerhaus Palais Thurn und Taxis, Bregenz A; Museum der Stadt Ratingen, A (Kat.)

2004
- Direkte Malerei, Kunsthalle Mannheim, Mannheim, D
- Central Station, collection Harald Falckenberg, La maison rouge – fondation Antoine de Galbert, Paris, F (Kat.)
- 150 Jahre, Staatliche Akademie der Bildenden Künste Karlsruhe, D
- Champs de vision, Musée des Beaux Arts, Rouen, F
- Close by - time space architecture, Mai 36 Galerie, Zürich, CH
- Monument to now, The Dakis Joannou Collection, Deste Foundation for Contemporary Art, Athens, GR

2004	- realityReal, Arbeiten auf Papier, Galerie Gebr. Lehmann, Dresden, D
	- Global World/Private Universe, Kunstmuseum, St. Gallen, CH (Kat.)
	- Treasure Island, 10 Jahre Sammlung Kunstmuseum Wolfsburg, D
	- Werke aus der Sammlung Boros, Museum für neue Kunst, ZKM, Karlsruhe, D (Kat.)
2003	- A New Modernism For A New Millennium: Abstraction and Surrealism Are Reinvented In The Internetage, The Logan Collection, Vail, USA (Kat.)
	- A Nova Geometria, Galeria Fortes Vilaça, Sao Paulo, Brazil
	- un-built cities, Bonner Kunstverein, Bonn, D (Kat.)
	- Die Sehnsucht des Kartografen, Kunstverein Hannover, Hannover, D (Kat.)
	- Heißkalt. Aktuelle Malerei aus der Sammlung Scharpff, Hamburger Kunsthalle, Hamburg; Staatsgalerie, Stuttgart, D (Kat.)
	- Frahm Ltd, London, GB
	- Outlook, „The Factory", Athens school of Fine Arts, Athens, GR (Kat.)
	- Supernova: Art of the 1990s from the Logan Collection, San Francisco Museum of Modern Art, San Francisco, USA (Kat.)
	- Berlin-Moskau/Moskau-Berlin, Martin Gropius Bau, Berlin, D (Kat.)
	- Chaotic Order, Houldsworth, London, GB
	- EU3, Stephen Friedman Gallery, London, GB
	- Hands up, baby, hands up!, Oldenburger Kunstverein, Oldenburg, D
	- Global Navigation System, Palais de Tokyo, Paris, F (Kat.)
	- Dreams and Conflicts - The Viewer's Dictatorship, Biennale di Venezia, Venedig, It
	- painting abstract now, Museum Morsbroich, Leverkusen, D
	- Franz Ackermann, Harald Klingelhöller, Meuser, Andreas Slominski, Galerie Georg Kargl, Wien, A
	- Love is a battlefield, New York, USA
	- There's no land but the land (up there is just a sea of possiblities), Meyer Riegger Galerie, Karlsruhe, D
	- Contemporary German Art: Recent Aquisitions, Washington University, St Louis, Missouri, USA
	- Painting pictures, Malerei und Medien im Digitalen Zeitalter; Kunstmuseum Wolfsburg, Wolfsburg, D (Kat.)
	- Away from Home, Wexner Center for the Arts, Columbus, USA
2002	- Psychodrome 02, Fundació Juan Miró, Barcelona, ES (Kat.)
	- En Route, Serpentine Gallery, London, GB
	- The 8th Baltic Triennial of International Art, Contemporary Art Center, Vilnius, Lt (Kat.)
	- Drawing now – eight positions; Museum of Modern Art, Long Island City, USA (Kat.)
	- Hossa. Arte Alemán del 2000, Centro Cultural Andratx, Mallorca, ES
	- Lila, Weiss und andere Farben, Galerie Max Hetzler, Berlin, D
	- Reverberator (kurat. Michael Archer), Houldsworth, London, GB
	- Nashville II, Kunstverein Harburger Bahnhof, Hamburg-Harburg, D
	- Kopfreisen, Seedamm Kulturzentrum, Pfäffikon und Kunstmuseum Bern, Bern, CH (Kat.)
	- XXV Bienal de São Paulo, São Paulo, BR
	- // Paralela; Galeria Fortes Vilaça, Casa Triângulo, Galeria Luisa Strina, Galeria Brito Cimino; São Paulo, BR
2001	- Rotativa, Galeria Fortes Vilaça, São Paulo, BR
	- Arte Contemporáneo internacional, Museo de Arte Moderno, Mexico, MEX
	- Brown Field, market, Glasgow, GB (Kat.)
	- EU; Stephen Friedman Gallery, London, GB
	- Form follows fiction, Castello di Rivoli, Turin, I (Kat.)
	- Patterns: Between Object and Arabesque, Kunsthallen Brandts Klaedefabrik, Odense, DK
	- Freizeit, Kokerei Zollverein, Essen, D
	- Musterkarte, Modelos de Pintura en Alemania, Goethe Institut/ Centro Cultural Condeduque/ Galeria Heinrich Erhard/ Galeria Elba Benitez, Madrid, E
	- Casino 2001, S.M.A.K., Gent, B (Kat.)
	- Tempted to pretend, Kunsthaus Kaufbeuren, Kaufbeuren, D (Kat.)
	- Field, Market, Glasgow, GB
	- hybrids, Tate Liverpool, Liverpool, GB (Kat.)
	- Germania. La costruzione di un imagine, Palazzo delle Papesse, Siena, I
	- mirror' s edge, Tramway, Glasgow, GB
	- Glee: Painting Now; Palm Beach Institute of Contemporary Art, Lake Worth, USA
	- close up; Kunstverein Hannover, D
	- painting at the edge of the world, Walker Art Center, Minneapolis, USA (Kat.)
	- comfort: reclaiming place in a virtual world, Cleveland Center for Contemporary Art, Cleveland, USA (Kat.)
	- brown field, Rob Tufnell, Glasgow, GB abstraction and hybridity, Tate Liverpool, Liverpool, GB (Kat.)

2000
- more works about buildings and food; Fundição de Oeiras, Hangar K7, Oeiras, P (Kat.)
- Glee: Painting Now, The Aldrich Museum of Contemporary Art, Ridgefield, USA;
- Palm Beach Institute of Contemporary Art, Palm Beach, USA (Kat.)
- home ist where the heArt is; Museum van Loon, Amsterdam, NL
- DAAD: weltwärts, Kunstmuseum, Bonn, D
- Salon, Delfina Project Space, London, GB
- Millefleurs, picture show, Berlin, D
- Malkunst, Fondazione Mudima, Mailand, I (Kat.)
- Kunst und Mode, Picture Show, Berlin, D
- Re_public; Grazer Kunstverein, Graz, A (mit Rirkrit Tiravanija)
- Loneliness in the City , Migros Museum, Zürich, CH (mit Rirkrit Tiravanija)
- M Art in (n), M Art in (n) c/o Martin Schibli, Helsingborg, S
- LKW, Lebenskunstwerke, Kunst in der Stadt 4, Kunsthaus Bregenz, A (Kat.)
- Bleibe, Akademie der Künste, Berlin, D
- [re:songlines], halle_für_kunst e.V., Lüneburg, D
- Close up, Kunstverein Freiburg, D, Kunsthalle Baselland, Basel, CH (Kat.)
- hausschau - das haus in der kunst, Deichtorhallen Hamburg, D (Kat.)
- CITY-INDEX, Festspielhaus Hellerau, Dresden, D (Kat.)
- Mysliwska, Künstlerhaus Bethanien, Berlin, D
- „Utopische Bürger"?, workweb.art, Köln, D

1999
- German Open, Kunstmuseum Wolfsburg, Wolfsburg (Kat.)
- Carnegie International 1999/2000, Carnegie Museum of Art, Pittsburgh, USA (Kat.)
- Mirror´s Edge, BildMuseet, Umea, SE; Vancouver Art Gallery, Vancouver, Can; Castello di Rivoli, I; Tramway,
  Glasgow, GB; Charlottenborg Exhibition Hall, Kopenhagen, DK (Kat.)
- Officina Europa, Galleria d´Arte Moderna, Bologna, I (Kat.)
- Malerei, INIT Kunst-Halle, Berlin
- Drawn from Artists´ Collections, The Drawing Center, New York, USA (Kat.)
- amAzonas Künstlerbücher, Villa Minimo, Hannover
- zoom, Sammlung Landesbank Baden-Württemberg, Stuttgart; Museum Abteiberg,
- Mönchengladbach, Kunsthalle zu Kiel, Kiel (K)
- go away: artists and travel, Royal College of Art, London, GB (Kat.)
- Dream City, Kunstverein München, D (Kat.)
- Otto&, Otto, Kopenhagen, DK
- <Anderswo 1>, Kunstraum, Kreuzlingen, CH
- Frieze, ICA Boston, USA (Kat.)

1998
- Franz Ackermann und Jonathan Meese, Sammlung Volkmann, Berlin
- Ferien, Utopie, Alltag, Künstlerwerkstatt Lothringer Straße, München, D
- Osygus, Produzentengalerie, Hamburg, D
- Deep Thougt. Part II, Basilico Fine Arts, New York, USA
- Painting: Now and Forever. Part I, Pat Hearn Gallery & Matthew Marks Gallery, New York, USA
- Hanging, Galeria Camargo Vilaça, São Paolo; Paco Imperial, Rio de Janeiro; Museum of Modern Art, Recife, BR (Kat.)
- sehen sehen, loop - raum für aktuelle kunst, Berlin, D
- Atlas Mapping, Kunsthaus Bregenz, A (Kat.)

1997
- Urban Living, Galerie Fons Welters, Amsterdam, NL
- Kunst...Arbeit, Südwest LB, Stuttgart, D (Kat.)
- Heaven, P.S.1, New York, USA
- Kunstpreis der Böttgerstraße in Bremen, Bonner Kunstverein, Bonn, D (Kat.)
- Time Out, Kunsthalle Nürnberg, D (Kat.)Atlas Mapping, Offenes Kulturhaus Linz, A (Kat.)
- Topping out, Städtische Galerie Nordhorn, D
- Giò Marconi, Milano, I
- Imbiss, Künstlerhaus, Stuttgart, D
- a summer group show, neugerriemschneider, Berlin, D

1996
- Wunderbar, Hamburger Kunstverein, Hamburg, D (Kat.)
- Faustrecht der Freiheit, Sammlung Volkmann, Kunstsammlung, Gera/ Neues Museum Weserburg, Bremen, D

1995
- En passant... Hamburger Kunstverein, Hamburg, D
- En passant... Akademie der Bildenden Künste, Wien, A

1994
- Cocktail, Kunstverein Hamburg, D
- Wiensowski & Harbord, Berlin, D

1991
- BP, Hamburg, D

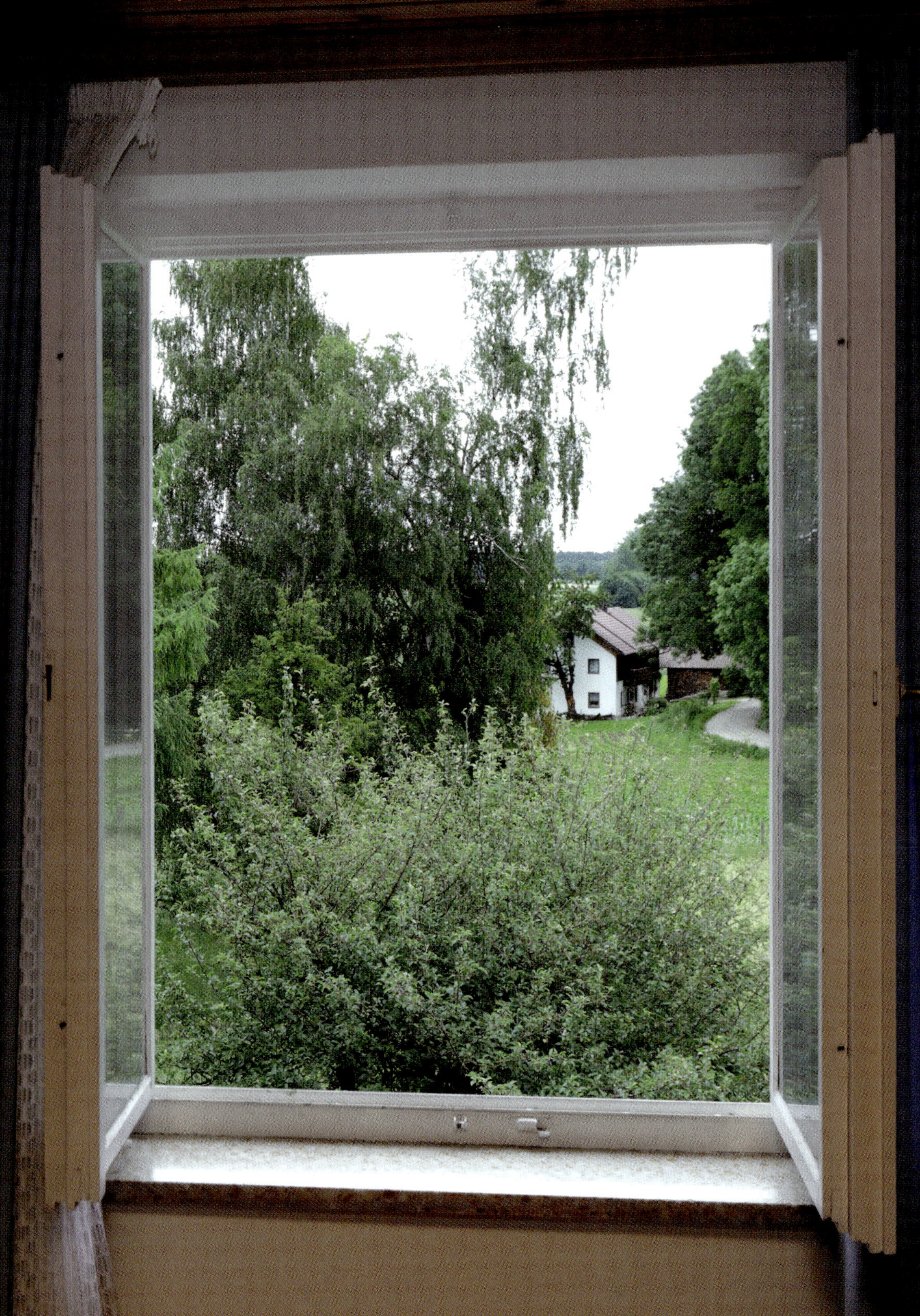

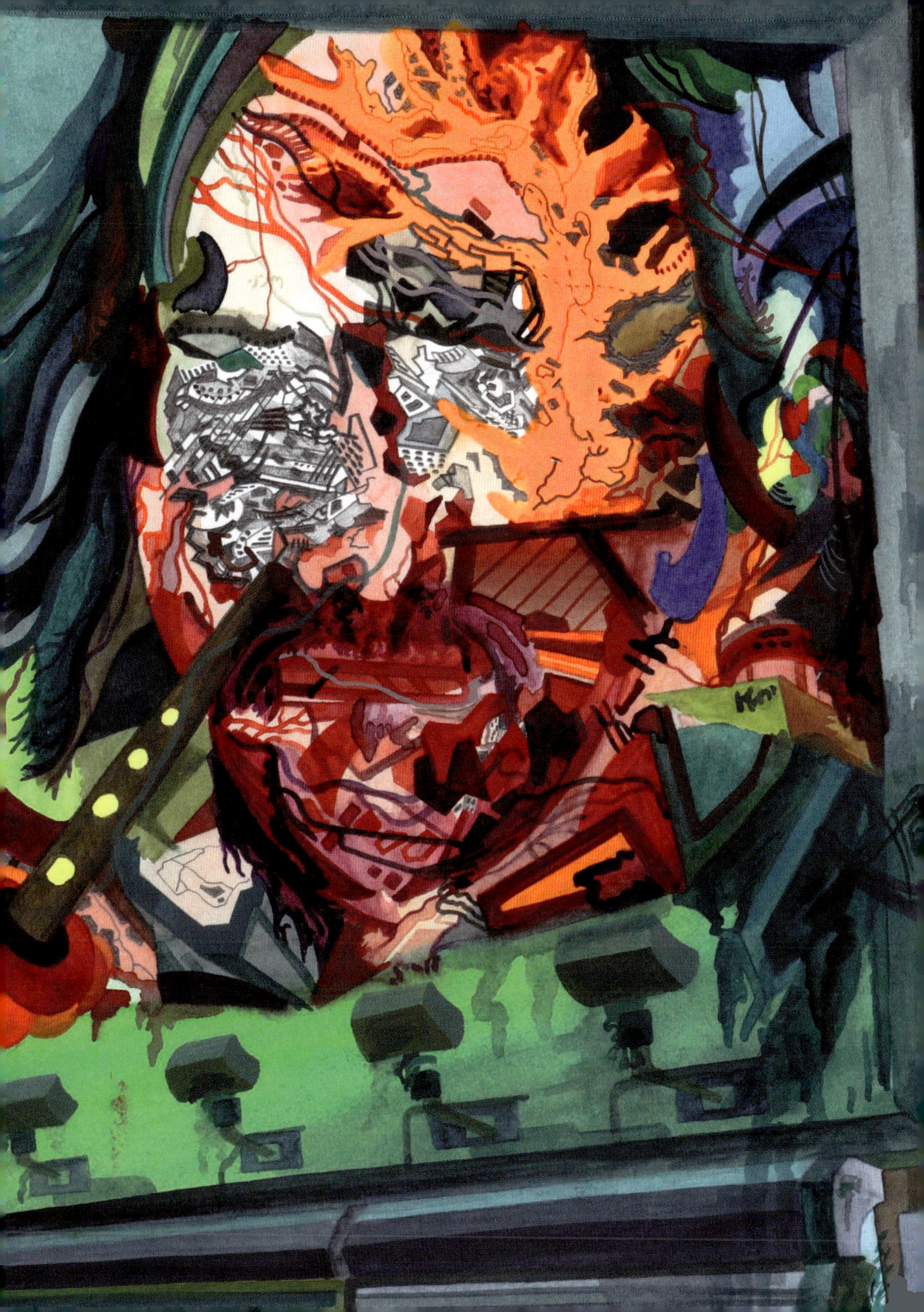

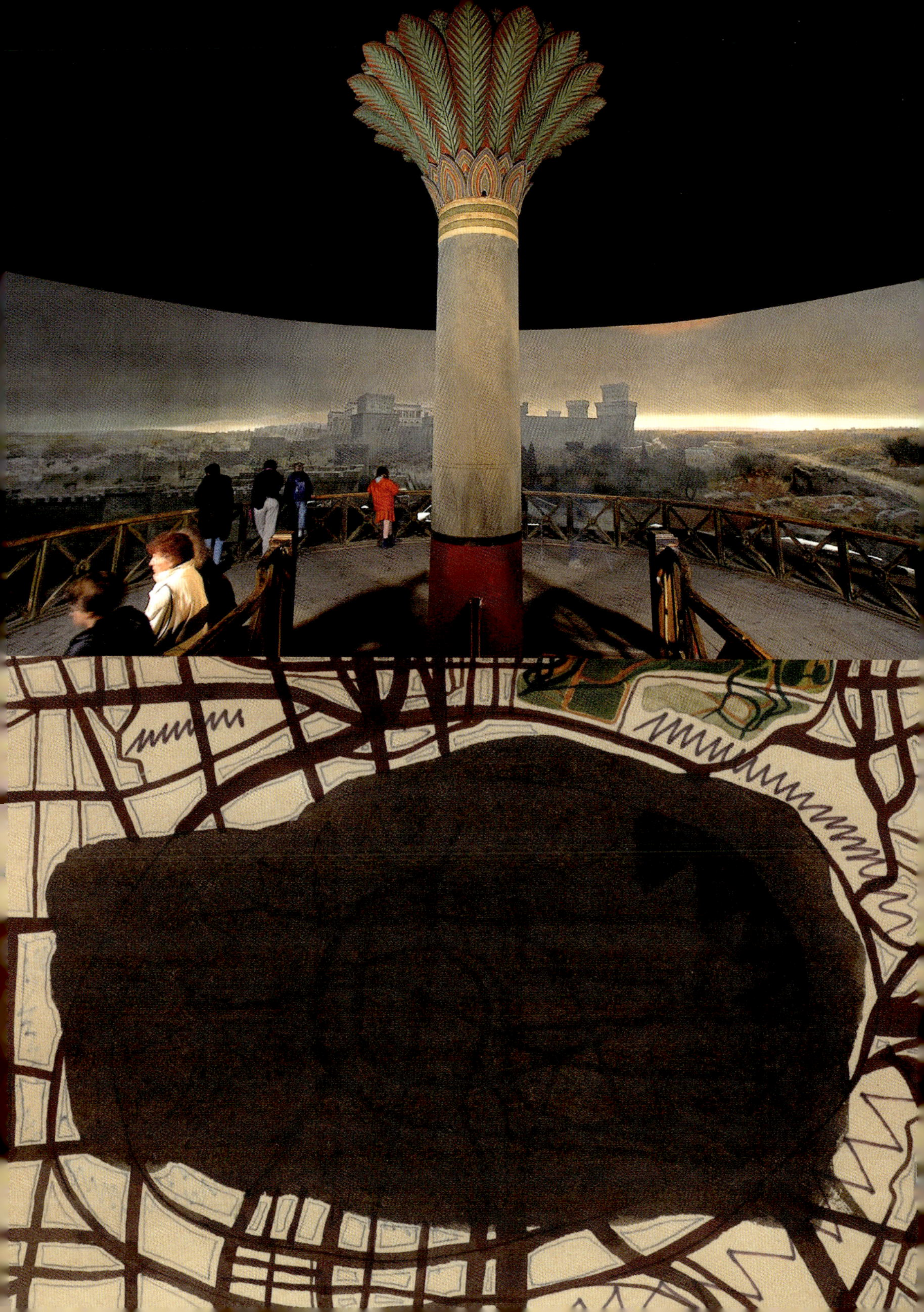

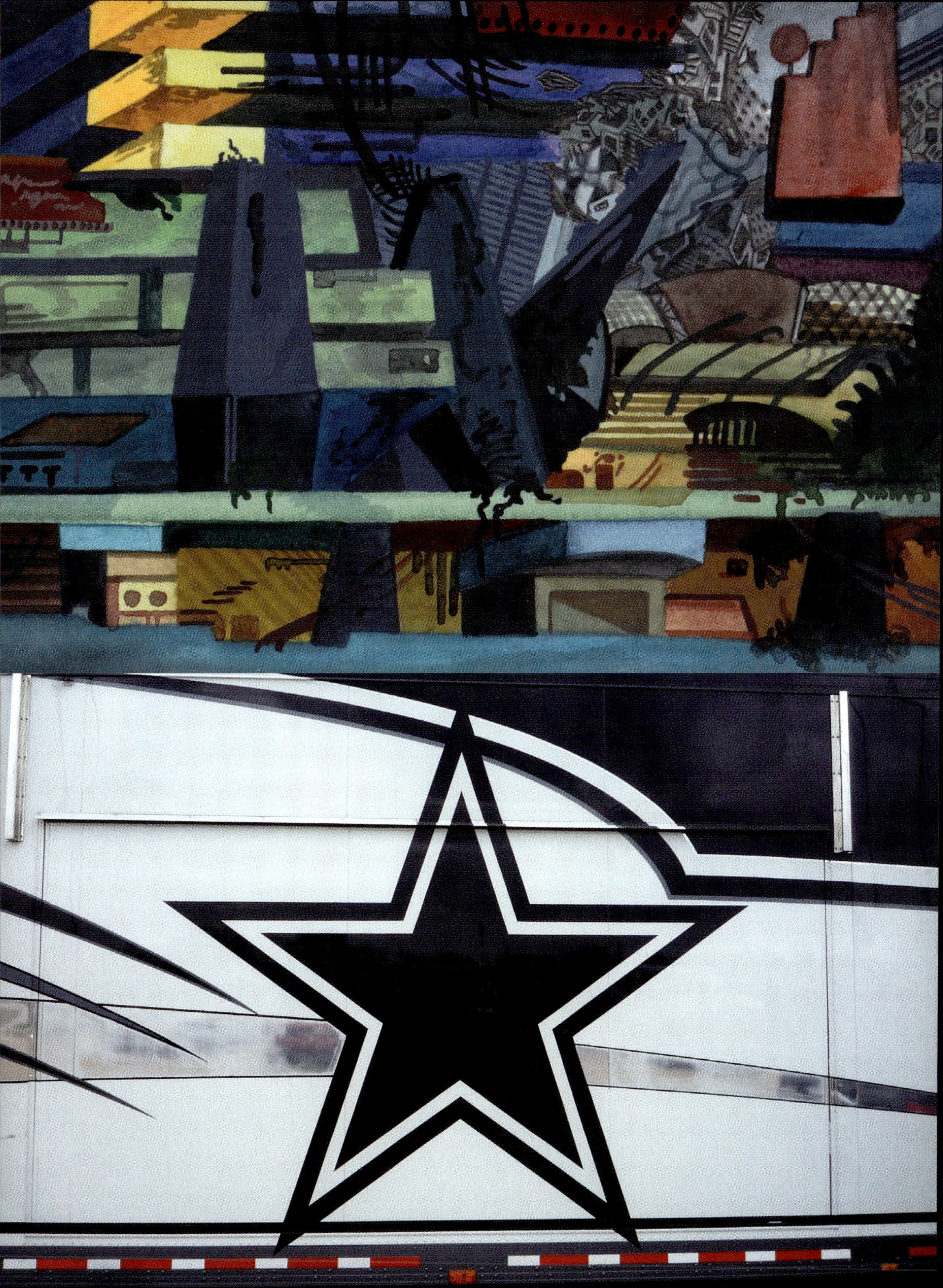

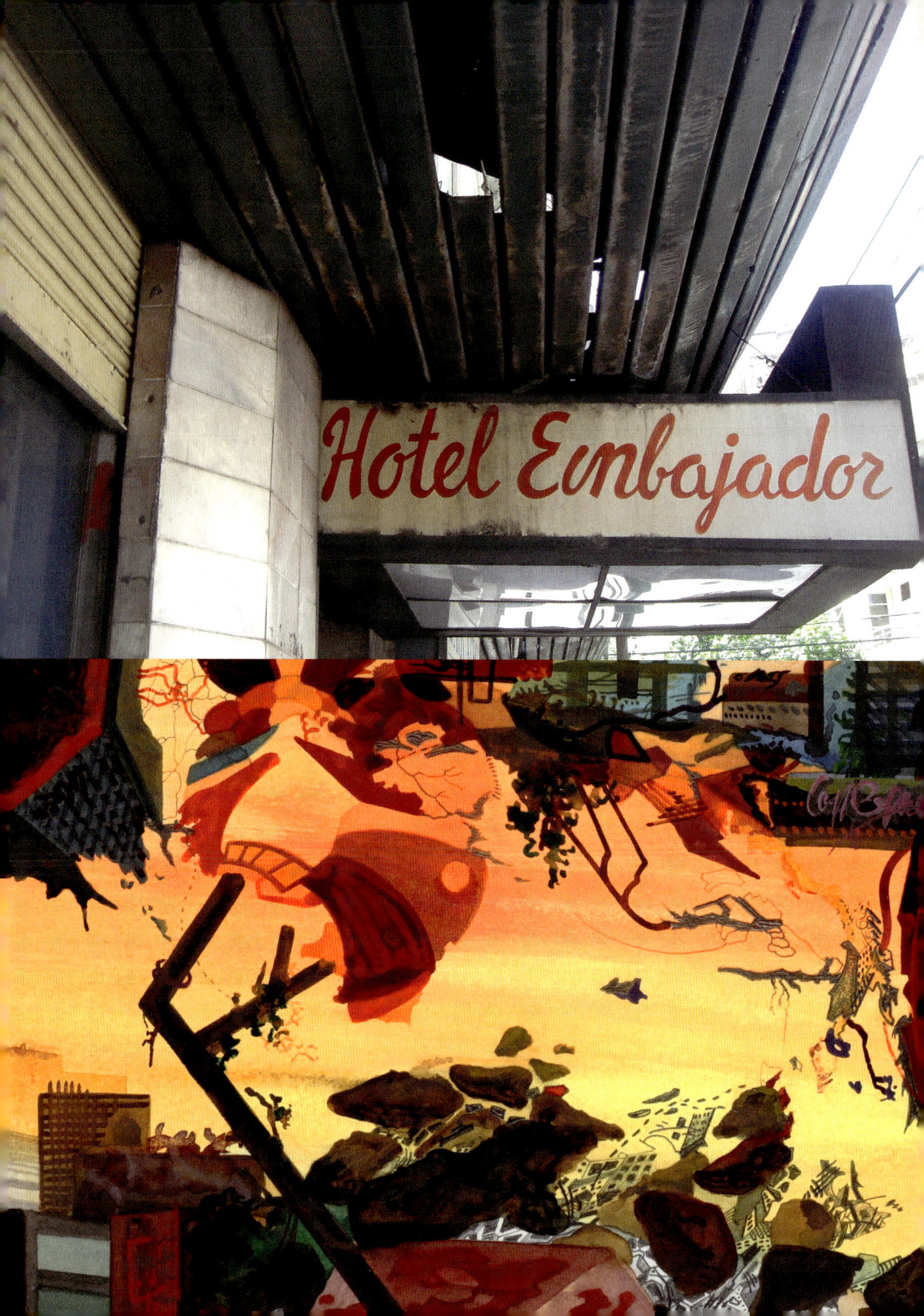
Hotel Embajador

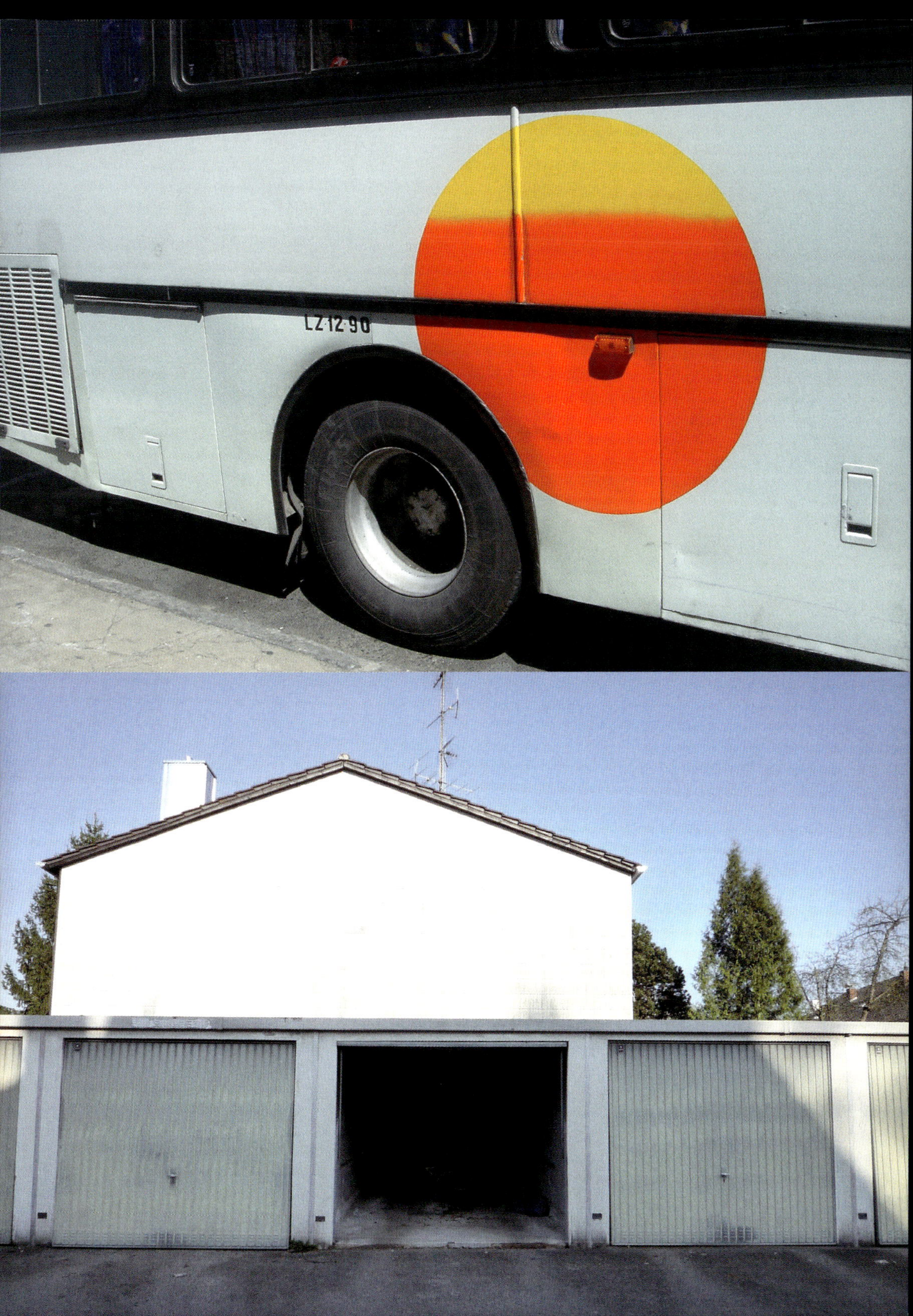
LZ·12·90

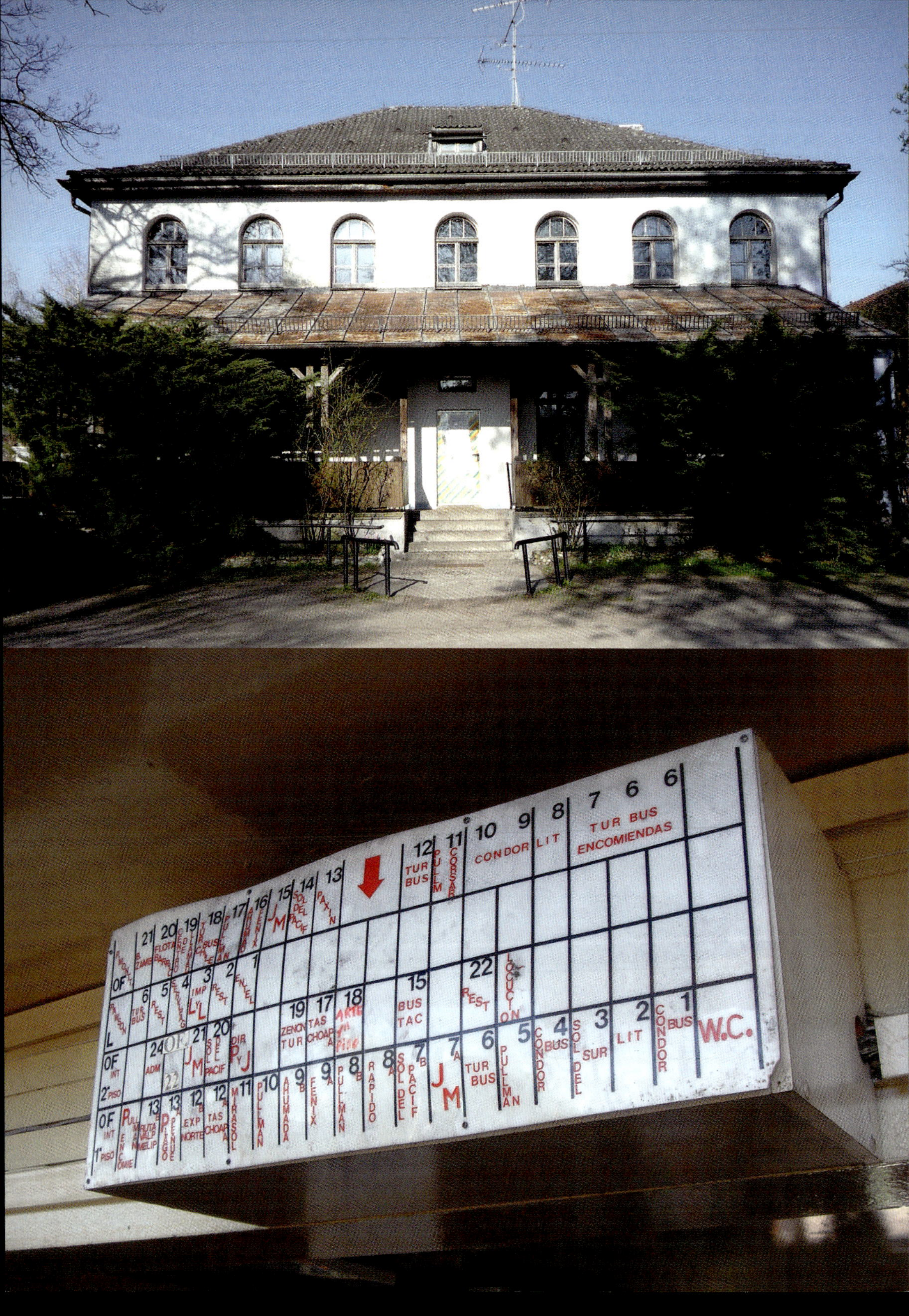

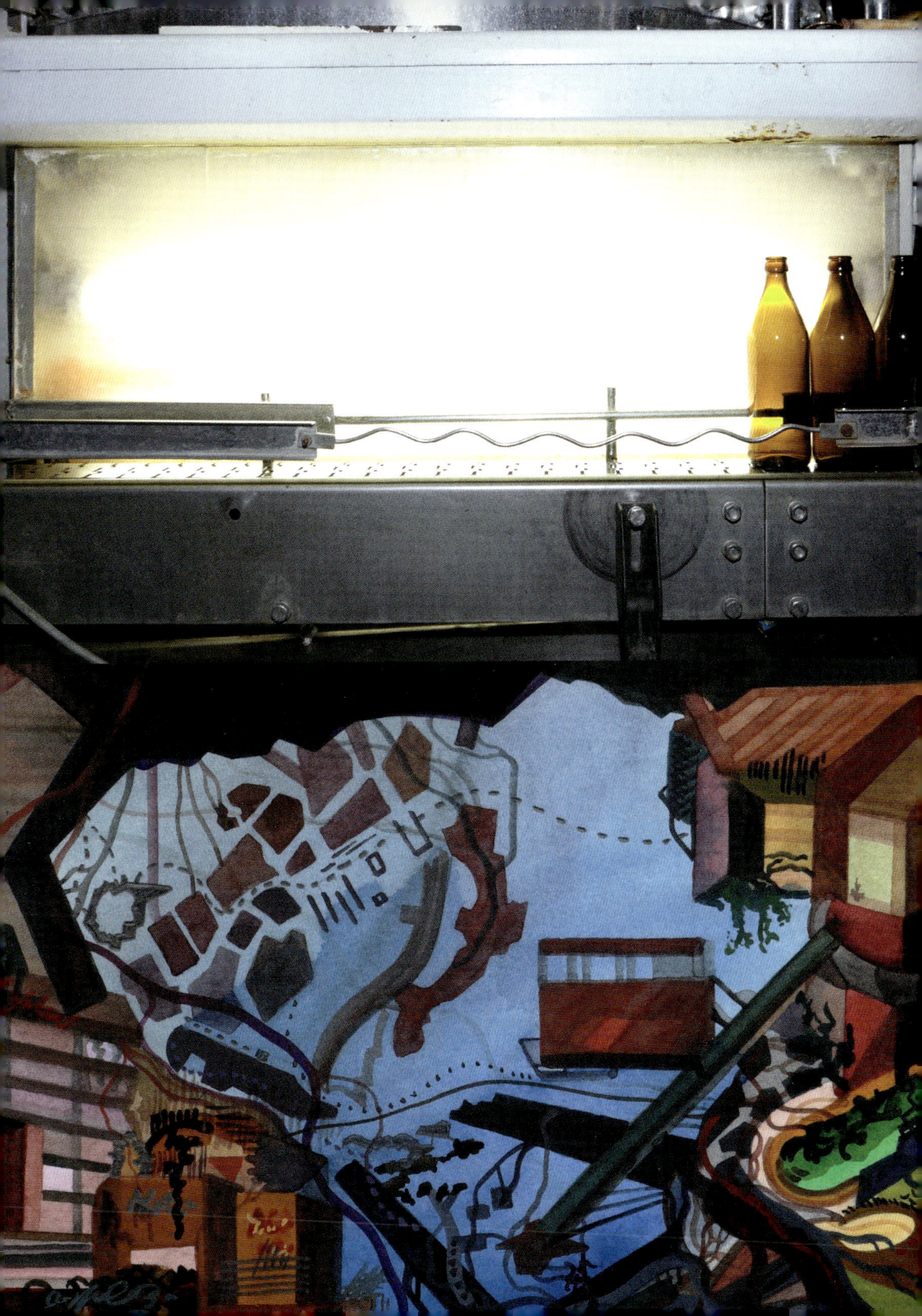

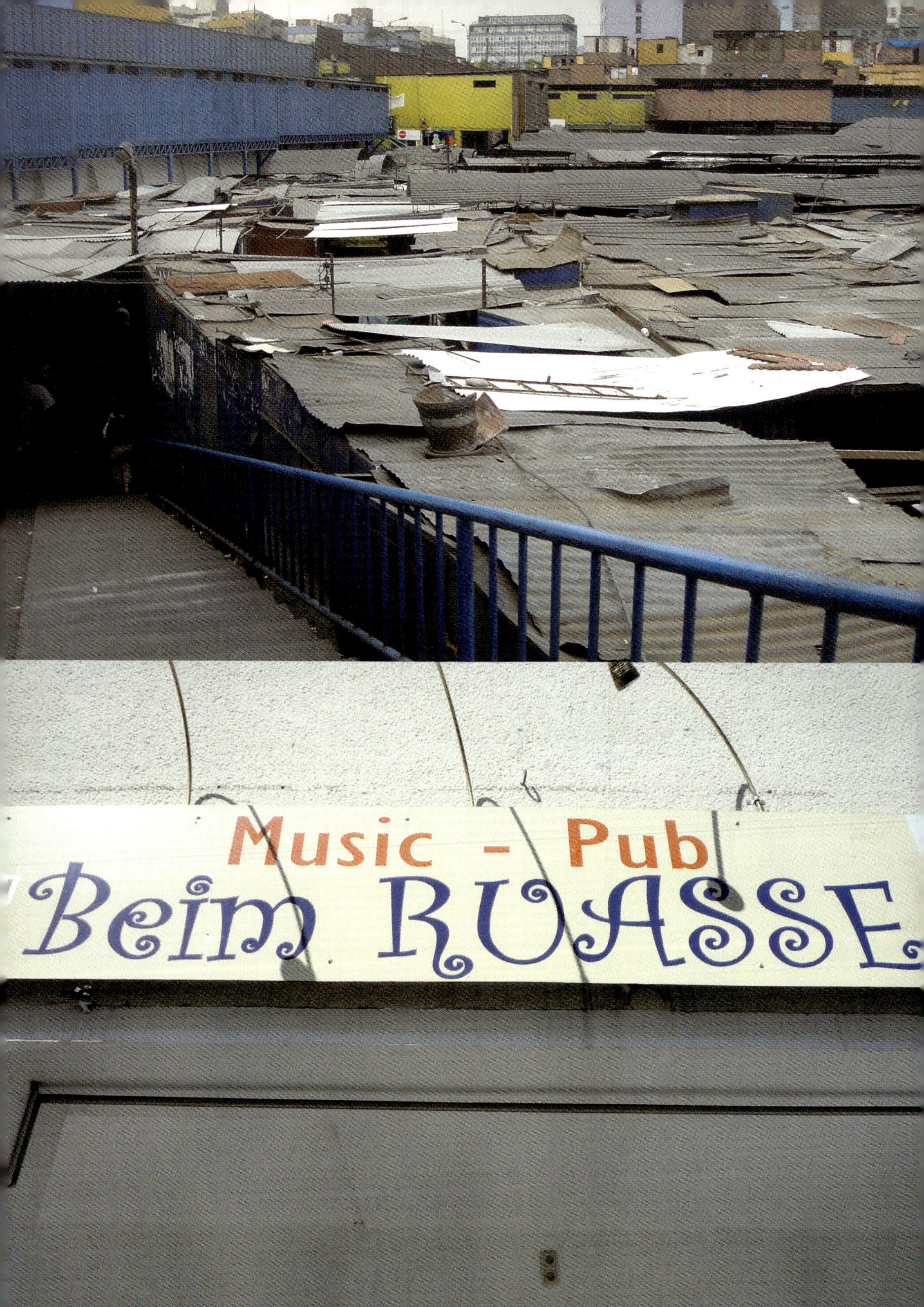
Music - Pub
Beim RUASSE

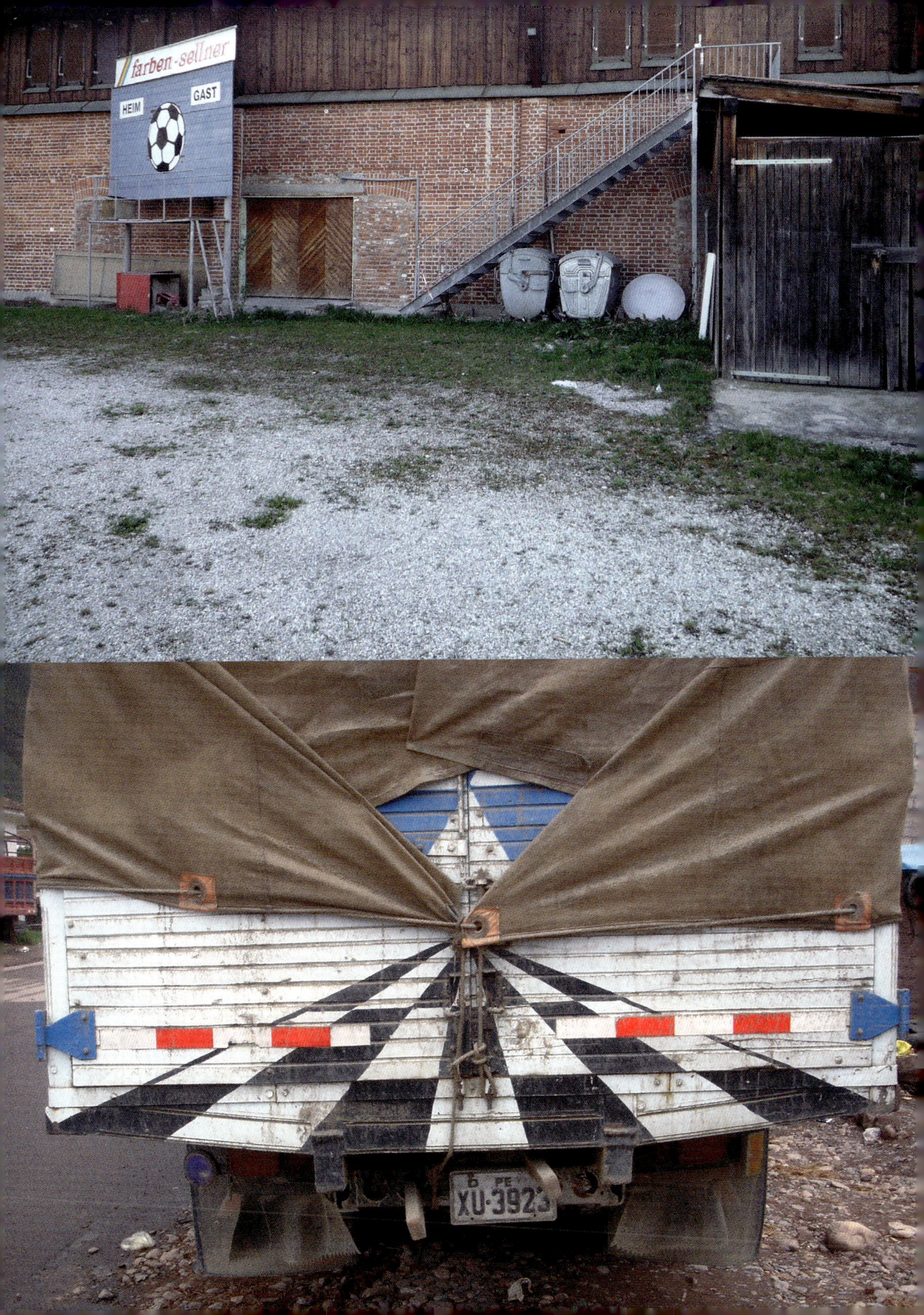

farben-sellner
HEIM   GAST
PE
XU·3923

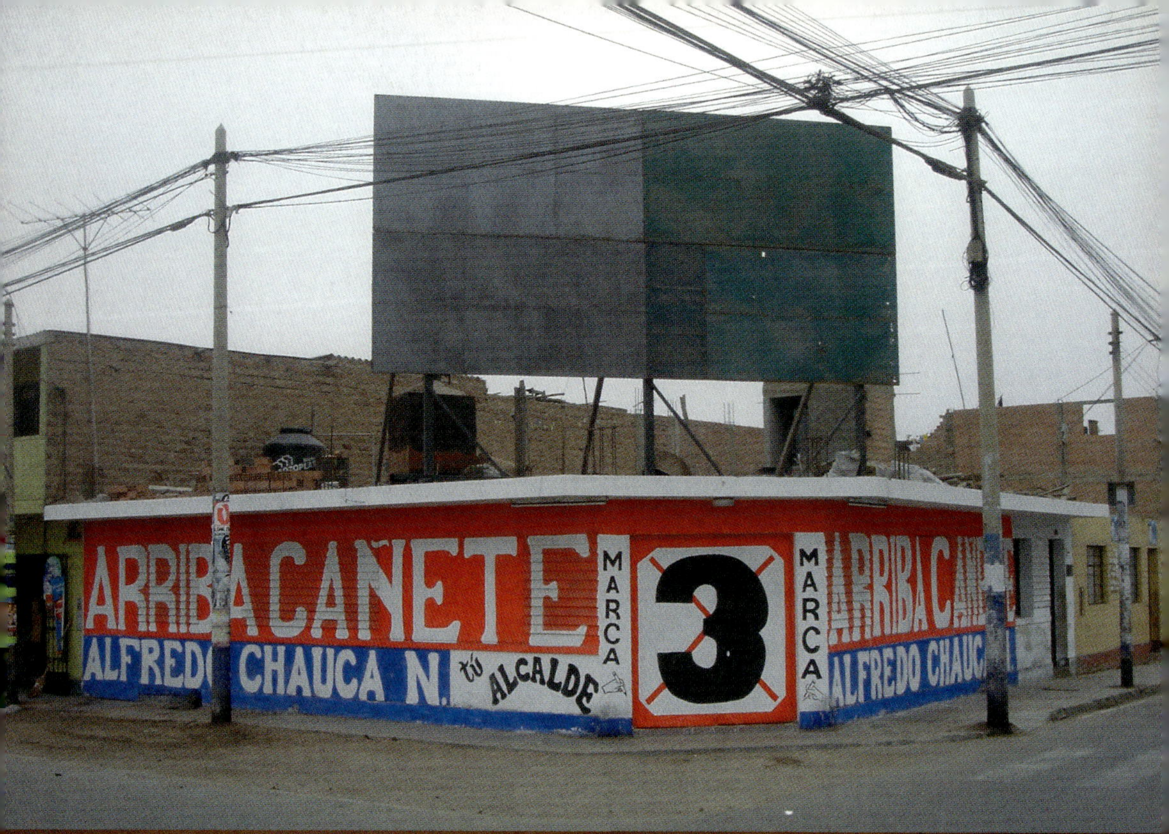

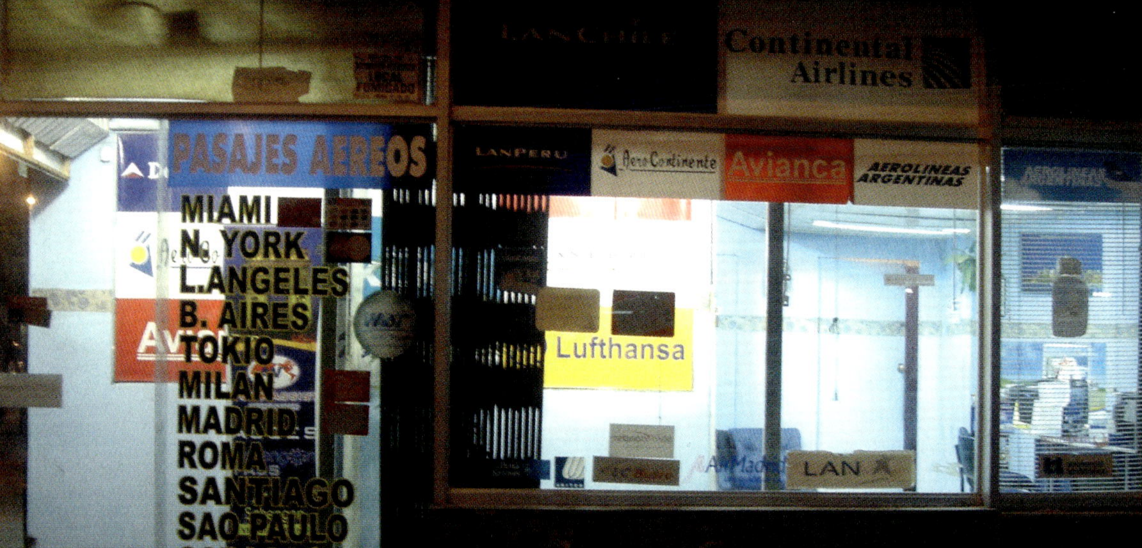
ARRIBA CAÑETE
MARCA
3
MARCA
ARRIBA CAÑ
ALFREDO CHAUCA N.
tu ALCALDE
ALFREDO CHAUCA
PASAJES AEREOS
MIAMI
N. YORK
L. ANGELES
B. AIRES
TOKIO
MILAN
MADRID
ROMA
SANTIAGO
SAO PAULO
CARACAS
BOGOTA
Continental
Airlines
LanPeru
Aero Continente
Avianca
AEROLINEAS
ARGENTINAS
Lufthansa
LAN

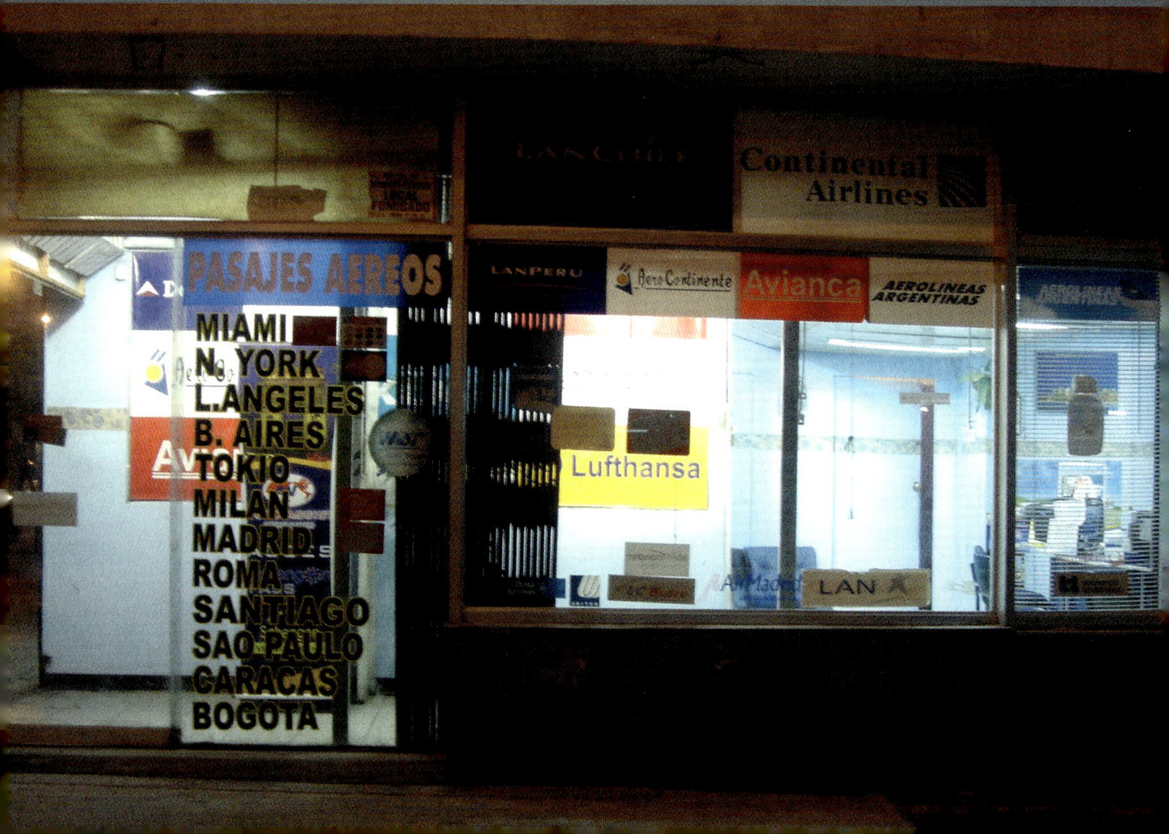

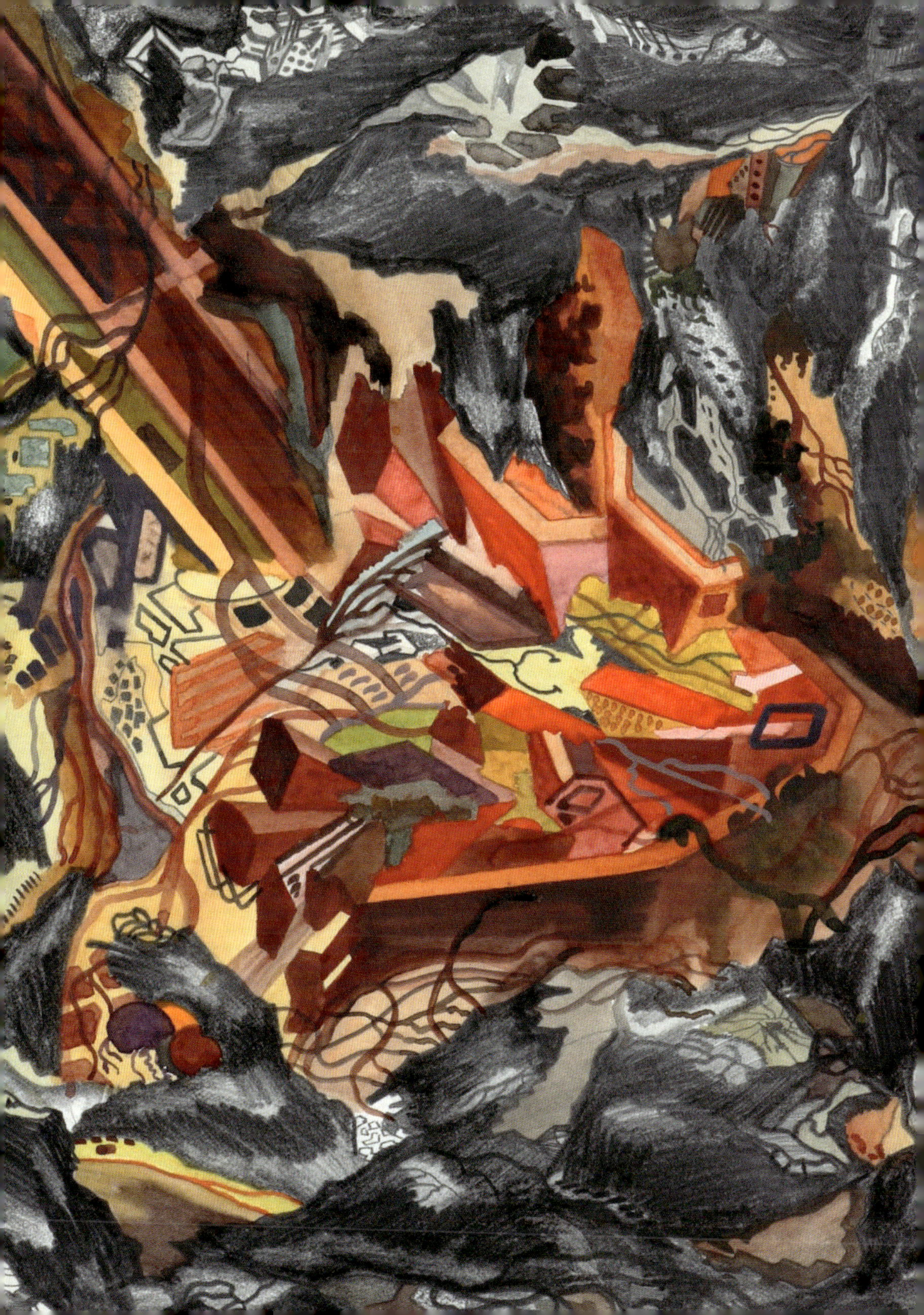

DANK | CREDITS

Herbert Hofauer, Herbert Bauer, Ulrike Kirnich, Prof. Dr. Rainer Metzger, Christopher Barber, Christopher Roth, Christian und Stephan Ackermann, Ralf Lücke, Franz Meyer, Sinta Werner, Judith Karchether, Christa Fülbier, Wolfgang Lugmair, Simone Wackershauser, Danielle Scheuer, MASO, Zetti, Familie Moritz, John Caldor, Joachim Plum, Igor Mishiev, Edith und Jean Majerus

Rosa Ackermann, Agnes Wegner, Rosi und Ludwig Leiser, Markus Wirl, Georg Reidl, Ruasse, Hubert „Bim" Rothmayer, Anton Dingl, Familie Detter, Konrad Schwanthaler, Hubert Bremen

neugerriemschneider, Berlin; Gavin Brown's Enterprise, New York; Mai 36, Zürich
und alle Leihgeber, and all lenders

und irgendwie für immer Norbert Huber

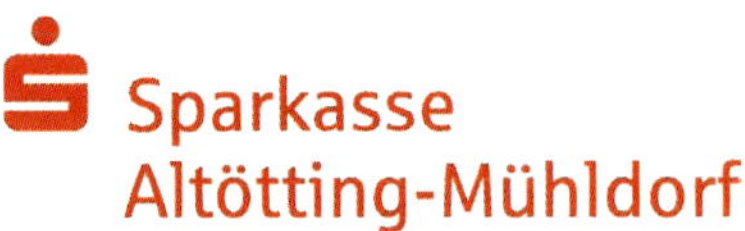

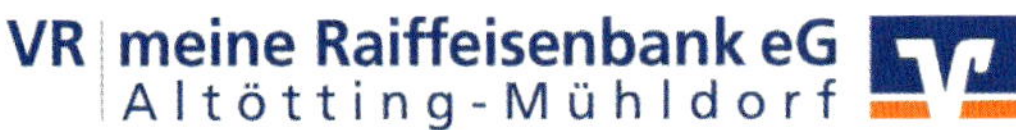

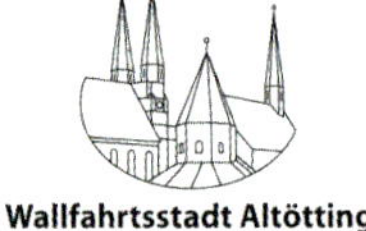

Wallfahrtsstadt Altötting

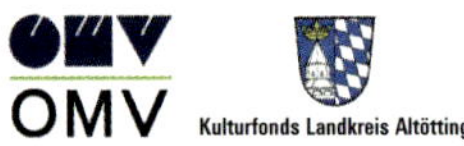

IMPRESSUM | COLOPHON

Eine Publikation der Stadtgalerie Altötting anlässlich der Ausstellung
Franz Ackermann. LIMA, ALTÖTTING (15. Mai – 26. Juli 2009)
This catalogue has been published by the Stadtgalerie Altötting
to coincide with the exhibtion
Franz Ackermann. LIMA, ALTÖTTING (15. May – 26. July 2009)

Herausgeber | Editor: Stadtgalerie Altötting, Papst-Benedikt-Platz 3, 84503 Altötting
Schirmherrschaft | Patronage: Herbert Hofauer, Erster Bürgermeister Altötting
Ausstellung und Katalog | Exhibition and catalogue: Franz Ackermann, Stadtgalerie Altötting
Autor | Author: Prof. Dr. Rainer Metzger, Karlsruhe
Textredaktion und Lektorat | Editing and Proof-reading: Rosi Leiser
Übersetzungen | Translations: Christopher Barber
Gestaltung | Graphic design: Franz Ackermann, Ludwig Leiser und Markus Wirl
Fotonachweis | Photo credits: Franz Ackermann, Jens Ziehe, Heiner Heine
Papier | Paper: Parilux 170g/qm
Schrift | Type: Univers Condensed BQ
Druck | Printing: Gebr. Geiselberger Altötting

Verwaltung | Administration: Wallfahrts- und Verkehrsbüro Altötting
Kapellplatz 2 a, 84503 Altötting
Tel.: 0 86 71/50 62-19 oder -38, Fax 0 86 71/85 85 8
www.altoetting.de
Leitung | Director: Herbert Bauer
Assistenz | Assistance: Ulrike Kirnich
Ausstellungstechnik | Installation: Stephan und Christian Ackermann, Franz Meyer, Ralf Lücke

Die Deutsche Nationalbibliothek verzeichnet diese Publikation in der Deutschen National-
bibliografie; detaillierte bibliografische Daten sind im Internet über http://dnb.ddb.de abrufbar. /
The Deutsche Nationalbibliothek holds a record of this publication in the Deutsche National-
bibliografie; detailed bibliographical data can be found under: http://dnb.ddb.de.

© 2009 Kerber Verlag,
Bielefeld/Leipzig
Autoren, Herausgeber und Künstler
Authors, Publisher and Artist

ISBN 978-3-86678-326-3
Printed in Germany

Kerber Verlag, Bielefeld
Windelsbleicher Str. 166–170
33659 Bielefeld/Germany
Tel. +49 (0) 5 21/9 50 08-10
Fax +49 (0) 5 21/9 50 08-88
info@kerberverlag.com
www.kerberverlag.com

Kerber, US Distribution
D.A.P., Distributed Art Publishers Inc.
155 Sixth Avenue 2nd Floor
New York, N. Y. 10013
Tel. +1 212 6 27-19 99
Fax +1 212 6 27-94 84

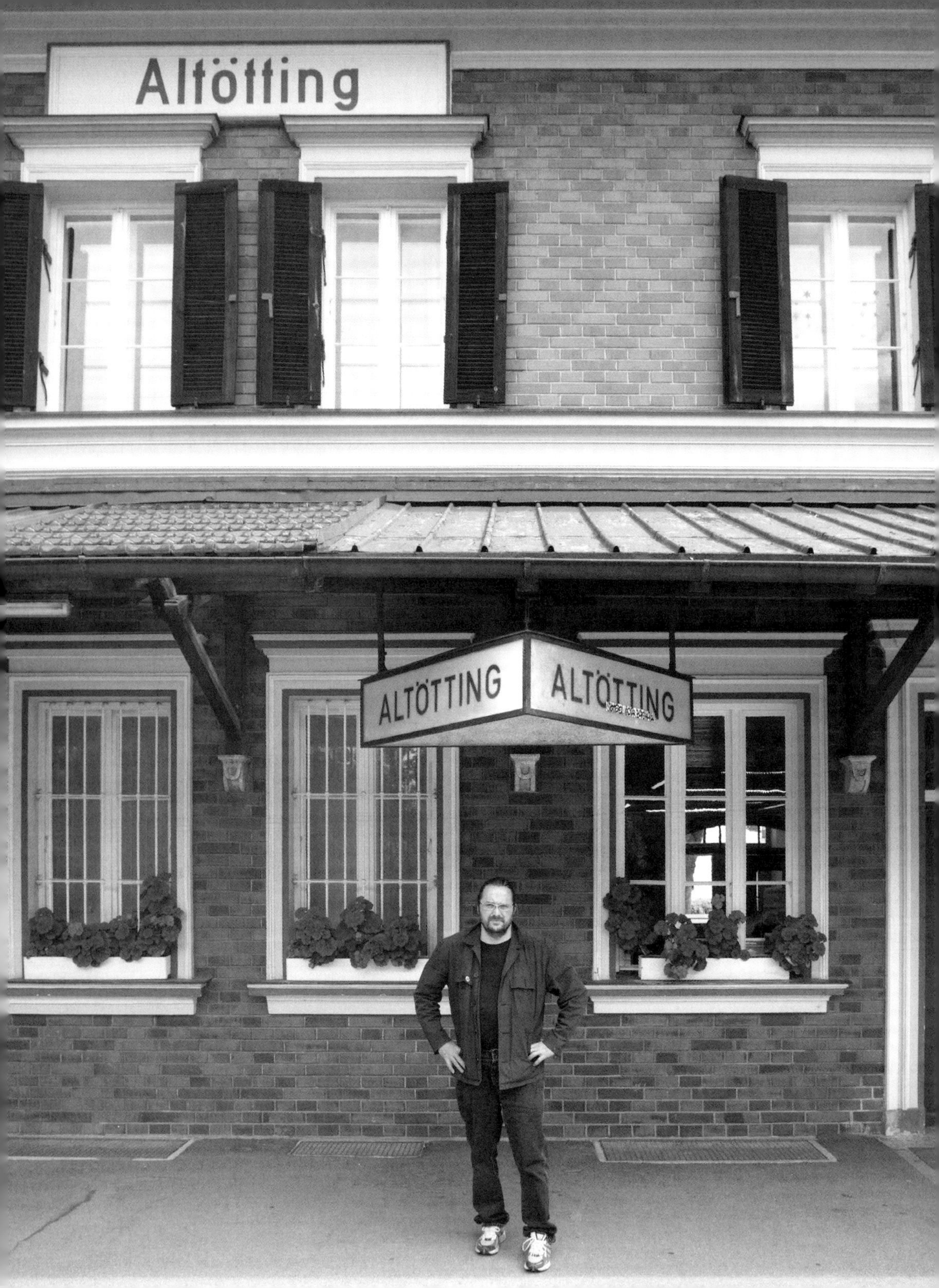
Altötting
ALTÖTTING ALTÖTTING